NEURAL NETWORK TIME SERIES FORECASTING OF FINANCIAL MARKETS

WILEY FINANCE EDITIONS

continued on back endpaper

NEURAL NETWORK TIME SERIES FORECASTING OF FINANCIAL MARKETS

E. MICHAEL AZOFF

John Wiley & Sons
Chichester • New York • Brisbane • Toronto • Singapore

Published 1994 by John Wiley & Sons Ltd,
                    Baffins Lane, Chichester,
                    West Sussex PO19 IUD, England

Telephone (+44) 1243 779777

Reprinted September 1994, May 1995, with corrections February 1996

Other Wiley Editorial Offices

John Wiley & Sons, Inc., 605 Third Avenue,
New York, NY 10158-0012, USA

Jacaranda Wiley Ltd, 33 Park Road, Milton,
Queensland 4064, Australia

John Wiley & Sons (Canada) Ltd, 22 Worcester Road,
Rexdale, Ontario M9W 1L1, Canada

John Wiley & Sons (SEA) Pte Ltd, 37 Jalan Pemimpin #05-04,
Block B, Union Industrial Building, Singapore 2057

Library of Congress Cataloging-in-Publication Data

Azoff, Eitan Michael.
     Neural network time series forecasting of financial markets /
E. Michael Azoff.
       p. cm. — (Wiley finance editions)
     Includes bibliographical references and index.
     ISBN 0-471-94356-8
     1. Futures market — Forecasting — Mathematical models.
     2. Timeseries analysis — Mathematical models.   3. Neural
     networks (Computer science)   I. Title.   II. Series.
     HG6024.A3A96   1994
     332.64'5 — dc20   93-42336
                                                      CIP

British Library Cataloguing in Publication Data

A catalogue record for this book is available from the British Library

ISBN 0-471-94356-8

Typeset in 10/12pt Times from author's disks by Laser Words, Madras
Printed and bound in Great Britain by Bookcraft (Bath) Ltd

To my parents

Contents

Preface

The field of neural networks has seen a recent surge in activity as a result of progress in developments of efficient training algorithms. For this reason, and coupled with the widespread availability of powerful personal computer hardware for running simulations of networks, there is increasing focus on the potential benefits this field can offer. The neural network may be viewed as an advanced pattern recognition technique, and the intention of this book is to provide an introduction to its application in forecasting, and in particular financial time series forecasting. Aimed at a numerate reader who may be drawn to the subject from a diverse range of possible backgrounds, the mathematics has consequently been kept to the essentials, and the text avoids unnecessary jargon, with an emphasis on explanatory notes. A high school level is sufficient for mathematical knowledge — more advanced material requiring calculus has been assigned to the appendix. Computer programming expertise is necessary if the novel ideas introduced here are to be implemented. It has been an objective to encompass a wide range of aspects that touch on the central subject matter of neural network forecasting, including; data preprocessing, random walk probability theory, fully specified benchmarks and code for implementing the benchmarks as pre-trained networks, an overview of futures trading, providing an entry point for readers with a non-finance background, and discussion of trading systems and risk management.

A traditional statistical treatment of time series would include tests for randomness, analyses of series into component parts, seasonal adjustments, smoothing, and the class of autoregressive forecasting models; these approaches complement the material here. However, direct tests for randomness can be fraught with problems, as recent advances in chaos and nonlinear dynamics theory have shown many traditional tests to fail for deterministic systems that only appear random. This is an active area of research, some pointers to the literature are provided. Also, nonstationary nonlinear time series, such as found in the financial markets, are more suitable for analysis by the general nonlinear mapping provided by a neural network, than by linear based autoregressive models.

Rather, the approach taken here is that significantly above random chance neural network forecast performance is a strong indication that deterministic information exists in the time series. Performance verification is a twofold procedure; neural network forecast accuracy is measured through out-of-sample tests, and secondly, forecast implementation within an application system will have its own particular success criteria, which are also verified in out-of-sample tests. A key financial market application is futures trading, and this forms the main focus in the discussion on forecast implementation.

The primary topics addressed here concern neural networks, covering important issues such as preprocessing and network design strategies for time series. The neural network is a highly flexible multivariate technique, with the possibility of composing input data from a number of time series and processed variables in the form of indicators. The network is trained in an adaptive manner over many iterations to extract patterns in the input in order to provide a forecast for the selected target time series. Possible contingencies can be accounted for between different input time series without preconceived assumptions on the dependent relationships.

The introductory chapter provides a brief history of neural networks followed by a literature review of published work on forecasting financial markets and neural network applications in that field. The introduction concludes with a definition of neural networks, including remarks on the different types of network architectures. This book then treats in depth one particular neural network, known as the multi-layer perceptron (MLP), found in the majority of successful applications, both research and industrial, and highly appropriate for forecasting time series. The widespread availability of the MLP in neural network software packages makes it the architecture the reader will be most likely to meet in practice.

Chapter 2 provides a tutorial on applying the MLP net to a simple, but deep problem, learning the logical function known as the exclusive OR. This problem had historical importance in neural networks research. All the elements involved in more complex problems are introduced within the context of this illustrative example. Chapters 3 and 4 deal with general issues concerning the MLP that are important in all applications, not just forecasting, and which are not often dealt with in sufficient detail elsewhere. Chapter 3 covers input data preprocessing, including normalisation and dimension reduction methods. Chapter 4 is concerned with the design of the network, and discusses strategies for training and testing, defining cost functions and error performance measures, defining the transfer function of the neuron, and explains the issue of network complexity. Design aspects for forecasting time series are also covered, such as selecting the look-ahead period and configuring networks in multistages, as well as a novel error reduction scheme with the autocorrelation error (ACE) neuron.

Pure random variable time series possess some interesting properties which are not immediately intuitively obvious. Whilst a time series is defined as a sequence of variables in time, the random walk, or Brownian motion, is a particular form of time series obtained by *accumulating* a sequence of random steps in time and is therefore the theoretical counterpart to a purely random financial market time series. The behaviour of the random walk tends to be counterintuitive as a result of the gradual accumulative process over a long series of steps. The motion tends to follow a diffusive process with a tendency to spend long periods away from the original start-point; chance fluctuations may take the walk to a certain point after a long sequence, with subsequent motion showing a bias towards that region, relative to the start point. In contrast to the random walk itself, the differences between the random walk positions (price differences in financial time series) tend to follow a Gaussian-like distribution, (Gaussian is used throughout for the statistician's normal distribution, to avoid confusion with normalisation of neural network inputs), this leads to possible exploitation of the *median forecast method*—a technique introduced here for predicting the next likely price difference *trend* with an above even chance reliability. These perspectives and techniques are expanded on in Chapter 5, forming a useful background to time series forecasting.

Fully specified benchmarks, not usually available, are of great benefit for anyone contemplating designing their neural networks using one of the many commercial simulators, or writing their own simulator. The benchmarks appearing in Chapter 6 are described in full detail, including generating input data and network parameter settings. Classic benchmarks are provided including the sunspot number series and problems from chaos theory. Two financial time series are treated; futures in the S&P 500 stock index and foreign exchange rate futures.

Futures trading forms one of the key application areas of financial time series forecasting, and hence it is the focus in Chapter 7 on forecast implementation. First, background material on this specialist field is provided, followed by the important issue of constructing historical time series from futures contract data. This material should also be treated as reference for the futures terms introduced earlier in the text where futures input data is discussed. The methodology of automated trading systems and their performance testing is next discussed and the important subject of risk (or money) management is outlined. The final chapter provides references on reading material for further study and useful information on journals, conferences, associations and neural network and related software tools.

As mentioned, the mathematical content of the book has been kept to a minimum, with references provided for more detailed material. However, certain essential areas are better served by a complete mathematical description and this applies to the derivation of backpropagation, which is provided in Appendix A. The next two appendices concern the benchmark solutions, providing weight solution tabulations and a recall mode MLP simulator, coded in FORTRAN, for implementing the pre-trained neural networks.

The recent developments in neural networks, reflected in the material discussed here, provides new opportunities in forecasting the stock and financial derivatives markets, as well as other financial and economic time series. Here will be found a firm foundation for practical applications of neural networks and upon which new ideas may be further explored.

Acknowledgements

Thank you to Chris Jennings for bringing this topic to my attention, a highly stimulating one indeed. My knowledge of neural networks benefited from the excellent meetings of the Neural Computing and Applications Forum. Many thanks also to Quentin Burrows and Martin Price for sharing some of their insights into futures trading. Thank you to Tony O'Hagan, who was kind enough to offer his views in a private correspondence. I'm grateful to Andre Koeckelenbergh, at the Sunspot Index Data Center, for supplying recent international sunspot numbers. Thank you to Richard Baggaley, at John Wiley, for bringing the book to press, and Lewis Derrick for the fine production. And a special thank you to my parents for their encouragement while I wrote this book, and to whom it is dedicated.

The manuscript was prepared using the LaTeX document typesetting system on a Tiny Computers 486 PC, with a Borland screeneditor. Camera-ready figures were produced on a Hewlett Packard DeskJet 500 using GRAFTOOL by 3-D Visions.

Communications to the author may be addressed to: *Themisto Numerics Ltd, Numerical Modelling Consultancy, 59 Colin Gardens, London NW9 6EP.*

Neural Network Software

Themisto Numerics will be launching a neural network forecasting tool, Prognostica, in the final quarter 1995, which includes features discussed in this book. Readers wishing to be placed on the mailing list are invited to either send their details to the above address or fax (+44) 115 9523207. Any comments on features you would like to see are welcome.

1

Introduction

Time series are a special form of data where past values in the series may influence future values, depending on the presence of underlying deterministic forces. These forces may be characterised by trends, cycles and nonstationary behaviour in the time series and predictive models attempt to recognise the recurring patterns and nonlinear relationships. Whilst linear models, such as those based on regression techniques, have been the basis of traditional statistical forecasting models, their drawbacks have led to increased activity in nonlinear modelling[30]. Neural networks are nonlinear models that can be trained to map past and future values of a time series, and thereby extract hidden structure and relationships governing the data[92].

The recent upturn in neural network research activity has been a consequence of the realisation that neural networks have powerful pattern recognition capabilities, surpassing those of other techniques in many applications — both for accuracy and/or computation speed. This new wave of neural network activity, building on work going back a few decades, started at the time of Rumelhart's et al[139] widespread dissemination of their research on the multilayer perceptron neural network architecture, with backpropagation training algorithm.

Although constrained nonlinear regression techniques are being developed[162], the unconstrained nonlinear properties of the neural network make it a preferred candidate in the realm of forecasting time series. To put neural networks in the context of traditional statistical methods, it can be considered as a 'multivariate nonlinear nonparametric inference technique that is data driven and model free'. Multivariate refers to the neural network input comprising many different variables whose interdependencies and causative influences are exploited in predicting future behaviour of a temporal sequence. Nonparametric, model free is a consequence of the lack of any presumptions regarding the relation between input variables and extrapolations into the future. Rather the network is trained by adaptation of *free parameters* to discover any possible relationships, devoid of model constraints, driven and shaped solely by the input data. Here nonparametric, in a statistical model sense, describes the fact that no predetermined parameters are required to specify the mapping model, which leads to the most general approach in processing data; not to be confused with the network training algorithm parameters. The *free parameters* are weights associated with the signal communication lines between neurons, and which attenuate the passing signals, or data.

An important aspect of neural networks is their capability to construct *nonlinear* relationships between the input data and target output. Linearity, ($p_t = a_1 p_{t-1} + a_2 p_{t-2} \ldots$, for a price time series p_t and constants a_i) only describes the most simple relationship that may occur in a time series. If historical prices affect future values then higher powers, cross-terms and functional dependencies may all be involved in a general time series. Techniques in nonlinear modelling have been developed, particularly in control engineering, that rely on polynomial series, known as Volterra and Weiner expansions[105,147], whose coefficients are adjusted to provide a least mean square error fit. However, high orders of the polynomial are required for general problems that are not polynomial in nature, making the method unwieldy as the number of coefficients increase.

Thus neural networks encompass many desirable features as a data analysis tool and within a relatively efficient implementation scheme — in terms of computation speed and computer memory requirements. The advent of such a powerful technique naturally attracted the interest of the finance community and economists, who have a history of tracking developments in artificial intelligence for application in their field. For example, many applications of rule-based expert knowledge systems are to be found on Wall Street.

The next section provides an introduction to the main concepts in neural networks and is followed by an overview of literature related to forecasting financial time series. Chapter 2 provides a tutorial on the most important neural network architecture, the multilayer perceptron.

1.1   NEURAL NETWORKS

A neural network may be considered as a data processing technique that maps, or relates, some type of input stream of information to an output stream of data. For example, the input may be in the form of a two dimensional image with missing or distorted segments, and the processing output may produce a corrected image. In time series applications of interest here, the input may be a one dimensional time series, and the output the best estimation of the next item in the series. In general, neural network tasks may be divided into four types of distinct applications:

1. *Classification:* Deciding into which category an input pattern falls into.

2. *Association:* Acts as a content addressable memory that recalls an output given some part of it as an input.

3. *Codification:* Encoding compresses an input by producing an output with reduced dimension. The opposite task, decoding, may also be of interest.

4. *Simulation:* The creation of a novel output for an input that acts as stimulus, the network having been exposed to a sample of possible stimuli.

Any particular task may involve a number of the above functions. For example, time series forecasting by the multilayer perceptron may involve an element of compression of the input data (encoding), an element of noise reduction (association), the capability of detecting recurring patterns that lead to predictable behaviour (classification), and the forecast of a unique event (simulation).

Neural networks may be implemented in either software or hardware. The former method results in a neural network simulation; it may be programmed in a conventional manner on a serial processor computer, or programmed in specialised languages and run on parallel architecture computers. The motive for a direct hardware implementation is the advantage of faster operation, or in industrial mass production, a cost efficiency in hard-wiring a single task implementation. However, the dividing line can be somewhat blurred with the rapid advances in software driven systems, which also possess the flexibility of software. Hardware implementations will remain the provenance of highly specialised tasks, whilst the majority of users will prefer the software route.

Some processing tasks performed by neural networks may also be fulfilled by traditional techniques, such as look-up databases or regression analysis. However none share the unique capabilities of neural networks, whose advantages may be summarised as follows:

- *Generalisation:* The neural networks are first established through a 'training' phase, whereby example inputs are presented and the network is trained to extract relevant information from these patterns. Subsequently the network has the capability to generalise, so that a hitherto unseen input pattern may also be processed.

- *Flexibility:* The range of tasks that the neural network can be applied to, vastly exceeds any one traditional technique.

- *Nonlinear Modelling:* The network mapping process involves nonlinear functions that can consequently cover a greater range of problem complexity. Although other nonlinear techniques exist, the neural network is superior in its generality and practical ease in implementation.

There are numerous neural network architecture designs, also called neural *paradigms*, however they can all be divided into three broad classes, on the basis of the technique used to iteratively train the free parameters in the network, known as weights. These learning classes are as follows.

- *Supervised Learning:* The network output targets are known during training, so that the error, the difference between the desired target and actual output, may be fed back to the network for improving the performance. Example architecture: the multilayer perceptron.

- *Reinforcement Learning:* Targets for each of the network input examples are not known (or not used), only a criterion as to whether the network performance is correct or not is utilised in feedback, no information regarding the actual correct output is available for training. In some cases the evaluative judgement is only available after a sequence of inputs have been presented, which creates a further separation between individual inputs and desired network performance. Examples exist in neural network driven robot designs[112].

- *Unsupervised Learning:* There is total lack of feedback as to whether the learning objective has been correctively achieved or not. Rather, these types of networks are self-organising, using correlations amongst the input patterns to categorise them according to self-discovered classes. Example network: Kohonen Self-Organising Maps[85].

This book treats comprehensively one type of architecture, the supervised network, and one particular example of such a network, the multilayer perceptron. A highly successful neural network design that is widely applied, it is also appropriate for time series forecasting — the supervised methodology makes optimum use of available information; during the training of the network each prediction is compared with the desired value, and this information is fed back to improve the network.

Historically, the study of neural networks has been in progress for a number of decades and originated in artificial intelligence research, whether as a means of understanding the brain or in creating a thinking machine. The first systematic investigations that attempted to define a computational model of the brain's thinking process started with the work of McCulloch and Pitts[109], Hebb[61] and Rosenblat[136], in the 1940s and 50s. However subsequent progress was gradual and suffered from the lack of efficient training algorithms, although unbeknown to the AI community, control engineers were developing the necessary methods in different contexts. The renewed activity in neural networks was largely due to the development in training neural networks with deep, or hidden layers, known as multilayer perceptrons (MLPs). This was the result of research by psychologists Rummelhart et al[139,106] who published in 1986 a new training method, named backpropagation. The rapid dissemination of this technique led to the burgeoning of a new wave of research activity. It was also realised that other researchers had independently co-discovered similar training algorithms[173,124,94]. The MLP, with backpropagation, is the most successful example of a neural network, with the majority of industrial applications implementing this design[101], despite there being a large number of alternative neural architectures.

The name 'neural network' derives from the neural structure in the brain, and was so termed by the biologists and physiologists who attempted to simulate and model the neurons in the brain. The subject today is interdisciplinary, ranging from the biologists and psychologists whose aim is to understand better the actual computation process in the brain, to physicists who have successfully formulated statistical mechanical models of networks, to engineers interested in massively parallel filter designs, to mathematicians, computer scientists and statisticians for whom foundation rigour, the logic of reasoning and pattern recognition are active areas of research. Each of these disciplines tackle the problem of artificial intelligence from their unique viewpoint and are also concurrently inspired by neurophysiological developments.

The viewpoint adopted here is that of treating the neural network as a signal, or data, processing tool, in contrast with research efforts in biological realism. Rather, a pragmatic approach predominates in designing a computational process that is optimum in achieving the desired aim of detecting patterns in time series data. However, one of the attractive aspects of this field is the wide variety of approaches being examined by the research community, which provides a rich source of inspiration.

The function of cells in a neural network is discussed in the tutorial, for terminology reference: *nodes* will be used to describe the neural network input cells, with the term *neuron* reserved for processing cells — the artificial equivalent of biological neurons, (not necessarily a realistic representation for purely engineering applications). Where no distinction is being made, the generic term *cell* will be used. Notation for the number of cells in a layer will often be given in the form, for example a three layer structure, $i - h - o$, for the number in the input, hidden and output layers respectively.

1.2 LITERATURE OVERVIEW

The financial industry has been a prime application area of artificial intelligence techniques, with the latest advances rapidly ingested in the drive to maintain competitive edge[53]. Thus expert system approaches have been explored by all the major banks, for an overview see Freedman[52], Miller[112], Pau[125] and Schmerken[144]. The analysis of market prices with a view to forecasting future behaviour presumes that such an approach is meaningful, whether its methodology is technical analysis (which assumes historical price studies alone are sufficient for prediction) or fundamental analysis (which studies general economic variables, company performance statistics, prevailing supply and demand etc.). Acceptance of the market as being governed by purely random forces leads to the efficient market hypothesis (EMH), and if strictly adhered precludes forecasting as a viable activity.

The EMH, in varying degrees of weak and strong forms, has been the central assumption in economic academic circles for a number of decades[36], its roots can be traced to the Gaussian random walk model of Bachelier[10]. According to the strong form of the EMH hypothesis, the 'true' price of a stock or commodity is its observed price if traders act rationally, have perfect relevant information (with no delays), and are all participating in the market[52]. However in the actual market deviations exist between true prices and market prices because not all traders have complete information, and do not always act rationally. Despite this realistic scenario, the EMH attracts continued support, since market prices have defied traditional statistical tests in attempts to detect significant nonrandom deviations (significant in the sense that trading costs and brokerage commissions invariably dissipate any unusual gains).

Different variations of EMH have been postulated, based on the degree to which information, of whatever form, may influence the market prices. In contrast to these established theoretical models, there is an increasing awareness that exceptions exist which may require a major re-think on the dynamics of price movement[47,71]. Any model that consistently produces above average returns implies a weakness in the EMH, the Value Line being a case in point[31,71]. Whilst the debate in academia is far from being conclusive, ideas from chaos theory are emerging that point to possible deterministic mechanisms underlying market behaviour, and which are not explicable by invoking market risk alone.

Brock[23] has surveyed the field of detecting nonrandom behaviour in prices and also addresses the problem of detecting patterns that turn out to be spurious. In particular Brock, Dechert and Scheinkman[24] have developed a sensitive nonparametric test, the BDS test, for detecting nonrandom behaviour in time series. The technique, though not infallible, is superior to many traditional statistical tests in detecting nonrandom structure. Brock lists the following criteria for a scientific measure of predictability of prices:

1. What is the probability that the successful prediction of a forecasting system is due solely to chance. Perform t-test and chi-test for assessment of significance.
2. The forecasting system must be a prescribed system, not requiring human interference/interpretation.
3. Compare to buy and hold: for example, what was % of S&P index rise over same period.

Structure in an apparently random time series may be due to chaotic dynamics of a deterministic process. Another possibility of nonlinear dependence between price changes at different times is that of exchange rate changes which are nonlinear stochastic functions of their own past. Hsieh[68] has used the BDS method to test foreign exchange rates and found evidence for an underlying nonlinear stochastic process.

Brock et al[22] analysed the use of technical analysis indicators, based on moving averages and trading range breaks, in predicting equity returns. They found evidence of above average performance that was inconsistent with the random walk model, as well as with linear statistical models, such as autoregression. The conclusion of this study was that nonlinearities exist in market prices and that technical analysis methods may pick up some of the hidden patterns.

Savit[141,142] has examined logistic nonlinear dynamic models with feedback as simplified models for market price time series, including options prices. Savit concludes that the consequence of chaos analysis on options price modelling could lead to strategies for improved forecasting.

Peters[126] has analysed market prices from the viewpoint of chaos theory and found evidence for nonlinear dynamic behaviour. A measure of nonrandom, fractal behaviour is the Hurst exponent, which lies in the range [0,1]. Low values indicate a noisy, random time series. Peters analysed the price return, defined in logarithms $ln(p_t/p_{t-1})$, for the S&P 500 stock index and concluded that the prices followed a biased random walk, with an anomalously high Hurst exponent of 0.78. Bonds and currency rates were also analysed. Peters argued that for dynamical analysis, price differences are inappropriate, since nonlinear serial dependence on past prices are eliminated, and this memory of historical past is important for projections into the future. However, it is argued that the data should be first detrended in order to remove the effects of inflation. Chen[35] also detrended data, assuming a constant rate of economic growth. Peters suggested a detrending factor, based on the consumer price index, that accounts for monthly fluctuations. Performing chaos theory analysis on the detrended S&P 500 index series revealed evidence for the stock index being governed by chaotic deterministic forces. The S&P 500 time series was found to have a chaotic attractor with largest Lyapunov exponent that was *positive*, indicative of sensitivity to initial conditions since the errors in prediction are exponentially amplified in time. The largest Lyapunov exponent conveys the rate of decay of known information about the time series.

Larrain[93] tested a model for T-Bill rates combining nonlinear past prices (technical analysis approach) with fundamental variables, including gross national product, consumer price index and money supply figures. The results indicated that interest rate series contain periods of chaotic behaviour governed by nonlinear dynamics, rather than being solely random.

A number of approaches have been taken in the research literature in searching for chaos in time series for forecasting purposes. The literature is vast, see Peters[126] and Casdagli[30] and references therein. In particular, Farmer and Sidorowich[48] use a local approximation method and Sugihara and May[155] use a simplex method for short-term prediction.

A final note on the detection of chaos in financial time series, or in fact for any time series. Ruelle[137] points out the pitfalls that can occur in applying the technique imprudently, in particular the time series should be of sufficient sample length N, that any correlation dimension, D_c, detected should satisfy

$$D_c < 2 \log_{10} N \qquad (1.1)$$

Anomalous behaviour in stock prices have been known to exist, one example being the January effect[58] a start of year phenomenon when small company stock values tend to rise. Hirsch[65] has produced an almanac for traders, documenting unusual patterns in stock market prices. Such patterns, of course, may arise solely due to chance in any random time series, however there may be causative deterministic influences in certain cases. Haugen and Lakonishok[58] provide evidence for the January effect. Thorp and Kassouf[161] found arbitrage opportunities by analysing stock warrants. Evidence for nonrandom behaviour in market time series is accumulating.

See also Lakonishok and Maberly[91] on the weekend effect and Ariel[6] on the phenomenon of high stock returns before holidays. Brock[22,23] reviews other evidence.

A number of writers have discussed the psychological aspects of trading and how this may affect market price behaviour[2,13,39,40]. Vaga[164] has developed a theory of price movement based on the effects of cumulative individual social interactions between traders. This approach formalises the psychology of trading, where herd-like movements are triggered by extreme waves of fear and greed[81,100]. Vaga's model extends earlier work by Callen and Shapero[28], whose *Theory of Social Imitation* used the Fokker Planck equation, well known in statistical mechanics, to model the effects of polarised opinions. Vaga concluded that financial time series were characterised by periods of true random walk interspaced with periods of coherence due to uniform crowd behaviour.

One of the first applications of neural networks in forecasting was performed by Lapedes and Farber[92]. They designed networks for forecasting chaotic time series generated by the logistic map and Mackey and Glass[100] equation. They also introduced sinusoidal transfer functions for neurons. Early applications of neural network forecasting to the stock market were reported as unsuccessful[120,174]. However more recent research has been increasingly positive in assessing the potential for successful financial forecasting.

Weigend et al[169,170] investigated foreign exchange rate prediction using a neural network with two output neurons, one for the return and the other for the sign of the return. The input vectors comprised absolute prices, returns and various indicators. Targets were restricted to Tuesday prices in the belief that trading patterns are dependent on the day of the week. Performance was assessed on the prediction accuracy, which indicated evidence of nonrandom behaviour. However there was no evaluation of an implementation of the forecasts in actual trading.

Chakraborty et al[33] applied neural networks to forecasting monthly flour price indices at three commodity exchanges. With data limited to 100 samples, their networks were very simple structures, and used the logarithm of the data as input in experiments with univariate and multivariate input combinations. The neural network performances were found to be superior to traditional statistical regression type models. Assessment was based solely on prediction accuracy, implementation was not discussed.

Refenes et al[132] described neural network strategies for foreign exchange rate predictions, using hourly tick data over one trading year. Their network used the previous 12 hours of data, fed into a 35 neuron hidden layer, which fed into a single neuron output layer, predicting the next currency value in the sequence. They compared single-step predictions with iterated-single-stepping, where the forecasts are used as input to forecast further ahead in time.

Bergerson and Wunsch[16] developed a hybrid neural network and expert system for predicting the S&P 500 stock index. The targets were selected as buy/sell/no-action signals by a human expert in a labour expensive exercise, in contrast to predicting every rise and fall of the index. A rule-based expert system governing the money management aspects of trading, such as stop positions and profit taking, as well as including market volatility indicators, overrode the neural signals whenever appropriate.

Wong et al[175] have integrated fuzzy logic reasoning and neural networks within an intelligent stock selection system. Apart from a separate neural network forecaster, a neural network was also incorporated within the fuzzy logic module in a combined FuzzyNet. Fuzzy input variables were processed by fuzzy neural gates that encapsulated the fuzzy logic operations and had trainable input link weights. The system was applied in selecting stocks from a database of 800 stocks, using a broad range of input information, including expert rules and fundamental data (financial ratios, earnings, turnovers, returns etc.).

In a similar application, Swales and Yoon[156] have developed a neural network for differentiating between well and poorly performing stocks. The input data included total returns, comprising dividends and stock price appreciation, and market valuation according to Fortune 500 and Business Week Top 1000.

Harston[57] discussed neural network applications in business. An enhanced associative neural network was described (see references therein) which was trained on fundamental data from a Value Line financial database. The network could then be requested to identify companies with specified financial characteristics for investment screening purposes.

Zaremba[176,158] emphasised the importance of accounting for traders' sentiment, in the form of professional traders' commitments (open interest data, i.e. the number of active futures contracts), and described three neural network forecasting models for S&P 500, US Treasury Bonds and Gold futures. The input variables consisted of data from the monthly Commodities Futures Trading Commission's (CFTC) Commitments of Traders in Futures Report and weekly futures prices (see Chapter 7 for an explanation of futures terms). The CFTC data utilised were the five reportable open interest (OI) figures for all contracts in the particular commodity: the total OI (TOI), noncommercial long and short positions (NCL, NCS) and commercial long and short (CL, CS) numbers. Large speculators make up the reportable noncommercial positions, large hedgers the commercial figures and small traders (nonreportable positions) make up the difference to form the total OI. Percentage sentiment figures are defined as follows, where the number of speculators $Nspc$, number of hedgers $Nhdg$, and number of small traders $Nsml$, may be $+$ or $-$, for net longs and net shorts respectively:

$$Nspc = \frac{50(NCL - NCS)}{TOI} \tag{1.2}$$

$$Nhdg = \frac{50(CL - CS)}{TOI} \tag{1.3}$$

$$Nsml = -(Nspc + Nhdg) \tag{1.4}$$

note the division by 2 and the last relation reflects the fact that futures trading is a zero sum game, the net number of short players balances net long players.

Zaremba's neural network input comprised 20 data elements, representing a four-month window, with five pieces of data per month. The five variables were the three CFTC trader sentiment percentages (these being sign sensitive, as noted above), and two variables representing weekly futures market change in prices (calculated as interpolations of two five-week centered averages and standard deviations). Prices were for the contract that currently held the highest open interest, as reported in Barron's. Zaremba considered the use of the change in price as a suitable compromise for absolute prices in constructing a long time series from concatenated futures contracts. The CFTC input channels were normalised as a group to preserve their zero sum relationship. The look-ahead period was monthly and a three-layer network cell structure of 20–41–1 was explored. Zaremba reported moderate success in actual trading but noted that the 2.5 weeks delay in CFTC data availability is an obstacle.

A number of articles have appeared in Technical Analysis of Stocks and Commodities on forecasting with neural networks. Shih[150] describes a neural network trained on long and short indicators. Fishman et al[50] trained a network on the S&P 500 price difference to predict a week ahead. In a later article[51] they discuss a hybrid system combining neural networks with an expert system. Katz[76] discussed development issues in neural forecasting, and advised the use of separate networks, one trained to predict top and the other bottom turning points. Kean[78] described training a net to predict the S&P 500 index. The journal Futures has also featured articles on the subject, Jurik[73] discussed aspects of preprocessing input data based on harmonic analysis (see also Section 6.3).

A workshop on nonlinear modelling and forecasting[30], held at the Sante Fe Institute in 1991, included wide ranging contributions on forecasting as well as papers on neural network approaches. An earlier workshop, The Economy as an Evolving Complex System[5], also discussed forecasting financial time series.

This completes the overview of the literature. Chapter 8 contains further references on books of interest, journals, and conference proceedings.

2
The Multilayer Perceptron: A Tutorial

The multilayer perceptron is a supervised neural network, by which is meant that the data used for training and testing the network is available paired with the desired response of the network, known as the target, or possibly targets for more than one output neuron. Knowledge of the desired response provides a starting point for iteratively modifying the network, by comparing the observed response with the targets and using the error to drive the network's free parameters in a direction that will minimise the error for repeated presentations of the training input data. This is the essence of the backpropagation method, which backpropagates the errors through the network, adjusting the weights, which are the free, modifiable parameters.

The training input data is assembled in the form of vectors or patterns, a collection of discrete values (also elements or variables). For each element in an input vector a corresponding input node is provided in the network input layer. For time series the input vectors will be produced by rolling a window, of some fixed length, along the series. Naturally for time series which are continuous in nature, a discrete series needs to be produced first, using a suitable sampling scheme, assumed here to be with equal time intervals. If the task is to forecast one element ahead, then for a window of length n elements, the target will always be the $(n+1)$th element.

Since the network is being trained by examples, the more example input vectors available, covering the whole range of possible input data behaviour, the more accurate will be the resulting network performance. The available data is divided, by an appropriate scheme discussed in detail in Chapter 4, into a training and a test set of vectors. Statisticians would describe the training set as the *in-sample* set and the test set as the *out-of-sample* set.

On completion of training and testing, the network is used in recall mode. This involves supplying input data in the format used for training the network, the signals are forward cycled through the network and the network output provides the solution mapping or forecast. Recall mode is very rapid compared to the training process, or indeed to other signal processing techniques, and is a key advantage of neural networks in applications where a pre-trained network is to be implemented.

The MLP is introduced here by way of a practical example, one that provides all the essential features of the standard design. The example is the training of the network to learn a logical function known as the exclusive OR, also written XOR; historically an important problem. Minsky and Papert[114] proved in 1969 that a perceptron with only one layer of nonlinear artificial neurons cannot perform the task of linear separability. This aspect will be returned to at the end of the tutorial. At least one hidden layer, with nonlinear transfer function neuron(s) is required.

Whilst the solution of this example serves as a useful benchmark, the nature of the problem also illustrates the different type of problems that the MLP network can tackle. In a time series problem the inputs are analogue values that can take an infinite range of values, whilst with logical functions the inputs are binary and the range of possible input vectors are thus finite and all available for training purposes.

2.1 THE MULTICONNECTIVITY MLP

The multilayer perceptron neural network, in a very compact design example, is shown in Figure 2.1. The network comprises three layers of cells, with interconnections between all combinations of cell layers (adjacent cells in the same layer are not linked). Such a complete forward path interconnectivity is known as a multiconnectivity MLP. Network designs with only adjacent layer connectivity are also commonly used, the benchmark chapter provides performance comparisons.

The first layer is the input representation, shown as squares, these nodes take on the value of the input data. One case, or pattern, of input node data values is known as an input vector, and the training set comprises many such vectors. Consider next the life-cycle of applying one input vector to the network.

The interconnecting lines indicate that the value output by a cell is passed along that line to the next neuron's input stream. When all the input layer data has filtered through to the last layer, known as the output layer, one forward pass, or cycle, has been performed. The interconnecting lines are shown with bracketed numerals, these are the *weight* values; weights are adjustable parameters which attenuate the data along their associated line (simulated by multiplying the data value with the weight). These weights are crucial aspects of the net. Initially assigned random values from a pre-set range, centered around zero, the weights are incrementally adjusted during the training phase so as to achieve the desired output result for given input data. Typical weight initialisations are in the range $[-1,1]$ or less.

The second layer, and all subsequent layers, contain processing nodes, known as artificial *neurons*, and shown as circles in the figure. Any layers between the

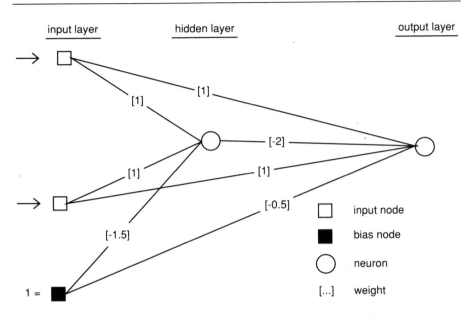

Figure 2.1   Multiconnectivity multilayer perception neural network. Weight values were obtained by inspection. Neurons have step transfer functions (sigmoid with large gain)

input and output layers are called *hidden* layers, in the XOR example there is just one hidden layer, containing one neuron. In general, network designs may contain typically one or two hidden layers with many neurons per layer (see Section 4.5). The processing performed in the artificial neuron may be divided into three steps.

1.   Data passing along the input lines to a neuron are multiplied by the line weights: the process of attenuation.

2.   All the attenuated data inputs fanning into the neuron are summed.

3.   The summation value is put through a transfer function, whose output represents the neuron's output value.

The simplest transfer function is the linear function, whose output equals the input. The use of nonlinear transfer functions is one of the distinguishing features of neural networks that underpin their power. The processing performed in a neuron is sketched out in Figure 2.2, which also shows the sigmoid transfer function used in the XOR example below, for various gradients. The choice of possible transfer functions is further discussed in Chapter 4.

Generally, a network design may deploy a different transfer function in each layer, or in each neuron, although in the XOR example all the neurons have the sigmoid function. The Chapter 6 benchmarks provide cases of mixed transfer

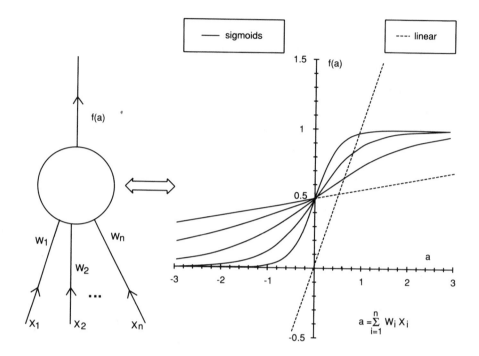

Figure 2.2 Processing performed by an artificial neuron. Data values, x, attenuated by weights, w, along lines ($i = 1 \ldots n$), are summed yielding value a. The transfer function takes in a (possible range $[-\infty, \infty]$) and squashes it to the range $[0,1]$ in the sigmoid case. Sigmoids are plotted for various gains, g: (starting with gentlest gradient) 0.25, 0.5, 1.0, 2.0, 4.0. Also shown is a linear transfer function with unit gradient: $f(a) = a$. The neuron output is $f(a)$

functions. Apart from the linear case, transfer functions have a squashing role in restricting the possible neuron output, which takes a value that may lie in the range $(-\infty, \infty)$ and constrains it to, typically, $[0, 1]$ or $[-1, 1]$. By definition a nonlinear transfer function represents its input in a series of powers of the input value, often given implicitly in the form of an exponential or trigonometric term. This is the basis for the greater generality of such neural networks.

Also shown in Figure 2.1 is a special node at the end of the input layer. This is the bias node, it has a fixed value of 1, and feeds into all the neurons in the network, with each line also attenuated by adjustable weights. The bias node is an explicit representation, or equivalence, of adjustable neuron threshold levels in the transfer function input; the nodal representation eliminates the need to treat threshold as a special neuron feature and leads to a more efficient algorithm implementation.

At the end of the forward cycle, the input data has been propagated to the output neurons, whose output is the final state of the network. The selection of the number of output layer neurons, and choice of their transfer functions, should be chosen with attention to the problem requirements (see Section 4.5). The XOR example requires only one output neuron.

The output state of the network is monitored after all the neurons have completed their processing in the forward cycle. There are neural net designs that introduce an element of time delay into the architecture, usually through a feedback loop, however these nets are not considered here. The MLP is known as a supervised network since, during training, each input data vector is paired with a corresponding target value for the network output. The observed neuron output values in the output layer are now compared with their targets, their difference being the output errors. In the XOR example there will be one such error, which is now *backpropagated* — sending the errors in reverse order through the network — in order to make corrections to the weights. A complete presentation cycle, or iteration, thus comprises the forward and reverse cycles. One set of presentations of all the training vectors constitutes an *epoch*. The order of presentations in each epoch is usually best randomised so that the weight updates do not fall into a set pattern. The process of exploring the whole of weight-space in random order leads to the name of this scheme: *stochastic weight updates*.

In an alternative training scheme, the reverse cycle is postponed until an epoch of forward cycles has been completed, with the accumulated weight corrections averaged and backpropagated once at epoch end. Such a scheme is often called *batch mode weight updating*.

2.2 THE BACKPROPAGATION ALGORITHM

A derivation of the backpropagation method for adjusting the weights requires a mathematical treatment for a detailed description, and is left for Appendix A.

The results are summarised in the following MLP network training algorithm, where the stochastic procedure of updating the weights after each pattern presentation is adopted, rather than accumulating the updates over an epoch:

1. Define a function of the weights in the network, $E(w)$, known as the energy or cost function, which it is desired to minimise. This is discussed in detail in Section 4.2, the half sum of square errors is chosen for this example, (also given is the first derivative of E required below):

$$E^{tot} = \sum_{\mu} \sum_{o} E(w) \qquad (2.1)$$

$$E(w) = \frac{1}{2}[T - O(w)]^2 \qquad (2.2)$$

$$\frac{\partial E}{\partial O} = -(T - O) \qquad (2.3)$$

where the summations are over patterns μ and output layer neurons o, T is the target and $O(w)$ is the observed network output, a function of the network weights w.

2. Define a transfer function, $f(a)$, for the neurons, here the sigmoid function is chosen for all the neurons in the example (with gain g, and no shift, hence f has range $[0,1]$):

$$a = \sum_{i=1}^{n} w_i x_i \qquad (2.4)$$

$$O = f(a) \qquad (2.5)$$

$$f = \frac{1}{1 + e^{-ga}} \qquad (2.6)$$

$$f' = g(1 - O)O \qquad (2.7)$$

where a is the input to the transfer function, being the sum over all neuron fan-in lines $i = 1 \ldots n$, of the product of weight w and input line value x, and $f'(a)$ is the first derivative of $f(a)$.

3. Define network performance measures; the percentage accuracy, PA, and root mean square (RMS) error will be mentioned here:

$$PA = 100 \frac{N_c}{N_e} \qquad (2.8)$$

$$\varepsilon_{rms} = \sqrt{\frac{\sum_{\mu} \sum_{o} (T - O)^2}{N_o N_e}} \qquad (2.9)$$

where N_c is the number of correct or true scores, N_e is the total number of patterns in an epoch, and N_o is the number of neurons in the output layer.

For each measure select a tolerance level for determining the point at which to cease the network training. (Alternative methods for training cessation are discussed in Chapter 4).

4. Initialise the weights randomly, drawing from a small distribution, here for example $[-0.5, 0.5]$. If momentum is used in the weight update rule below, then also set Δw initially to zero.

5. Initialise the epoch order list, the order of presentation of each training pattern, using a randomisation procedure. Take the first pattern indicated in the list and present to the input nodes of the network.

6. Propagate the input node values forwards through the network: Evaluate for each neuron its transfer function input a. Evaluate the transfer function output $f(a)$, this is the neuron's output value which can be propagated forward along the neuron's fan-out lines. This process is continued until the output

layer neurons have been reached and the network has a new observable output state.

7. Compare the observed output layer neuron values, O, with the target values, T, and update the performance measures with the result.

8. Calculate the δ_i value for each output layer neuron i, defined as follows

$$\delta_i = -f'(a_i)\frac{\partial E}{\partial O} \tag{2.10}$$

$$\delta_i = g(1 - O)O(T - O) \tag{2.11}$$

9. Backpropagate the deltas through the network to the preceding layer of neurons j, connected to the output neurons i, and calculate new delta values

$$\delta_j = f'(a_j)\sum_i w_{ij}\delta_i \tag{2.12}$$

Thus for a particular neuron j in the hidden layer below the output layer, the weight connecting it to the output layer neuron i is multiplied by the latter's delta value and summed over all the i output layer neurons. This sum is then multiplied by the derivative of the j neuron's transfer function $f'(a_j)$. This process is continued back through the network until deltas have been calculated for each neuron.

10. The weight connecting any two cells is updated by the product of the preceding layer cell's output, V_p, and the proceeding layer neuron's delta value, δ_q:

$$\bullet_p \longrightarrow \bullet_q \tag{2.13}$$

$$\Delta w_{qp} = \eta\delta_q V_p \tag{2.14}$$

$$w_{qp}^{new} = w_{qp}^{old} + \Delta w_{qp} \tag{2.15}$$

where the arrow indicates the forward path structure, and η is the learning coefficient. All the weights are updated according to this rule.

11. The above weight update expression for Δw may be modified with the addition of a momentum term:

$$\Delta w_{qp}^{new} = \eta\delta_q V_p + \alpha\Delta w_{qp}^{old} \tag{2.16}$$

where the momentum coefficient α takes a value in the range [0,1]. The consequence of this is to give the weight update a memory of its last update, providing a smoothing of the forces affecting the weight changes.

12. If the epoch list has been exhausted, continue to the next step, otherwise present the next training pattern to the input layer and go back to step 6.

13. Having completed an epoch, and accumulated the errors over all the patterns, the error scores are evaluated and compared with the tolerance levels. If the network has not converged then go back to step 5, otherwise stop training.

Note that whether weights are adjusted after each pattern stochastically or in batch mode, a further variation is possible. Since the weight adjustments in a layer make use of weight values in the next forward layer, there is the possibility during the reverse backpropagation cycle, of updating the weights instantly in sequence from output layer down, so that weights in deeper layers are affected by the newly updated values. The method adopted here calculates all the weight changes using existing weight values in the update rules, and then performing the actual updates.

2.3 EXCLUSIVE OR EXAMPLE

The truth table for the XOR logical function with two inputs, shown in Table 2.1, summarises the possible input states and the required output for the function. To give the example a context, consider a discrete time series made up of binary values. The task is to train a neural network to signal a warning whenever the series changes state, i.e. from 0 to 1 or 1 to 0. Clearly the input 'window' sampling the series need only be two elements wide, hence the XOR function of Table 2.1 provides the necessary logic for the task, since it signals a high whenever the inputs are different from each other.

The training set thus comprises the four possible input vectors, and a random number generator will draw up a random order of presentation for each epoch, using a select and discard procedure (that is, no repeats are allowed in an epoch).

A possible solution to this example may in fact be found by inspection, the weight values shown in Figure 2.1 were so determined and represent a valid solution. It is a worthwhile exercise to apply each of the input vectors in Table 2.1 to this network and follow through the forward cycle, verifying the desired results.

Naturally our concern is with automated calculations of the weights, Figure 2.3 shows a backpropagation solution. There is no unique solution for the task, even for a given network design, and much depends on the initial random distribution of weight values. This problem is used as a benchmark in Chapter 6 where various enhancements to the standard algorithm are compared.

Returning to the historical issue concerning this problem in the theoretical development of neural networks. The XOR inputs form a two-dimensional space, with

Table 2.1 XOR binary function truth table

Input layer states		Network output
Node 1	Node 2	State
0	0	0
0	1	1
1	0	1
1	1	0

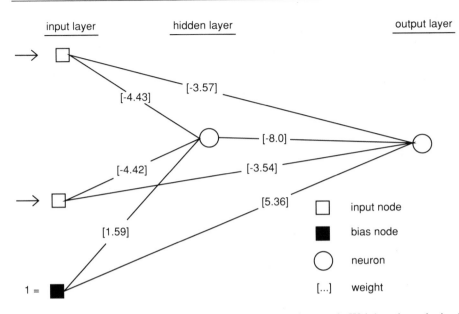

Figure 2.3   Multiconnectivity multilayer perceptron neural network. Weight values obtained by backpropagation solution. Neurons have sigmoid transfer functions (unit gain)

each input node representing one dimension. The valid points in the input-space are (0,0), (1,0), (0,1) and (1,1), representing the corners of a square. Now the XOR function output is one dimensional, the regions of input-space where it is required to be 0 are around (0,0) and (1,1), and it is required to be 1 around (0,1) and (1,0).

Consider an XOR network with an input layer and one neuron layer (comprising one neuron). The network output, given by the sole neuron, and regardless of whether its transfer function is linear or nonlinear, separates regions of 0 and 1 that can be mapped to the input-space. The boundary between these regions forms a straight line for a 2D input-space, or in general a curve (hypercurve) for higher dimensional input-spaces. Now, it is being required of the network to separate these regions using the one boundary line. A little experimentation with paper and pencil will soon convince you that this is impossible, at least two lines are needed to create the boundaries in the input-space between the 0 and 1 regions that correspond to the network output.

If the neurons being considered have linear transfer functions then inserting hidden neuron layers does not help, a multilayer network with linear neurons can be coalesced into a single neuron layer network. However, if nonlinear transfer function neurons are used, then inserting a second neuron layer will transform the capability of the network. In this case the output of the second layer neuron will form what are known as convex regions when mapped to the input-space, these being regions whose boundaries are the lines/curves defined by the previous layer output decision boundaries. (In a closed (completely bounded) or open convex region, any two points may be linked by a straight line without crossing the boundary). Now the input-space can be divided by more than one curve.

This type of problem is known as *linear inseparability*[96], and was methodically proven by Minsky and Papert[114] for perceptrons, concluding that at least two layers of nonlinear neurons are needed to emulate XOR logic. Further developments established that three nonlinear neuron layers can solve any input-space separability problem, and in most cases two layers are sufficient — this question of whether two or three layers are sufficient is still actively debated in the research literature.

The limitations of the single layer network were recognised and also known to be circumvented by multilayer nonlinear networks, but training the weights in multilayer nets was only possible with the advent of backpropagation. This completes the tutorial, in which aspects in the design and training of an MLP network have been touched on. The next three chapters enter into these issues in greater depth and expand on design issues.

A note on the terminology used here: the term *observed* network output refers, in all the applications here, to the output from the sole neuron in the output layer. For time series forecasting, this observed value corresponds to the neural network *forecast*. Similarly, the *target* refers to the actual time series data.

3

The Preprocessing Stage

Preprocessing the input data should be a serious consideration prior to training the network. While it is not essential in certain cases, it is vital in others. The conditions involved in selecting a suitable data manipulative technique is discussed together with the choice of methods available.

3.1 DATA INTEGRITY

The first step is a validation of the raw input data. This involves checking that your assumptions regarding the data are indeed true. The following check list is essential for time series data.

1. Plot the time series from start to finish to obtain a global overview of the data range and trend. Any erroneous data point in a sufficiently large deviation from the general trend will stand out by visual inspection. For example, commodity prices may be zeroed on exchange holidays by the data supplier.

2. Evaluate the standard deviation of the time series steps and then compare the series steps against various multiples of the standard deviation. This provides a quantitative monitoring of the deviations from the trend. For example data items that fall outside the $\pm 5\sigma$ levels may be suspicious and deserve checking. The manner of evaluating the standard deviation depends on the time series being considered. In the case of daily commodity prices, the standard deviation of the day's high minus low provides a suitable measure of the volatility, which can be used to monitor the change in closing price from one day to the next.

3. Time series for which the time, or date, per data item is known, and which are periodic, can be further checked with respect to any missing or duplicated elements. For example, daily commodity prices should be filed with the date for each element. A calendar program can then be written which checks day of the week consistency, by keeping track of the last date and checking the new

element's date against the calendar. This check is especially essential if the data is being trained with sensitivity to the particular date (day of the week, month etc.), in which case missing days due to holidays must be filled in by the last available market price, otherwise the data will be out of phase and hence corrupted.

4. If the data is available from a number of sources, it is prudent to acquire segments of data from second and third sources and make comparisons with your primary source. This again tests any assumptions made regarding the data. For futures price series, the question of how to treat the end of a contract and start of a new series is problematical — it is discussed in Section 7.1. Suffice to say here that acquiring data on the understanding that the time series switches to the next nearest contract in the delivery month, it should be checked with particular attention over the switching period.

3.2 DATA REPRESENTATION

The choice of input and target data should be selected with due consideration paid to the final *task* the network is to perform. A number of ways to achieve a desired task may be explored, which entail radically different choices for the data inputs and targets.

Thus, if the task is to predict whether a price series will rise or fall, the target may be selected as the actual price, or a price difference with respect to the previous price, or a binary 0, 1 or −1, 1 for fall and rise of the target.

The selection of input data should be viewed as a model construction process. Given a particular choice for the target, the input data may be composed of data in the same form, or in conjunction with prices and price differences. The input data need not necessarily be restricted to the time series being forecast. In fact this is one of the strengths of the neural approach, in that any data, of whatever form, that is considered to be contingent in some manner to the target time series, whether through being a direct causative agent, or indirectly related, can be incorporated in the model.

The following is a list of inputs worth considering for inclusion in an input vector, including functional preprocessing.

1. The time series itself: p_t, for some window length n, where $t = 1, \ldots, n$.
2. Variable difference: $p_t - p_{t-1}$.
3. Relative variable difference: $(p_t - p_{t-1})/q$, where possible choices for q are p_{t-1}, $p_{t=0}$ (very start of series), σ (the standard deviation of $p_t - p_{t-1}$ over the whole series).
4. Natural logarithm of relative variable: $\ln(p_t/p_{t-1})$ (suitable only for positive p).
5. Square root of variable: $\sqrt{p_t}$ (suitable only for positive p).
6. Trigonometric function: $\cos(p_t)$, $\sin(p_t)$.

The distribution of values in a time series may be skewed towards either low or high values. Thus it may be worth considering a transformation that reduces the asymmetry[171]; the square root transform is effective in this respect, as is the following (suitable for positive valued data only)

$$\hat{p} = \log_{10}(p + c) \tag{3.1}$$

where c is a constant.

In addition to the historical prices, fundamental data, such as economic indices and interest rates, are worth considering as input variables.

Indicators may also be applied as neural network input variables; the construction of these is one of the most popular approaches in analysing futures prices in technical analysis methodology. Indicators are a processed form of historical prices, which may include for instance the open, high, low and close daily prices, that are designed to emphasise specific features in the time series. For example a buy/sell indicator may be based on the crossover of short and long term moving averages. These ideas are well accounted in the technical analysis literature, and will not be repeated here, refer to standard references[77,116].

A data search approach in formulating indicators and suitable input data, may involve the use of fuzzy logic, genetic algorithms and also control engineering tools such as Kalman filters. This subject area is an important one, but too broad to be discussed here, pointers are provided in the software tool lists in Chapter 8, see also Goonatilake and Treleaven[53].

Two indicators used in the benchmarks will be described here.

3.2.1 The Random Walk Indicator

Consider a time series, with time step intervals τ; if the price moves are governed by purely random motions (the random walk) then statistical analysis reveals that such a price move will deviate from its starting point in proportion to the square root of the number of τ intervals elapsed — this is proven in Chapter 5. Conversely, a strong market trend imposing its force on the random market noise will appear as a persistent departure from the random walk expectation. Note that such departures will occur as a natural consequence of random events, it is only a persistent departure that indicates the *possibility* of nonrandomness. Also, the concurrent appearance of certain patterns in other indicators and in the target time series, may all work to enhance the detectability of any existent nonrandom features.

Poulos[127] has suggested the construction of an indicator, the random walk index (RWI), that monitors departures from random motion. The indicator discussed here is similar. For a price time series sampled at time intervals τ, the average price step is first evaluated, $\overline{\Delta p_t}$, then

$$RWI = \frac{\Delta p_t(N\tau)}{\overline{\Delta p_t}\sqrt{N}} \tag{3.2}$$

where $\Delta p_t(N\tau)$ is the price difference over the time interval $N\tau$.

A set of RWIs evaluated for various look-back periods may be used as inputs to a neural network. RWI will be sign sensitive, depending on whether prices fell or rose over the $N\tau$ interval.

3.2.2 The Volatility Indicator

Commodity price data vendors normally quote four figures for daily prices: OPEN HIGH LOW CLOSE. With the availability of a complete tick price time series, a similar quartet of prices may be assembled for any intra-day period, such as per hour. For periods greater than one day, the daily prices may be combined. Thus, whichever sample period is used for the time series, the four figures may be provided as a field set for each point in the time series.

It should be noted that the *daily* OPEN and CLOSE prices have special significance in that they correspond to the open and close of a day's session in the exchange, and thus may have additional *psychological* importance as well as being influenced by some traders not wishing to hold contracts overnight. That said, the four figures may be constructed for any period and encapsulate the market activity in that period. Naturally with the availability of tick data, the field may be extended further with other summaries of the market activity (for instance the time order of the high and low prices may be definitively calculated for daily quotes).

The volatility indicator is a straightforward monitor, based on the price quartet figures, of the extent of market volatility, defined as follows:

$$VI = \frac{(P_{HIGH} - P_{LOW})(P_{CLOSE} - P_{OPEN})}{|average\ of\ numerator|} \tag{3.3}$$

The indicator will be positive for rising prices and negative for falls. Normalising by the average magnitude of the VI numerator, over a long history of data, provides a measure of activity that is unusually high. The indicator may be used directly as input to the neural network, or first averaged using simple moving averages or exponential moving averages.

3.3 INPUT NORMALISATION

The input data in the majority of cases will require normalising, a process of standardising the possible numerical range that the input vector elements can take. The exception is for data that is already in a sense normalised, such as binary data, or data that is all composed from the same time series and presented in the same form. Even in this latter case, normalisation is advisable since the network training parameters can be tuned for a given range of input data, and can be carried over for similar tasks. Given that normalisation is advisable, the method adopted requires consideration to the nature of the input data, there is no 'correct' normalisation as such, the ultimate measure is whether the network is successful.

There are four approaches to normalisation:

1. *Along channel normalisation:* Consider an input data vector of dimension n, that is, the elements in the vector run from $i = 1, \ldots, n$. Then the kth channel refers to an element in the $i = k$ position in any vector in the input set. Normalisation *along* the channels is performed by taking each channel in turn, and normalising all the vectors only along that particular channel. A variation is to combine a number of channels and perform normalisation on the group, as if the data were in one channel.

2. *Across channel normalisation:* Each input vector is normalised in isolation to any other vector. For each vector, the normalisation is performed across all the elements $i = 1, \ldots, n$. Again, a variation is to group elements within one vector and perform normalisation separately for each group.

3. *Mixed channel normalisation:* Various mixtures of *along* and *across* normalisation may be performed. Thus some elements may be normalised *along* the channel and the remaining elements grouped into one or more sets and normalised *along* within each group. Some groups may be *across* normalised (meaning that for those elements involved, *across* normalisation is performed unique to each vector). This type of approach accommodates the wide variety of input variables, where some variables may be related in special ways.

4. *External normalisation:* Prior to constructing the input vectors, the data, such as a time series, is first normalised to lie within a specified range. This is the least disruptive form of normalisation since the structure between channels is preserved and is equivalent to performing the group variant of *along* channel normalisation for all the channels combined. Note that as a result of using the maximum and minimum of the whole series for transforming variables to, say, $[-1,1]$, then some channels may have elements that never hit the extremes -1 and 1.

The choice of method depends on the composition of the input vector. Certain rules can be applied in confidence: If the elements consist of data from more than one source, or preprocessed into more than one form, even if from the same series, then *along* channel normalisation should be used for all or subgroups of the channels.

If all or a subgroup of the elements are from the same time series, and are of the same form, such as adjacent samples from the series, then the temporal order is useful information that should be considered preserving. This can be achieved through either *external* normalisation or the group variant of *along* channel normalisation or *across* channel normalisation.

In conclusion, the only circumstance for using solely *across* channel normalisation is for uniform data: one source, one form. A further advantage exists then that each vector is normalised independently of other vectors, and there is no need to carry normalising parameters for processing new vectors.

Three types of *along* channel normalisation processing that should cover most applications are as follows; the first two involve finding the maximum and minimum element in each channel, max, min, the third only the absolute maximum, *amax*, where $amax = |max|$ if $|max| \geq |min|$, otherwise $amax = |min|$.

- *Along Norm* [0,1]: The elements, p_i^j, for channel i and total N sample vectors $j = 1, \ldots, N$, are normalised to the range [0,1].

$$\hat{p}_i^j = \frac{p_i^j - min}{max - min} \qquad (3.4)$$

- *Along Norm* [−1,1]: The elements, p_i^j are normalised to the range [−1,1].

$$\hat{p}_i^j = 2\frac{p_i^j - min}{max - min} - 1 \qquad (3.5)$$

- *Along Norm 0-offset:* The elements, p_i^j are normalised to either the range $[min/amax, sgn(max)]$ or $[sgn(min), max/amax]$ depending on whether $|min| < |max|$ or $|min| > |max|$, respectively, where sgn is the sign operator with unit magnitude.

$$\hat{p}_i^j = \frac{p_i^j}{amax} \qquad (3.6)$$

Note that *along* channel normalisation should be performed on the totality of available data vectors in a single procedure. Normalising the test set over only its own data set is a pitfall, since it is usually the case that the test set is a smaller sample set than the train set and such a normalisation can severely distort the test vectors. Using the normalisation *parameters* of just the train set to subsequently normalise the test set, runs the risk that the test data will fall significantly outside the range of the train data (small departures from the range are not a problem). This can happen for time series where the test data is sampled from the most recent period of the series, and may take the series to new highs or new lows. The training and test sets should therefore be combined during normalisation, the single set of normalisation parameters should then be preserved and applied to new vectors during the forecasting applications. A pre-trained network used in this fashion should be re-trained after a period, if only to update the network with a possibly extended data range.

Zero offset along channel normalisation is particularly useful for vector elements that are processed variables whose sign conveys useful information. For example, a price difference will convey a rise or fall in the series, purely on the basis of its sign. Along normalisation, which offsets the variable by $-min/(max-min)$ for [0,1], and $-(max+min)/(max-min)$ for [−1,1], will destroy the meaning in the sign. This is less important for standard MLP designs, where the input layer is connected only to the adjacent hidden layer, however in multiconnectivity designs the input nodes are also directly connected to the output neurons, the sign information can then be significant.

In the case of *across* channel normalisation, max and min are now found amongst the elements of each vector, and the same processing equations given above apply, except that the normalisation is performed across the vector.

The choice of whether to normalise to the range [0,1] or [−1,1] may be a natural choice, depending on the data, otherwise would require experimentation. Thus, if the vector elements can take on values in the range (−∞, ∞), then the [−1,1] norm is appropriate. If the elements are only positive valued, it may still be worthwhile to consider [−1,1]. Note that the weights may be negative as well as positive, so the question concerns which range of the inputs are to be presented to the centre region of the transfer function input (assuming for the sake of this argument that all weights are unity). For positive valued raw data, a [0,1] norm will present the extreme low value end to the centre region of the transfer function input, whilst [−1,1] will present the mid values to the centre of the transfer function input. Try both approaches and select the one giving better results.

3.4 TARGET SELECTION AND NORMALISATION

The choice of target is critical to the success of the problem solution. The first guideline is to minimise the number of targets required for the problem. A multi-connectivity neural network whose output neurons are reduced from two to one, will have half the number of network weights required, with important consequences for the generalisation capability of the network, see Section 4.5 on complexity issues. A single output neuron is the ideal, as the network is focused on one task and there is no danger of conflicting outputs pulling the weights in opposing directions during training.

Time series forecasting is well suited for a single network output state. The choice is then whether to train the network directly on a price value or to a derived indicator of it, such as a price difference. Particularly where forecasting a rise or fall is sufficient, it would be tempting to use the latter type of target. However, there are hazards in using such derived variables, such as the destruction of fragile structure inherent only in the original time series. The use of direct price values is favoured here.

Factors considered in normalisation of the targets are quite independent to the input vector normalisation procedure. The main consideration is the output range of the output neuron's transfer function. Thus a neuron with asymmetrical output range [0,1], should have targets normalized to [0,1], whilst outputs symmetrical about the origin can be normalized to the range [−1,1]. All the targets for a particular output neuron are normalized in one group, and the parameters max, min retained for normalising new targets in the network recall mode.

Consideration should also be given to whether the output transfer function is one with asymptotic limits, such as the sigmoid, which only reach the limits of the range [0,1] for inputs at $\pm\infty$. In this case typical outputs may only reach [0.1,0.9], so a suitable target normalisation should be chosen to that range, or even [0.15,0.85] should be considered.

The normalisation equation for the range $[a, b]$ is given by

$$\hat{p}_o^j = \frac{(p_o^j - \min)(b - a)}{\max - \min} + a \tag{3.7}$$

where j is the vector sample number and o is the output layer neuron.

Note that as a result of normalising the targets, the observed output of the network will correspond to the normalised scaling. In order to interpret targets in the original scale, the normalising parameters need to be preserved for de-scaling the network output. For targets that are relative values, denoting say the rise or fall of a time series, then the scaled output can be interpreted without de-scaling being necessary.

3.5   DIMENSION REDUCTION

The number of elements in an input data vector, its dimension, can reach large proportions for certain problems; particularly where due to lack of precise knowledge of which inputs matter, an 'include all' approach is adopted, or where there is a legitimate need to include large amounts of data which all have a bearing on the target time series. It is a general rule that large neural networks are more difficult to train, even under the best conditions. If there is a shortage of historical data available for a time series, the use of a large input dimension compounds the problems.

One approach to alleviate this problem is to introduce a preprocessing stage that takes in the large dimension vectors, extracts relevant information and produces a reduced dimension vector, discarding redundant information that inevitably exists in the original data. Three methods to achieve this end are discussed here, the first exploits a neural network, whilst the others are purely analytical.

3.5.1   Data Compression

There is a unique MLP design, known as the autoassociator, which performs a data compression task by encoding the input data in a hidden layer with fewer neurons than nodes in the input layer. The design is a three-layer network, whose output layer has the same number of neurons as nodes in the input, shown in Figure 3.1. Note that there is no multiconnectivity, only adjacent layer connections are enabled.

The target vectors are identical to the input vectors, thus the network is trained to reproduce its own input. Due to the bottleneck design, the hidden layer therefore learns to compress the input data vector. There will usually be some residual error depending on the degree of compression performed. Note that if the error cannot

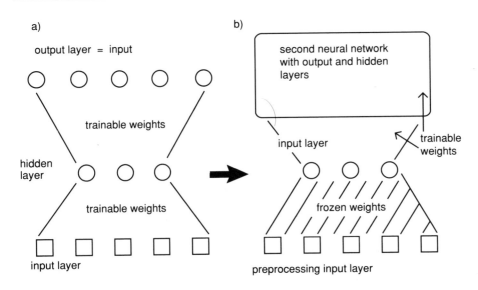

Figure 3.1 Autoassociator MLP with adjacent layer connectivity. After training the top part is removed and the hidden nodes act as input nodes to a secondary neural network

be reduced to an acceptable level, then it implies that data reduction is not suitable for the problem, or perhaps for the input data selected.

At the end of training the output layer is removed and the hidden layer output provides the reduced dimension vectors. The input-to-hidden layer weights are now frozen and the structure is substituted for the input layer of the forecasting network, as shown in Figure 3.1. There has been some theoretical work reported in calculating the autoassociator weights using linear algebraic techniques[21].

3.5.2 Principal Component Analysis

The overriding criterion in selecting the input variables that constitute the network input vector, is their relevance to the target. It is inevitable, therefore, that the resulting mix of variables may overlap in information content. This duplication in the input data, technically known as correlation between the input variables, can slow down the training of the network, as weights try to adjust to the most relevant input variables. Sharpening the boundaries between the type of information each variable provides, eases the training of the network, as weights tune in on precise data variables. The process of sharpening these boundaries is known as decorrelating the input variables (the optimum being a zero correlation coefficient between any two variables). The decorrelation process may be visualised as rotating the cartesian axes of the input-space (a hyperspace for more than three input variables), so as to minimise the dependence of the data vectors on a maximum number of directions, that is zeroing (or reducing) as many elements in the vector as possible.

Given input variables that have been decorrelated, there arises the additional advantage of gauging which of the new variables have the greatest information content, and thereby discarding the least influential variables. The decorrelation property therefore also leads to a dimension reduction possibility. This section describes an analytical technique, based on linear algebra, that can achieve these tasks, known as principal component analysis[72] (PCA), making it a powerful pre-processing tool.

A statistical measure for 'information content' in a decorrelated variable is the magnitude of its variance, this property reflects the extent to which the variable is active over all the input vectors. For example, at the inactive extreme, a decorrelated variable with zero variance will be a constant throughout the new input vectors, and will therefore have no useful influence on predicting the target, a ripe candidate for discarding and therefore resulting in a dimension reduction.

The new set of variables that result from a PCA analysis are known as principal components; component being another term for variable, or element, in the vector. A number of points remain concerning the use of principal components. Although engineers have their own equivalent technique to PCA (Karhunen-Loèv transform and Hotelling transform), it is traditionally a statistician's tool. As such the literature almost universally takes a zero-mean transform of the variables (normalising by an additive constant $-\Sigma_i p_i^j$), in order to calculate variances, and often further standardisation is performed by normalising with the standard deviation. This approach permits further theoretical statistical analysis on the principal components. It should be mentioned, however, that these steps are not preliminary requirements to perform PCA, it can be performed on nonuniform mean and variance variables (nonstandard variables), using other normalisation schemes or none at all.

There will be advantage in normalising the variables prior to PCA if an input vector comprises data from a variety of sources, and with widely differing ranges. This is best left for consideration in individual cases. Whichever the approach taken, the resulting principal components will not be normalised, in the sense of having uniform ranges, in fact the tail end components will generally be very small. However, the decorrelation property sufficiently makes up for this deficiency.

It is possible to normalise the principal components without corrupting the decorrelation property[7]. This is achieved by using the *along norm 0-offset* method, since it is the offset that would otherwise destroy decorrelation. There is another advantage in performing this type of normalisation on principal components. The backpropagation algorithm, using gradient descent methods, is affected by a property of the input variables, known as their spectral condition number (or more properly the spectral condition number of the input correlation matrix). The *along norm 0-offset* normalisation has the additional effect of improving the spectral condition number[7].

The PCA analysis will produce an 'eigenvector' matrix which will need to be preserved for transforming any new input vectors into the principal component vector space. This matrix can also be combined with the normalisation matrix so that all new vectors undergo just one matrix product.

Finally, to summarise the data compression aspect of PCA, the principal components that result from this preprocessing, have had distilled into the first few components (often only these are referred to as the principal components in the statistics literature) most of the information content in the original data, as previously spread throughout the original components. Thus the tail-end group of principal components may be discarded. The order of the components is established by a property that arises from the analysis, known as their 'eigenvalue'. The *principal* components have the highest eigenvalues. See Chapter 8 for details of statistics software packages with PCA options.

3.5.3 The Wavelet Transform

The wavelet transform has caused excitement in the mathematics and signal processing communities in recent times[167]. Whilst research in time-frequency analysis of nonstationary nonlinear signals has been an ongoing pursuit, the discovery by a number of researchers of classes of functions, known as wavelets, that serve as basis functions, has re-awakened interest in the subject[134]. (Basis functions are fundamental building blocks which, when combined, completely represent any arbitrary signal).

Given a set of neural network input vectors of some dimension d, the principal component analysis above rotated the cartesian axes in the multidimensional input domain-space, such that the new variables would be orthogonal. The eigenvectors formed the new basis vectors for the rotated space. Similarly a wavelet transform provides a new representation of the data, with wavelets forming the basis vectors, although wavelets need not be orthogonal. A key feature of the wavelet transform is that for a time series that is invariant to a time shift, $t \rightarrow t - t_0$, and/or scale change, $t \rightarrow at$, the wavelet transform is the same.

The coefficients of the wavelet transform correspond to various degrees of detail in the original data, thus by utilising a subset of these coefficients a means of data compression is obtained. The transform coefficients have a one-to-one correspondence to the original data vectors (i.e. there will be d coefficients) and are equivalent in this sense to the spectra of a Fourier analysis. Thus, as in Fourier analysis where a small set of spectral components may describe the important features that occur in the time domain, a subset of wavelet coefficients may also provide the key signature to the nonstationary nonlinear data.

One particular feature of interest is in those wavelets that possess compact support. The Fourier transform utilises sinusoidal basis functions which start at an infinite past and extend to an infinite future. A localised basis function is said to have compact support, i.e. it is nonzero only over a finite range of the function.

This property allows representation of the original signal in both frequency and time, thus the transform coefficients are two-dimensional.

Whilst all permissible wavelets can be recomposed to form the original signal exactly (the inverse transform), some are better approximations than others when truncation is exploited for data compression. The compression possibility is a consequence of the sparseness of the coefficients in the transformed domain. Different wavelets trade-off localisation properties to smoothness in the recomposition of the time series: compact wavelets better represent discontinuous time series, while noncompact, and hence smooth, wavelets provide higher numerical representation accuracy. Further aspects of the wavelet transform are discussed in Section 3.8. See Chapter 8 for details of software packages with wavelet transform features.

3.6 DECORRELATION

In the section on principal component analysis, it was pointed out that the method decorrelates the input variables. The resultant decorrelated variables are distinct from each other, representing the most unique attributes of the input data, as compared with any information that is common amongst all the original input variables.

Another term for decorrelation is orthogonalisation. If one considers the 3D cartesian system (x, y, z), each axis is mutually at $90°$. An arbitrary input vector set will not in general have the axes of the vectors orthogonal to each other. Decorrelation of the vectors will result in the orthogonality condition being satisfied for all the input variables.

Apart from PCA, there are direct orthogonalisation methods possible, such as the Gram-Schmidt method. An interesting development by Orfanidis[121] has been the insertion of an adaptive Gram-Schmidt preprocessor at each layer of an MLP, with consequent improved training performance reported.

3.7 NOISE FILTERING

The autoassociator network can also be used for smoothing a time series by filtering out noise which has a random origin[82]. In this application, the degree of smoothing is controlled by the dimension reduction factor. The training is performed as outlined in Section 3.5.1. Some experimentation will be required in selecting suitable transfer functions, Klimasauskas[82] recommends using sine functions.

On completion of training, the network is used in recall mode as follows; the time series is fed sequentially through the input layer and the *last* neuron in the output layer is monitored. The redundant output neurons are stripped away and the weights fixed for subsequent application. As the time series slides through the input, the selected output neuron will produce a filtered time series. The filtered series can subsequently be used in place of the raw data.

Finally, note that a forecasting network also performs a noise filtering function, however the use of the autoassociator as a preprocessing stage provides an initial smoothing function.

3.8   SPECTRAL ANALYSIS FOR NONSTATIONARY SIGNALS

This section introduces important new developments in signal processing that have a bearing on time series analysis and signal detection. Taking a preprocessing viewpoint, any type of mathematical transform of the original time series that suppresses noise and highlights the onset of deterministic patterns, is an important consideration. Taking the transform of a rolling window on the time series, provides a unique signature that may be used to train the network in place of, or in conjunction with, the original input vectors. The new developments concern the analysis of real-world signals, that contain nonstationary, or time-varying signals.

In one sense nonstationarity is known to occur in constructed futures time series, due to the finite lifetime of a contract; new contracts are typically launched every three months. The discontinuous nature of futures prices are often resolved by concatenation of contract life histories; for example the time series of the nearest active futures contract for a given roll-over date (see Section 7.2). The resultant periodic imprint on the series, of the life-birth cycle of the contract, is a nonstationary feature, however the cause and timing is known in advance.

The type of nonstationarity that is of most interest concerns the search for an underlying cause for prices to rise and fall. A herd-like behaviour amongst market traders to leap onto a fast rising bull market with buy orders and sell during a plunging bear market, may be revealed as a nonstationary deterministic process. The onset of these tendencies may occur at irregular times, but distinct market price patterns may trigger such mass behaviour by traders. There can be much speculation on underlying *hidden* causes for market moves, but if they exist it can be assumed that they will have a nonstationary nature. Techniques for analysing nonstationary signals are therefore quite relevant for financial time series.

A traditional approach to spectral analysis is to assume that the time series can be composed of sinusoidal signals of varying frequency and amplitude, known as Fourier analysis. This involves representing the original time-domain series in the frequency-domain, providing a global view of the series' spectrum, or frequency components. Knowledge of the frequency components provides a means of estimating where in the cycle the present time series has reached, with important consequences for predicting future behaviour. Thus a Fourier spectrum indicates the frequencies, and their strengths, inherent in a time series. However this assumes the signal, or signals, to be stationary. For a general nonstationary time series the Fourier transform provides no information on the time localisation of spectral components, rather the frequency spectrum would reveal wide band features characteristic of noise. A single abrupt change in the time series would, for example, affect all the components of the frequency spectrum. A transform designed for stationary signals cannot resolve features of a nonstationary signal.

Consider the simplest nonstationary example, where a signal has a constant frequency up to time t_0, and thereafter shifts to a lower frequency. A transform that can analyse a time series and produce a graphical representation of the time-frequency behaviour for ready interpretation would be very useful. A whole class of time-frequency transforms have in fact been developed, from within a number of disciplines, and there is a strong unifying trend in current research to harmonise this diverse body of results[66,134].

The concept of instantaneous frequency (IF) was introduced to provide a one-dimensional time dependent frequency $\hat{f}(t)$, see Boashash[20]. However for general signals the IF averages different spectral components in time. A more accurate approach exploits a two-dimensional representation of the time series in a combined time-frequency domain. A time-frequency representation is akin to a musical score, which in a 3D graph would have a surface indicating which spectral components are present at which time.

There are two important classes of time-frequency transforms (TFTs), those with a linear dependence on the original signal and those with a square dependence. Linear TFTs have the advantage of satisfying the superposition principle. That is, in decomposing a time series into two separate series, taking the linear TFT of each and combining the results is equivalent to taking the linear TFT of the original. The two most important such linear TFTs are the short-time Fourier transform (STFT) and the wavelet transform (WT), introduced in Section 3.5.3. In practice, the main difference between these transforms is that while the STFT time-frequency resolution is the same for each frequency analysed, the WT analyses higher frequencies with better time resolution but poorer frequency resolution. At very high frequencies the WT time resolution surpasses the STFT time resolution. At very low frequencies the WT frequency resolution surpasses the STFT frequency resolution. Neither transform can simultaneously achieve arbitrarily good resolution of time resolution and frequency resolution, a manifestation of Heisenberg's uncertainty principle: $\Delta t \Delta f \geq 1/4\pi$.

Quadratic TFTs are also highly versatile transforms and are appropriate for signals which represent the energy of an underlying source. The Wigner Distribution transform is one such widely used example. The best TFT to apply for a given problem often depends on some knowledge of the time series and fine tuning of the transform parameters. In analysing general, real-world, time series with time-varying signals, these transforms are powerful tools for suppressing noise and detecting the onset of deterministic signals.

Whilst spectral analysis of nonlinear nonstationary time series may be the most relevant to financial markets, there may still be interest in spectral techniques more appropriate for nonlinear stationary time series. This is justified by applying the analysis to a rolling data window on the whole time series. The data in each window may then be considered as locally stationary, with spectral variations tracked from window to window and thus providing a global nonstationary analysis.

In this vein, alternative approaches to Fourier analysis exist, such as fast orthogonal search techniques. Whilst the Fourier expansion of a signal involves the breakdown of the series into a superposition of harmonic sinusoidal signals, alternative nonharmonic sinusoidal expansions are also possible, such as parsimonious sinusoidal series. Such techniques offer superior frequency resolution to conventional Fourier series analysis and are applicable to highly nonlinear stationary time series. See Korenberg[88] for more details.

Finally, a note of warning regarding spectral preprocessing of data that has *already been preprocessed*, for example by moving averages. Any processing step applied to the raw data is equivalent to applying a filtering operation. Subsequent further spectral processing will combine spectral features of not only the processed data, but also characteristics of the filter. An example of how such filter features were mistakenly attributed to the time series is reported in Howrey[67], where a moving average operation, which acts as a low pass filter by smoothing short-term high-frequency fluctuations, created low-frequency cycles in the spectral features of an economic time series. Since the filtering operation is known, its features can be accounted for in the final analysis and removed before presenting to the neural network[17,67].

Marple[103] also warns against the dangers of performing de-trending and zero-mean preprocessing prior to spectral power density evaluation, and illustrated this with the example of artifacts entering the spectrum as a result. Marple suggests that sample mean and trends should only be removed in cases where they are clearly dominant or expected for physical reasons, and advises against the practice for transient signals.

4
Designing the Neural Network

The design stage of working with neural networks involves a number of aspects: designing the network structure, selecting neuron transfer functions, selecting a method for updating the weights and selecting a training cessation scheme. The sections in this chapter explore in greater detail the choices available and the advantages and disadvantages associated with each choice. The final sections deal specifically with neural network design issues for forecasting applications.

4.1 TRAINING AND SAMPLING

The training set of input vectors should include representative samples of the possible range variables may assume. One method is to randomly select the training samples. In the case of the two-input XOR problem, only four possible cases exist, so the representation problem does not arise, since all the cases are used for training. In the case of financial time series, it is prudent to include training data that features typical market behaviour, including bull, bear and sideways moving markets.

The training vectors should be presented in a random order during each epoch in stochastic weight update schemes. This ensures that the sequence of input presentation does not affect the weight values. Note that for most problems, after presentation, a vector should be set aside so as not to be drawn again in the same epoch.

In certain cases where the problem contains distinct boundaries it may be advantageous to select a preponderance of training patterns that cover the boundary regions, in preference to other regions of the problem space. For classification problems involving multinode output layer neurons, where an uneven distribution of classes exists in the population of possible cases, and the distribution is known, then a strategy of representing the in-samples in accordance with this distribution may on occasion be a successful strategy.

It is advisable to re-train networks a number of times using different random weight initialisations, in order to ensure that the network solution has not been trapped in a local minimum. This is the reason for repeating each benchmark problem 10 times in Chapter 6, using different weight initialisations each time.

The question of selecting suitable input vectors for time series is discussed further in Section 4.4.

4.2 COST FUNCTIONS

The backpropagation method is a technique for adjusting network weights in order to minimise a global parameter of the neural network, known as the cost, or energy, function. The cost function should be chosen so as to best represent the particular problem to be solved, since the functions emphasise different aspects of the training data. Naturally the function should be based on the error term, since ultimately the aim is to minimise the error. However, there are a number of ways to measure the error.

The most common cost function is the half sum of square errors, since it tends to lead to the most rapid training. However this quadratic function is highly sensitive to outliers in the training target data, which in real-world problems may be due to errors in measurement, and which are therefore best ignored.

The following list of cost functions discusses the chief merits of each approach, and also gives the derivative for inserting into the backpropagation algorithm. The global cost function, E^{tot}, is the summation over an epoch of patterns μ and over all the output layer neurons o, of the cost function kernel E:

$$E^{tot} = \sum_{\mu} \sum_{o} E \tag{4.1}$$

1. *Quadratic:* The most commonly used cost function is a square of the error term, (the one half factor is introduced for convenience, as it simplifies the derivative). This results in equal significance attached to all errors in updating weights, including the outlier errors. This function is also sometimes called the *Euclidean* energy function.

$$E = \frac{1}{2}(T - O)^2 \tag{4.2}$$

$$\frac{\partial E}{\partial O} = -(T - O) \tag{4.3}$$

2. *Absolute:*

$$E = |T - O| \tag{4.4}$$

$$\frac{\partial E}{\partial O} = -sgn(T - O) \tag{4.5}$$

The absolute cost function is the least sensitive to the extremes in the distribution of the target data, usually associated with noise.

3. *Non-Euclidean:* A generalisation of the square-error, or quadratic, cost function[151].

$$E = \frac{|T - O|^p}{p} \tag{4.6}$$

$$\frac{\partial E}{\partial O} = -\frac{|T - O|^p}{T - O} \tag{4.7}$$

where $1 \le p \le 2$

The effect of p is to control the sensitivity of the cost function to outliers in the training target data. $p = 2$ is very sensitive (quadratic error), whilst $p = 1$ (absolute error) is least sensitive.

4. *Cross-Entropy* $[-1,1]$: This version of the cross-entropy cost function is suitable for output neuron transfer functions with range $[-1,1]$.

$$E = \frac{1}{2}(1 + T) \ln \left[\frac{1 + T}{1 + O} \right] + \frac{1}{2}(1 - T) \ln \left[\frac{1 - T}{1 - O} \right] \tag{4.8}$$

$$\frac{\partial E}{\partial O} = \frac{O - T}{1 - O^2} \tag{4.9}$$

Cross-entropy is suitable for probability, or binary decision type problems, with targets trained on $T = 1$ for true and $T = -1$ for false, with $(1 + T)/2$ interpreted as the binary term. Similarly for output layer neuron output O, with $(1 + O)/2$ interpreted as the binary output.

5. *Cross-Entropy* $[0,1]$: This version of the cross-entropy cost function is suitable for output neuron transfer functions with range $[0,1]$, for example sigmoid. The cost function is defined as follows.

$$E = T \ln O + (1 - T) \ln(1 - O) \tag{4.10}$$

$$\frac{\partial E}{\partial O} = \frac{T - O}{(1 - O)O} \tag{4.11}$$

4.3 CONVERGENCE METRICS

A criterion needs to be chosen for determining the point at which the neural network provides a satisfactory performance and training should be ceased. The most common method is to measure the performance of the training data as a function of its error, and then set a tolerance level below which the network is considered to be sufficiently well trained.

Various measures may be selected depending on the nature of the problem, the merits of each method are discussed in the following. Note that the choice of error monitoring is quite independent of the choice of cost function to be minimised. Thus it is permissible, for example, to choose a cross-entropy cost function and monitor the normalised RMS error.

Some performance measures discussed here are designed for classification problems where the targets form distinct classes. In a general case with multinode output layers, the classes may be mutually exclusive, that is only one output high may be correct for any given target vector, in which case the threshold criterion needs to be augmented by a highest high, winner-takes-all rule. Conversely, targets with multiple high neurons need only be ruled by thresholds on a per neuron basis. The classification performance measures can then be applied to each output layer neuron separately.

Classification problems should be couched in terms of a binary class problem whenever possible; this choice is preferable in simplifying the network structure in accord with the complexity criterion, covered in Section 4.5. Furthermore, a mutually-exclusive binary problem (i.e. either one case or the other is true, but not both at the same time) is best modelled by a single neuron, with the extreme ends of the output range representing the classes, rather than with two neurons, one for each class. Again this is based on complexity arguments.

In the case of time series, it is often the case that what is required is a prediction of the movement of the series rather than a precise forecast of the next element in the series. Such a problem can than be described by a mutually exclusive binary class problem, with an output layer neuron high representing a rise in the series, with respect to the most recent element in the time series, and an output low representing a fall in the time series.

Note that there can be a discrepancy in the value of the error as measured during, or on completion of, the training process, and the subsequent value measured when presenting one epoch of the training set in recall mode. The problem can occur when the method chosen for updating the weights in the network is performed at the end of each forward cycle, stochastic updating, or after n cycles, where n is less than the epoch size. In such a case the network is continually changing during an epoch and the accumulated errors no longer correspond to the same network. The difference in the errors is usually slight, if at all noticeable, for a converged network. Particularly for RMS error measures, a small difference will be inevitable for this choice of weight updating. However, a large discrepancy, where the post-training training data error measure is much higher than the tolerance level, is a useful indication that the network is unstable and has not properly converged.

4.3.1 Percentage Accuracy

The most straightforward method of keeping a network accuracy score is to tally the performance on a hit or miss basis. For binary problems, such as the XOR function task, a threshold for the output neuron is set, for which output values above the threshold constitute a 1, and values below the threshold a 0. A threshold value of 0.5 is thus suitable — threshold is further discussed below.

In the case of time series problems where the task is to predict whether the next item in the series is above or below the last item, a tally of the trend accuracy can be kept. For a target time series $p_t : t = 1, 2, \ldots$, and observed network output series O_t, a trend may be evaluated as a 'sign of argument' function T_R:

$$T_R = sgn\{(p_t - p_{t-1})(O_t - O_{t-1})\} \qquad (4.12)$$

T_R will be negative for an incorrect prediction and positive for a correct prediction, unless either the network prediction or the target make a perfect sideways movement, in which case T_R will be zero.

A further refinement is to keep separate scores of the trend accuracy for up and down movements, giving three figures of merit: an overall percentage, a percentage of correctly predicted up movements, and a percentage of correctly predicted down movements.

An alternative to percentage figures are direct classification error rates, defined as the ratio of number of errors to the number of cases for the different types of errors, see Section 4.3.4 where classification errors are treated in detail.

One pitfall to avoid in time series forecasting, is to rely solely on PA measures without consideration of the timing quality. Thus accurate predictions of large movements in the time series result in large payoff ratios, the need to correctly predict all the smaller movements is therefore diminished. In fact an accurate quality timing system yielding a payoff ratio of two (correct forecasts are twice as large, on average, as incorrect forecast movements) may be profitably exploited in market trading with PA down to 33.4%. This is discussed further in Chapter 7.

4.3.2   Mean Square Error

The most commonly used criterion for convergence makes use of the quadratic error measure. A number of variants may be used.

$$\varepsilon_{ms} = \frac{\sum\limits_{\mu}\sum\limits_{o}(T - O)^2}{N_o N_e} \qquad (4.13)$$

where N_e is the number of training vectors in an epoch, and N_o is the number of output neurons. Taking the square root gives the RMS error, which has the same dimension as the output error $(T - O)$.

$$\varepsilon_{rms} = \sqrt{\varepsilon_{ms}} \qquad (4.14)$$

A meaningful refinement is to divide ε_{ms} by the variance of the target data, since this gauges the extent to which the error differs from using the mean target value for each observed output neuron, and also removes any dependence on the range of the target data (useful when comparing results from different training sets). The variance can be calculated over the complete data field, combining both training and test data for this purpose, although it is often more convenient to calculate these separately for each set. The square root may also be taken, where the standard deviation is

$$\sigma = \sqrt{\frac{\sum\limits_{\mu}\sum\limits_{o}(T - \bar{T})^2}{N_e N_o}} \qquad (4.15)$$

$$\varepsilon_{rms} = \frac{\sqrt{\varepsilon_{ms}}}{\sigma} \qquad (4.16)$$

this measure is known as the relative or normalised RMS error.

4.3.3 Threshold Error

The threshold error monitor is introduced for targets that take on fixed discrete values, such as binary classifications of 0 and 1, or -1 and 1. In many cases a single threshold suffices for demarcating between either extreme classes. However, a couple of variations are also worth considering.

One can set two thresholds, giving a tighter criterion for a correct hit, such as 0.6 for the high end and 0.4 for the low end of a [0,1] binary classification.

The single or dual threshold method is monitored by the percentage accuracy. An alternative method uses an RMS error as monitor, accumulating the error only for those output layer neurons that are on the *wrong* side of the threshold, measuring the error as the difference between the observed output and the *threshold* value, rather than the target. Again either a single or dual threshold may be implemented.

4.3.4 Contingency Tables

The error rate in classification problems can be more distinctly categorised into the different types of errors. Tables that display these errors are variously termed confusion matrices, contingency tables, and classification tables. For problems involving a large number of classes, tabulating the error rates of observed classes against the target classes, reveals characteristics of the neural network that an RMS error measure alone does not. Each output layer neuron is characterised by its own classification table.

In the case of a mutually exclusive binary classification, since many problems fall into this category, the individual entries in the table have been given distinct names, shown in Table 4.1. Note that $N_+ = TP + FN$, $N_- = FP + TN$, $O_+ = TP + FP$

Table 4.1   Binary classification error rate table

	Target Positive (N_+)	Target negative (N_-)
Observed Positive (O_+)	True Positive (TP)	False Positive (FP)
Observed Negative (O_-)	False Negative (FN)	True Negative (TN)

and $O_- = FN + TN$. The total number of cases is given by $N = N_- + N_+ = O_- + O_+$. The results from Table 4.1 are commonly presented in terms of statistical ratios:

1.   Sensitivity $= TP/N_+$. Also known as the True Positive or Precision rate.
2.   Specificity $= TN/N_-$. Also known as the True Negative ratio.
3.   False Alarm $= 1 -$ Specificity. Also known as the False Positive ratio.
4.   Positive Prediction $= TP/O_+$. Also known as the Recall rate.
5.   Negative Prediction $= TN/O_-$.
6.   Accuracy $= (TP + TN)/(N_+ + N_-)$.
7.   Total Error $= 1 -$ Accuracy.

A plot of the Sensitivity ratio against the False Alarm rate is known as a ROC curve[43], for Receiver (or Relative) Operating Characteristic. For a given network training strategy these ratios are plotted for a range of threshold values, one ROC curve for each output layer neuron. A typical ROC curve is schematically shown in Figure 4.1.

The ROC curve is an accuracy performance measure that permits comparison with a perfect score and has the advantage of being insensitive to the probability distribution of the classes in the training and test sets. A minimum of about 5 to 9 points are required for a reasonably smooth curve. The central diagonal in the graph defines the worst possible case, for which the neural network shows no discrimination capability. This corresponds to a random network performance $TP = FN = FP = TN = N/2$, resulting in Sensitivity equalling False Alarm rate. Perfect discrimination ability is characterised by the ROC curve collapsing to the point $(0,1)$, which is obtained for $FN = FP = 0$ and hence Sensitivity equals 1 and False Alarm rate equals 0. Note that perfect non-discrimination, $TP = TN = 0$, can be converted into perfect discrimination by swapping the definitions of O_- and O_+, i.e. simply reinterpreting the network outputs. Therefore, with the optimum labelling of the network outputs, the curves will always lie within the top half region above the diagonal. A ROC curve enables the characteristics of a network to be gauged for varying output decision threshold levels. Plotting a number of ROC curves for different network parameter settings facilitates performance comparisons. A single parameter equivalent for the curve may be quoted, by measuring the area under the ROC curve[108]; a perfect score will have area 1 (the ROC curve is considered in the limit to lie along the left vertical and upper horizontal axes), the worst score will have area 0.5.

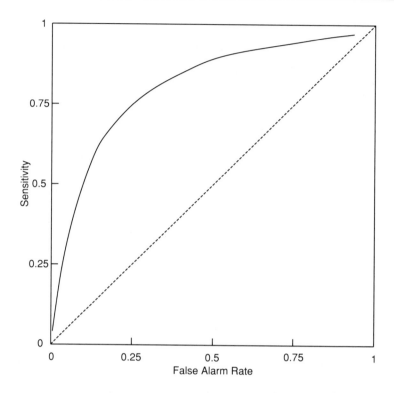

Figure 4.1   Relative Operating Characteristic (ROC) curve example. Diagonal shows worst possible case, ROC curves thus appear above the diagonal. *Sensitivity* is also known as the *True Positive* rate, and *False Alarm* rate as the *False Positive* rate

4.3.5   Correlation

A useful indication of the convergence of a neural network is the monitoring of the correlation between the target and observed output layer values over each epoch during the training. For each output layer neuron, the linear correlation coefficient, also known as Pearson's correlation, measures the strength of linear association between two variables, here the target and observed values, and is defined as follows:

$$
r = \frac{\displaystyle\sum_{\mu=1}^{N_e} T_\mu O_\mu - N_e \overline{T}\,\overline{O}}{\sqrt{\left(\displaystyle\sum_{\mu=1}^{N_e} O_\mu^2 - N_e \overline{O}^2\right)\left(\displaystyle\sum_{\mu=1}^{N_e} T_\mu - N_e \overline{T}^2\right)}}
\tag{4.17}
$$

where N_e is the epoch size (total number of training vectors), $\overline{O}$ is the average observed output over the epoch, and $\overline{T}$ the average target value.

The coefficient r will lie in the range $[-1,1]$. A small value, near 0, implies no association (observed outputs are random), a large absolute value implies a strong association; with a positive sign indicating the best agreement and a negative correlation indicating antithetical behaviour. Note that a neural network performance with a tendency towards strong negative correlation can be corrected by reverse labelling the network output.

The significance level for correlation, either side of 0, is given by

$$1 - erf \left(\frac{|r| \sqrt{N_e}}{\sqrt{2}} \right) \tag{4.18}$$

where a small value for this quantity implies significant correlation. erf is the error function, available in statistics tables[1] or evaluated numerically[128], (see Section 4.6 for a definition).

An alternative evaluation of r in terms of standard deviations will involve less computation, if these quantities are evaluated separately for use in normalising the RMS error metric and are thence already available for r.

$$r = \frac{\sum_{i=1}^{N_e} T_i O_i - N_e \overline{T} \, \overline{O}}{\sqrt{N_e \sigma_O \sigma_T}} \tag{4.19}$$

where σ_O and σ_T are the observed and target standard deviations respectively.

The factor of N_e implies a population correlation coefficient, since the correlation is over the training set only. The standard deviations should likewise be population space measures. However, in the RMS error normalisation the standard deviations should be sample space calculations, with a factor of $N_e - 1$: these are pedantic points, N_e should be large enough for these subtleties not to matter!

4.4 GENERALISATION AND TESTING

So far measuring the error of the network has been discussed on the basis of training set performance, such a measure is known as the *apparent* error. The *true* error, however, must take into account the generalisation performance of the network, that is, the error for input data new to the network and not used in the training. For finite space problems, such as the XOR logical function, where all possible permutations of the input data are known and finite to within a practical size, this question of generalisation does not arise, since the complete set of possible inputs are all used for training.

However, in the case of analogue inputs, where an input node may range over the real numbers, the training set represents only a sample of possible inputs. The problem can then arise of overtraining the network on the limited sample space of the training set, fitting the noise in the data for example. The generalisation performance of the network should therefore be measured by the use of either a validation data set or a test set.

A validation data set is a set of input vectors set aside specifically for measuring the error of the network during the training phase, but not used in the actual training set. The performance of the network is therefore gauged according to independent samples and provides a useful criterion for determining the iteration at which training should cease. The generalisation performance of the network is then measured against a third set, the test set. In cases where the sample size is limited, the validation set may be bypassed, and the training error used to determine the training stop criterion. However, the generalisation capability of the network should always be measured against a test set not used in the training of the network.

Experiments in particular cases will reveal at which point to set the tolerance level for the training phase error monitor, one which gives the optimum test set performance. A general characteristic of the test set error is of a U shaped curve; initially error decreases leading to a saturation level, beyond which the error rises as the network is being overtrained. Having established a suitable tolerance level, it should then remain fixed for the duration of the series of train and test trials recommended in the section on re-sampling. This avoids the danger of an indirect use of test set data in structuring the network.

4.4.1 The True Error

A general guide for the magnitude of the test set error is that it will be typically twice the training set error. The question arises, however, of how well the test set error is a correct measure of the true generalisation error of the network for the problem, measured over all possible samples — not just those available for the training and testing.

An unbiased estimate of the true error is best achieved by a re-sampling technique, discussed below, with the number of test set samples in the region of 1000 and upwards. This conclusion is based on statistical arguments[172]. Despite the precaution of using independent train and test sets, the size of the test set is important and, even with re-sampling, will tend to be on the optimistic side for less than 1000 samples.

The deviation of the measured test error rate $\hat{p}$, for N samples, from the true error is measured by the standard error statistic[117]

$$\sigma_{\hat{p}} = \sqrt{\frac{p(1-p)}{N}} \tag{4.20}$$

where p is the *true* error rate. An estimate for $\sigma_{\hat{p}}$ is possible by substituting the measured test error rate in place of the (unknown) true error.

For data limited problems, the accuracy of the generalisation error becomes a particularly acute concern, and the best recourse is the adoption of a re-sampling technique designed for small samples.

4.4.2 Re-sampling Techniques

Where the availability of data is plentiful, a suitable training method is the *holdout* method, whereby the sample data is split two thirds, one third for train and test sets respectively, with ideally upwards of 1000 samples used in the test set, 5000 test samples providing a safe unbiased estimate without the need for re-sampling. The minimum number of samples required for the train set is dictated by the number of free parameters in the neural network, this will be the number of weights and is discussed in Section 4.5.

In many real-world problems, availability of samples will be restricted, so re-sampling becomes essential. In the case of the holdout method, one approach is to ensure that every sample takes its turn as a test sample, with the train and test procedure repeated N_H times, where $N_H = Total\ Sample\ Size/Test\ Size$. Another approach is to randomly select the candidates for the train and test sets afresh with each new trial, for N_H, or more, trials. This approach is also known as random subsampling. In all re-sampling techniques, the final generalisation error is obtained by averaging the test error over all the repeated train/test trials.

The case of highly limited sample sizes, e.g. 100, has been the focus of recent research, with approaches based on re-sampling, concluding that cross-validation techniques provide the best error estimates. One such being the leave-one-out method: Training is performed on all but one of the available samples, with the isolated vector forming a single member test set. The procedure is repeated with each vector taking its turn as the test vector. Although this method tends to be expensive in computation time for large sample sizes, it provides a virtually unbiased estimate of the performance, and is the best recourse for limited data. Further examples of cross-validation techniques can be found in the literature, see the review by Weiss and Kulikowski[172] and also references 41, 44.

In the final analysis, only a large test set sample size can mitigate the effects of bias in estimating the true error. The question of sufficient data is a key issue and should be uppermost in consideration where a choice of forecasting problems exists, and should guide the forecaster to select problems where data is plentiful so that (i) forecasting performance measures are thence realistic estimates of the neural network capability, and (ii) the neural network structure size is not limited by the train set size and is sufficient to produce a solution.

4.4.3 Time Series

The question of sampling the data for the provision of training and test sets in the case of time series, poses new questions due to the temporal nature of the problem.

A unanimous approach taken in the literature is to choose the training vectors from within a fixed period of the series, and group the remaining vectors into two test sets, an early and a recent period. Often, particularly where the available sample size is limited, the use of an early period test set is dispensed with.

Whilst the random selection of training vectors from the available time series is also a valid approach, the former method allows for a testing technique that reflects the practical utilisation of the network in actual forecasting problems. This method is known as testing by *auto-single-stepping*. In order to provide a forecast for the next element in a time series, all the most recent data will be used in real-world circumstances, and so auto-single-stepping reflects this by training the network with all the vectors available over some period.

With training converged to within an acceptable error measure, the auto-single-stepping test procedure is as follows. A test is performed on the first vector, in a temporal sense, in the test set and the error measured. This vector is now added to the training set and the network re-trained. This procedure is repeated for each vector in the test set, single-stepping temporally through the set and accumulating the error scores. This procedure should be repeated for a number of training set periods, if possible, to eliminate error bias. For time series of limited length, where only one training and test set is available for the single-stepping exercise, it may well be preferable not to use the technique in place of the other methods discussed.

Another variant of single-stepping encountered in the literature is *iterated-single-stepping*. In this case no re-training is performed, as the existing network weights are used to provide a forward time series of forecasts, by processing each forecast into a new input vector and using this to produce a forecast for the next item in the series. The series of forecasts are then compared with the test set time series for a performance measure. This approach provides a good indication of the longevity of a trained network. Again, the procedure should be repeated over a number of training set time series periods. However, unless the network will be used in this manner in practice, to provide long range forecasts, the iterated technique is not a preferred test procedure.

Due to the continual re-training required, the auto-single-stepping method is computationally expensive, simply *single-stepping* usually suffices for most applications, and is used here in the benchmarking. This involves one time unit ahead forecasting through each of the test set vectors (for example, as set aside in the holdout method), without re-training.

In selecting the appropriate technique for measuring the performance of the network, bear in mind the practical use of the network. For applications where the network will be continually re-trained in preparation for each forecast, auto-single-stepping is the appropriate measure. However, if a pre-trained network is utilised for five consecutive forecasts, such as a week's daily forecasts with re-training over the weekend, then a five-fold single-stepping holdout method is the right choice, with re-training performed after every five forecasts.

4.5   NETWORK STRUCTURE AND COMPLEXITY

The procedure for designing the neural network structure can be subdivided into three distinct stages: input layer, hidden region, and output layer. Before discussing each of these stages, there is one global design criterion that should be mentioned first, and this concerns complexity.

Given two networks which produce the same performance figures over the *test* set, the natural choice under the complexity criterion is to choose the simpler network, the one with fewer free parameters. This is an application of Occam's Razor principle, and is guided by the fact that for a given performance level, the smaller network will be the superior generaliser. The fewer weights in the network, the greater the confidence that over-training has not resulted in noise being fitted.

This principle becomes obvious if an extreme case is considered where the number of weights in the network is greater than the number of training examples. Then there are enough weights available for the network to perfectly learn each input vector's target requirements, resulting in near perfect training performance. However since the training process has not forced the weights to extract meaningful data, the presentation of new input vectors will result in random outputs.

It is thus quite common to train complex networks to superior performance levels compared to simpler nets. However, the reverse in performance will occur for the corresponding test sets. Striking a balance between training performance and network complexity is a key issue in network design, whose ultimate objective is optimum generalisation performance. A number of guidelines can be applied, and will be discussed below for the three design stages.

An automatic method for including a complexity criterion in the training process is naturally a possible approach. In this vein, an aspect of complexity that has received notable attention is the concept of minimum description length (MDL), see Rissanen[135]. The idea is to end up after training with a network that provides a minimal description of the input data, in the sense of the number of free parameters required to describe the network. In the context of neural networks, this concept can be applied by adding terms to the cost function that penalise network complexity. Thus, in addition to an error measure, a factor that counts the number of weights in the network would satisfy an MDL approach:

$$\text{cost function} = \text{error measure} + \text{number of weights}$$

Unless the training involves weight pruning, this particular additional factor will be a constant, so the explicit inclusion of the factor is unnecessary, rather the principle can be applied through the guidelines to be mentioned below. However, explicit inclusion of additional terms can be applied for factors that force a given set of weights to take on certain features that are in accord with MDL. An example of such a factor includes weight decay.

Weight decay encourages weights that play little part in the evolution of the network during training to take on small, near zero, values, thereby causing an effective decrease in the number of weights. These weights would otherwise become available for fitting noise during the latter stages of training and are therefore undesirable. Such terms are not without side-effects however, since a tendency to reduce justifiably large weights may occur. For further details of this and related methods, see reviews in Hertz[64] and Hush[70].

One caveat regarding complexity should be mentioned. Recent research has shown that some neural network problems display a symmetry breaking phenomenon, such that test set performance improves dramatically as the number of free parameters is *increased* to a specific level. Naturally if the number of free parameters is too small, then meaningful test set performance will not be obtained, but these research examples have been obtained for comparatively good training set performances. These exceptions, however, have been found for relatively small size networks, the difference of one or two extra weights in the network should not be construed as acting against the spirit of the complexity criterion — which is foremost a general guideline and not fine enough to distinguish between networks that vary only slightly in number of weights. The best course is to explore different network sizes in any particular application to discover whether symmetry breaking phenomenon exist, and test set performances being equal, select the minimum network size.

Turning now to general guidelines for the three design stages. Note that the terminology used here refers to the input as the first network layer, whereas it is also common to find in the literature that the first layer refers to the first hidden layer, or layers meant with reference to weight layers.

- *Input Layer:* Here design is largely dictated by considerations of which input variables are necessary for forecasting the target, since the number of variables in the input vector correspond to the number of input nodes. From the complexity viewpoint it would be desirable to reduce the number of input nodes to an absolute minimum of essential nodes. Preprocessing the input vectors by dimension reduction techniques (Section 3.5) is therefore worth considering.

- *Hidden Region:* The maximum number of layers in a network, and number of neurons therein, required to solve a general problem has received attention through mathematical studies with the objective of setting upper bounds on these design parameters. Lippmann's[96] review recommended that three layer networks, with just one hidden layer, were sufficient to solve arbitrarily complex input-output mappings, with typically at most three times as many hidden neurons as input nodes. Hecht-Nielsen[62] and Lippman[96] consider a theorem due to Kolmogorov which suggests a three layer net with $2N + 1$ hidden neurons, and with continuously increasing nonlinear neuron transfer functions, can compute any continuous input function of N variables (input nodes). This is still an active area of research[70,90]. Whether multiconnectivity is used or not, it is usually sufficient to have at most two hidden layers, and very often only one. The optimum number of neurons in the hidden layer(s) is highly problem dependent and a matter for experimentation. Note that some problems work well with a bottleneck structure, where there are fewer neurons in the hidden layer than nodes in the input layer.

Since these issues also determine the number of weights in the network, it should be borne in mind that an upper limit on the weight number is dictated by the number of training vectors available. A rough guideline, based on theoretical considerations of what is known as the Vapnik-Chervonenkis dimension[70], recommends that the number of training vectors should be ten times or more the number of weights. Where input data availability is not limited, then the main constraint on network size is a practical consideration of the time needed to train the network, since this grows disproportionately with network size. For data limited problems, breaking the one tenth weight number guideline can result in generalisation deficiencies.

These consideration have motivated research into MLP networks that start with a minimum structure and grow during training, by the insertion of extra neurons or layers. See references[64,70] for further details on a developing field, and also related, the ACE neuron, discussed in Section 4.7.

- *Output Layer:* The number of neurons in the output layer should be the minimum that satisfies the problem requirements. For time series forecasting it is unusual to need more than one neuron; it is sufficient for an absolute value, such as predicting series values, and is sufficient for predicting trends, by utilising the extremes of the output to represent the binary decision. On occasion it may be worthwhile investigating the use of additional neurons, such as one for absolute value and one for binary classification[169]. However, caution is warranted in selecting suitable targets, as there is a danger of backpropagating conflicting messages during the training.

  The choice of transfer function for the output neuron should also be made with consideration to the choice of target. Thus for absolute target values a linear or piece-wise linear transfer function is appropriate, particularly with a gradient less than 1 for increased sensitivity.

4.6 NEURON TRANSFER FUNCTIONS

The transfer function is the rule for mapping the neuron's summed input to its output, and, by suitable choice, is the means of introducing nonlinearity into the network design. A range of possible transfer functions may be utilised, the necessary condition being that they should be differentiable functions. In practice the functions are also chosen to be monotonic and to saturate at the two extremes of $[0,1]$ or $[-1,1]$. Exceptions are cyclical functions and Gaussian functions.

In general a network design may utilise a different transfer function for each neuron. The functions also have a free parameter, the gain, which needs to be heuristically set. A common strategy is to set a different gain level for each layer. See the benchmark chapter for examples.

The notation a will be used to denote the input to the function, representing $a = \Sigma wx$, the sum over all input lines of the product of weight and input line value, and the derivative of the function by f', where $f' = \partial O/\partial a$. The gain parameter, g, varies the slope of the transfer function.

- *Step-function:* Early research work in the field utilised step-functions. This function is more suited for binary class problems, that take on one of two possible values. The step function has zero derivative everywhere except at $a = 0$, where it is infinite, so it is not appropriate for the backpropagation method, which requires the transfer function to be differentiable. However, it can be well approximated by a number of transfer functions, including the sigmoid function, by setting a high gain.

- *Sigmoid:* The sigmoid function is a commonly used function which squashes the input value in the range $a \in [-\infty, +\infty]$ into an O output range $O \in [0, 1]$. The slope of the transition region depends on the gain, a large value will cause the sigmoid to resemble a step function. The sigmoid output can be shifted by the shift parameter S: $O \in [-S, 1-S]$, a value $S = 0.5$ will make the sigmoid symmetrical about the origin. The sigmoid, and its derivative, are defined as follows:

$$O = \frac{1}{1 + \exp(-ga)} - S \qquad (4.21)$$

$$f' = g(1 - S - O)(S + O) \qquad (4.22)$$

- *Tanh:* The tanh function resembles the shifted sigmoid, it is a squashing function symmetrical about the origin, with output range $[-S, S]$.

$$O = S \tanh(ga) \qquad (4.23)$$

$$f' = g \left(S - \frac{O^2}{S} \right) \qquad (4.24)$$

- *Piece-Wise Linear:* The piece-wise linear transfer function is defined by

$$\begin{aligned} \text{if} \quad &a > C \quad &\text{then } O &= LC \\ &< -C \quad &&= -LC \\ \text{else} \quad &&&= La \end{aligned}$$

where L is the gradient of the transition region, and the points on the abscissa $-C$ and C are symmetrical about the origin, at which the plateau regions extend to $-\infty$ and ∞ respectively. The derivative is given next.

$$\begin{aligned} \text{if} \quad &a > C \quad &\text{then } f' &= 0 \\ &< -C \quad &&= 0 \\ \text{else} \quad &&&= L \end{aligned}$$

- *Linear:* The linear transfer function is defined by $O = ga$ and has derivative $f' = g$. Usually $g = 1$ in this case.
- *Sine and Cosine:* The sinusoid transfer functions are defined by

$$\Theta = ga \bmod 2\pi \tag{4.25}$$

$$O = \sin \Theta \tag{4.26}$$

$$f' = g\sqrt{1 - O^2} \tag{4.27}$$

$$\Theta = ga \bmod 2\pi \tag{4.28}$$

$$O = \cos \Theta \tag{4.29}$$

$$f' = -g\sqrt{1 - O^2} \tag{4.30}$$

where mod is the modulo function which yields the remainder when the prior argument is divided by the post argument. Note that Θ is in radians.

A particular feature of the cosine function is that it has a maximum at $a = 0$, whereas squashing-type transfer functions are increasing monotonic with typically zero value at $a = 0$. Thus it is well suited for a network design using a combination of transfer functions.

- *Gaussian:* The Gaussian transfer function has a special role in Radial Basis function networks[70]. However, it may also be used in MLP networks in combination with other types of neurons. It shares the same feature as the cosine transfer function in having a maximum at $a = 0$, although this can be shifted by using a nonzero mean μ:

$$O = exp\left[\frac{-(ga - \mu)^2}{2\sigma^2}\right] \tag{4.31}$$

$$f' = -\frac{g(ga - \mu)}{\sigma^2}exp\left[\frac{-(ga - \mu)^2}{2\sigma^2}\right] \tag{4.32}$$

- *erf: Error Function:* The error function displays sigmoid transfer characteristics similar to the tanh function.

$$erf(z) = \frac{2}{\sqrt{\pi}}\int_0^z e^{-t^2} dt \tag{4.33}$$

$$O = erf(ga) \tag{4.34}$$

$$f' = \frac{2g}{\sqrt{\pi}}H_0(ga)e^{-(ga)^2} \tag{4.35}$$

where H_0 is the zeroth order Hermite polynomial. Subroutines for calculating *erf* may be found in Numerical Recipes[128].

- $x/(1 + |x|)$: This transfer function has no special name, it is another variety of a sigmoid characteristic:

$$O = \frac{ga}{1 + |ga|} \tag{4.36}$$

$$f' = \frac{g}{1 + |ga|} - \frac{|ga|}{(1 + |ga|)^2} \tag{4.37}$$

The sigmoid and linear transfer functions have been plotted in Figure 2.2, the above transfer functions are displayed in Figures 4.2 and 4.3, for varying gains $g = 0.25, 0.5, 1, 2$ and 4.

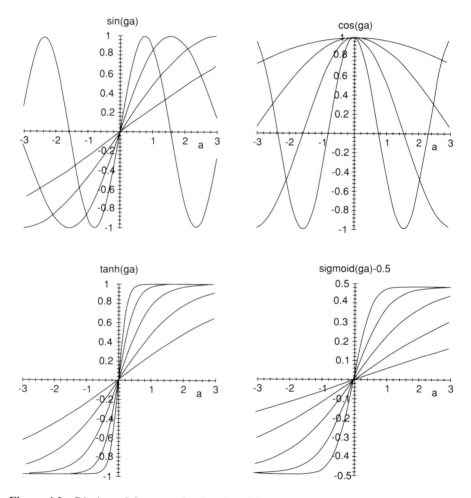

Figure 4.2   Display of four transfer functions: sin, cos, tanh and shifted sigmoid. Plots show varying gain g: 0.25, 0.5, 1, 2 for all functions, and a further $g = 4$ for tanh and sigmoid. Gentlest slope in all cases corresponds to $g = 0.25$

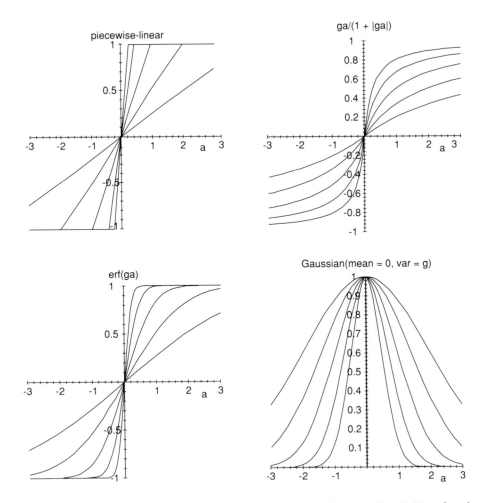

Figure 4.3 Display of four transfer functions: piece-wise linear, $x/(1 + |x|)$, *erf* and Gaussian. Plots show varying gain g: 0.25, 0.5, 1, 2, 4. Gentlest slope is 0.25

4.7 THE AUTOCORRELATED ERROR NEURON

The total time series forecasting error may be decomposed into noise and autocorrelation error. Random noise inherent in the data will result in random forecasting error and is best treated as a pre- or postprocessing filtering problem. However, any imperfect modelling of deterministic forces present in the data will result in non-random, structured forecast error, characterised by the error being autocorrelated:

$$\epsilon_t = T_t - O_t \qquad (4.38)$$

$$\epsilon_t = f(\epsilon_{t-1}, \epsilon_{t-2}, \epsilon_{t-3}, \ldots) \tag{4.39}$$

where ϵ_t is the error at time t, T is the target or actual series value, O is the observed network or model value, and f is a general nonlinear mapping function.

The presence of autocorrelation error implies that further development of the model may yield improved performance. One approach involves a growth or construction network, whereby neurons are added to the network in stages, see Hertz[64] for a review of the various proposed schemes. In many real-world problems with data limited conditions, minimal type networks form a constraint in order to keep the number of training patterns to weights ratio (TWR) high. As discussed in Section 4.13, it is recognised that for many complex problems a high TWR figure is essential to prevent over-training and produce good network generalisation. A growth-network method is discussed here that involves the addition of one neuron to the penultimate hidden layer of the network. This neuron is introduced in order to reduce model induced error, and is therefore named the autocorrelation error (ACE) neuron[8].

The ACE neuron is added to a trained network, as depicted in Figure 4.4. Stage one in the figure shows a three layered multiconnectivity MLP network, with cell structure 3-2-1. After training the ACE neuron is added to the penultimate hidden layer and multiconnected to all the preceding neurons (should they exist in multi-hidden layer networks) and the input nodes. Note that network designs utilising more than one output neuron can also be included: an ACE neuron is added for each output neuron, adjacent to the first ACE neuron, with the ACE neuron output linked exclusively to its corresponding output neuron. The weights linked to the ACE neuron, randomly initialised within a small range, are then trained in a second stage training procedure, with the first stage weights kept frozen, shown in stage two in Figure 4.4.

Let the training set RMS error for the first stage network be ε^j_{rms} for the jth output layer neuron, then the transfer function for the jth ACE neuron is a *tanh* function with saturating amplitude ε^j_{rms}. Whilst a unity amplitude tanh may also be used, the former provides smoother, dampened, characteristics. Training the ACE weights is rapid, often accomplished within 20 epochs. Thus the ACE transfer function is defined by

- *ACE tanh:* Output is symmetrical about the origin, with output range $[-\varepsilon_{rms}, \varepsilon_{rms}]$, the RMS error of the *converged* trained net in stage 1.

$$O = \varepsilon_{rms} \tanh(ga) \tag{4.40}$$

$$f' = g\left(\varepsilon_{rms} - \frac{O^2}{\varepsilon_{rms}}\right) \tag{4.41}$$

where g is the gain and a is the input to the transfer function as above.

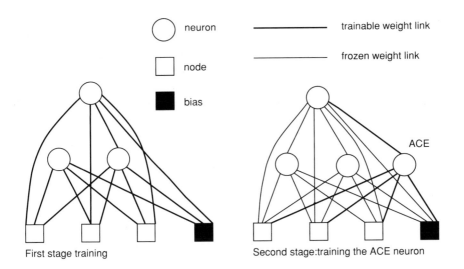

neuron   trainable weight link

node   frozen weight link

bias

ACE

First stage training   Second stage:training the ACE neuron

Figure 4.4   Training the ACE neuron. Stage 1: original network is trained. Stage 2: weights are frozen and the ACE neuron added to the penultimate hidden layer, and multiconnected (but only to one output neuron for multineuron output layer networks). Weights linking the ACE neuron are now trained

Experience with various neural network backpropagation training schemes has revealed that error reduction by the ACE neuron is more likely to be realised for the pre-ACE network (first stage) trained by the steepest descent method with stochastic weight updates per training pattern, (Appendix A discusses the various backpropagation methods). This observation holds irrespective of the backpropagation method used to train the ACE weights. When realised, the benefit of RMS error reduction for the expanded network is achieved for both training and test sets of data, and is in the region of a 10% improvement. See the benchmarks for examples of the ACE neuron.

4.8   THE LEARNING COEFFICIENT

Standard backpropagation with steepest descent minimisation of the cost function requires the specification of a learning coefficient. Although a momentum term is also often heuristically added to the weight update scheme, it is not advocated here for time series problems. More sophisticated minimisation schemes have the advantage of automatically selecting the optimum learning coefficient for each epoch, such as conjugate gradient methods, variable metric methods, and stiff ODE solvers[14,64,122,128].

In the case of backpropagation with steepest descent, continual adaptation of the learning coefficient during training is recommended. First initialise the network with separate learning coefficients, η_j, for each neuron layer, or each individual neuron. Also advised[64] is dividing η_j by the fan-in of the neuron (the number of neuron input lines).

Hertz et al[64] describes the following adaptation scheme. Monitor the change in cost function, $\Delta E(t) = E_t - E_{t-1}$, for each weight update cycle t. If E has decreased on average over several weight updates then it is safe to increase η by a small constant, a_1, otherwise decrease it geometrically (for a rapid decrease), with rate a_2:

$$
\begin{aligned}
\Delta\eta &= a_1 & \text{if} & \quad \Delta\overline{E}(t) < 0 \\
&= -a_2\eta & \text{if} & \quad \Delta E(t) > 0 \\
&= 0 & \text{otherwise} &
\end{aligned}
\tag{4.42}
$$

The averaging can be performed by exponential moving averages for example, with constants $b_1 = 0.9$ and $b_2 = 0.3$:

$$
\Delta\overline{E}(t) = b_1 \Delta\overline{E}(t-1) + b_2 \Delta E(t)
\tag{4.42a}
$$

Chen and Mars[34] suggest the following adaption scheme

$$
\eta(t) = \eta(t-1)[1 - \Delta\overline{E}(t)\sqrt{E(t)}]
\tag{4.43}
$$

4.9 TRAINING WITH NOISE

A limited amount of random noise added to the input variables during training has been reported[27,64] and found to improve the generalisation performance of networks. In the case of classification problems, such improvement is understandable, since a slight measure of noise in the input has the effect of ironing out any idiosyncrasies in the network training set. This is again a matter for experimentation, particularly for absolute value targets. Elman and Zipser[45] recommend the following method for adding noise to each input vector element p_i.

$$
p_i \longrightarrow p_i(1 + r)
\tag{4.44}
$$

where r is randomly selected from the range $[-0.5, 0.5]$ The noise term is re-evaluated each time the vector is selected for presentation to the network.

4.10 ROBUST COST FUNCTIONS

The concept of robustness concerns insensitivity of the network to small perturbations in the underlying distribution of the input data[89]. In practice, this leads to the curtailing of the effects of outliers in the data, these being unusual data points that significantly stand out from the main distribution of the data. As mentioned in Section 4.3, mean square error cost functions are sensitive to outliers, and this motivated the consideration of alternative cost functions.

Another approach is to implement the mean square error cost function, and then heuristically damp the resultant error term that appears in the backpropagation algorithm, (through the derivative of the cost function), by an error suppressor. Kosko[89] summarises a number of possible suppressor functions. The following example for infinite-variance probability density data has been found to be effective on occasion.

$$\epsilon \longrightarrow \frac{2\epsilon}{1 + \epsilon^2} \qquad (4.45)$$

where $\epsilon = T - O$, is the output layer neuron error: Target minus observed value.

4.11 WEIGHT PRUNING

The desire to optimise a network structure has motivated a number of approaches to the problem. One is to initiate training with a minimal, skeletal structure, and then let the network grow by splitting neurons, or adding neurons to existing layers, or introducing new layers. See Hertz[64] for a review of these methods. An alternative approach is to design and train the network according to conventional lines, and then par down the neuron connections which play little part in the network performance during training vector recall. This approach is also in accord with the concept of complexity and minimum description length, discussed in Section 4.5.

Whilst there can be confidence that large value weights will have a strong influence in the network, small weights can also play an important role, so a pruning method based solely on the weight magnitude risks degrading the network performance. A criterion that accounts for the sensitivity of the cost function to a particular weight would provide a better measure. One such approach is the Optimal Brain Damage (OBD) method by Le Cun et al[95].

In OBD the sensitivity of the cost function to a perturbation in any particular weight, w_{ij}, linking neurons i and j, is calculated analytically. Appendix A, Section A.3 provides a detailed analysis of second order effects, only the results will be quoted here. First, the total change in cost function E for perturbations in all the weights is approximately given by the sum of changes in E for any one particular weight perturbation:

$$\delta E \approx \sum_{ij:pairs} \delta E_{ij} \qquad (4.46)$$

$$\delta E_{ij} \approx \frac{1}{2} \frac{\partial^2 E}{\partial w_{ij}^2} \delta w_{ij}^2 \qquad (4.47)$$

The *saliency*, s_{ij} is now defined as follows

$$|\delta E_{ij}| = \frac{1}{2} \frac{s_{ij}}{w_{ij}^2} \delta w_{ij}^2 \qquad (4.48)$$

$$s_{ij} = \left| \frac{\partial^2 E}{\partial w_{ij}^2} \right| w_{ij}^2 \qquad (4.49)$$

The saliency is a measure of the degree of sensitivity of the cost function to the weight perturbation δw_{ij}. In order to calculate s, the second derivative of the cost function with respect to each weight is required. The appendix provides a derivation for a three layer network. The extension for deeper layer networks is then straightforward.

The implementation of OBD is performed as follows:

1. construct a network according to usual design rules,
2. train the network to convergence,
3. evaluate the saliency for each weight, summing over an epoch,
4. rank the saliency in order of magnitude,
5. remove weights of low saliency (in practice freeze weights at zero). The number of weights to be removed requires experimentation,
6. now go back to 2 and repeat this cycle a few times.

Pruning may be performed mid-training, or training re-started after each prune with surviving weights initialised to their original random setting. The number of weights that can be successfully removed depends largely on the size of the original network, with large networks having greater scope for reduction. Also for large networks, certain patterns may emerge in the saliency ranking, suggesting the possibility of removing a whole layer that has proved redundant. Cost function sensitivity methods have also been devised which monitor the effect of removing links and prune accordingly. The research literature is active in this field.

4.12 INPUT SENSITIVITY ANALYSIS

Training a network to forecast a time series to within an acceptable convergence criterion satisfies the forecasting problem, but leaves open the question of which precise relationships have been learnt by the neurons. Successful convergence implies the existence of these relationships, however they remain as implicit features of the network. Sensitivity analysis provides one approach in gauging certain aspects of these inherent input-output mapping 'rules'.

Perturbing each input node variable by a small value results in the network output altering in proportion to the influence of that variable, for a particular state of that and *all other* input variables. The perturbed output will depend not only on where in the range the particular input node is perturbed, but due to the complex inter-relationships between the inputs, the current settings of all the other inputs must also be accounted for.

Clearly, building a database of perturbation responses takes on huge proportions for real-world problems with numerous inputs. The very size of the resultant data poses a new problem in analysing and interpreting the information. One possible recourse is to automate the perturbation analysis and use another neural network to find patterns in the data for interpreting the primary network's input-output relationships.

Fortunately there is a short-cut method for gauging the sensitivity of the output for any particular input, and this makes use of the weight values. The weights in a converged network inherently represent the desired information to be retrieved. Although it is true that small weights can have a large influence, an estimate of *input node* influences is to monitor large weights linked to the input layer. The following method extracts the information relevant for any particular input node.

1. On completion of a successful training task, create a table as shown schematically in Figure 4.5, where the weight *magnitudes* of connections from each input node are entered against the receiving neurons; in a multiconnectivity MLP these will be all the neurons, whereas in an adjacent layer connectivity MLP these will be only the first hidden layer neurons.

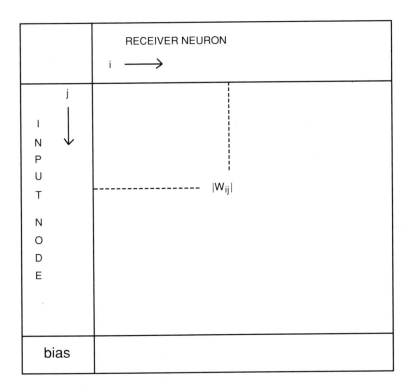

Figure 4.5 Input Sensitivity Table: shown schematically

2. Repeat the training of the network, starting with a different initial random distribution of weight values, and upon convergence, add the weights to existing entries in the table. Repeat this procedure a few times to average out any anomalies.

3. Now normalise along the columns by dividing each entry for a particular receiving neuron by the maximum value along that column. This creates a uniform weighting, so that the maximum entry for any particular receiving neuron is 1.

4. Now for each input node, sum the weights along the rows, giving a single figure for that node, which represents its influence in the network.

5. Finally, rank the input nodes according to their figure of influence.

Although large weight values almost always imply that the transmitting cell is highly influential, small weights can also be important. The column normalisation ensures that regardless of the neuron's transfer function and layer it appears in, the ranking of weights for any given receiving neuron is assessed equally. The repeated trials for different random generator seed in initialising the weights, ensures a fair assessment of the influence of any particular input node. Finally the row summation takes into account the influence of an input node throughout the network. This approach also mitigates against the neglect of any particular small value weight that happens to be important. See Section 6.2.1 for an example.

An alternative for weight magnitudes in the table entries is to use the saliency, discussed in Section 4.11. The saliency takes into account small valued influential weights.

4.13   DESIGN ASPECTS FOR FORECASTING

Many of the design topics raised so far are appropriate to a range of neural network applications. In this section time series forecasting will be the sole focus of attention. First, a brief recap of certain design aspects introduced above.

A suitably discretised time series will require to be sampled in order to construct the data vector sets for training and testing. The window size is the number of consecutive data points sampled for each vector, with each vector element requiring a node in the input layer. An input vector may comprise data from more than one time series, and may involve in addition a number of indicators. The number of input layer nodes largely dictates the design of subsequent layers. If the total number of weights in the network are too few then the network will not have the capability to solve the forecasting problem. Conversely, a model with a large number of weights can map the input vectors' corresponding target outputs, without necessarily extracting any meaningful relationships. The key factor is the ratio of input training vectors to weights, TWR. This figure of merit represents the extent to which the network can generalise from the training set as opposed to fitting the noise. The higher a TWR figure the better, a TWR less than five can produce suspect results. A recommended figure is 10 upwards.

Data limited time series can pose problems in fulfilling an adequate TWR figure, and this can be exacerbated when a reasonable sized test set is required to be set aside. One remedy is to use preprocessing techniques to increase a low TWR, for example: data compression by principal component analysis; compression by autoassociator neural network; weight pruning methods, such as optimal brain damage; cost function penalty terms that reduce complexity.

4.13.1 Prediction Look-Ahead Period

An important consideration is the forecast look-ahead time interval. Close examination of a typical market price time series shows a self-similarity characteristic found in fractal studies of natural phenomena. Thus plots of a price time series on different time scales show similar random-like patterns. Neural network experiments on predicting a chaotic time series, such as the Henon map and Mackay-Glass equation[92], reveal that a neural network trained on inputs that are spaced by a time interval, T, will have the capability to predict a time T ahead, irrespective of the length of T.

This should not be confused with the question of predicting a period nT ahead, for some multiple n, on a network trained on data inputs spaced T apart. The consequence will be a deterioration in accuracy as n increases. Studies of the effects of chaos on nonlinear dynamic problems reveal an exponentially diverging tracking of a time series as the look-ahead period is increased. There is good reason to presume that this analysis carries over to market price time series[126].

The important question is what length should T be. Circumstances may necessitate the selection of certain forecast periods according to requirements. Thus economists investigating general economic trends over many decades will find monthly or quarterly time series suitable for their purposes. Market traders however face a different type of problem in that a newly developed trading system requires real-time verification (at least should so in principle), and in order to build up a statistically significant sample size of trades for evaluation, the look-ahead period needs to have an appropriate bound.

Long term traders may differ on this point — but the risk aspect must be taken into consideration. Thus, training a neural network to provide a monthly forecast of market prices, or similarly, to seek out trading opportunities which occur about once a month. No matter how good the training *and test* performances, no forecasting system *involving high risk* should be acted on, unless it has been verified in real-time, and the forecasts found to be in accord with expectations. For the monthly system that would require a few years of monitoring, since 30 trades is a minimum effective sample size. A possible way round this for the long term trader, is to trade the same system in parallel markets, assuming it is flexible enough to cater for a variety of commodities/financials.

Possibly the most common setting for T is a daily look-ahead, with short term traders also favouring hourly tick data. One advantage of tick time series is that data is plentiful and covers a short window in the time scale of economic trends and cycles. In fact the effects of the economy can often be considered stationary processes for intra-day trading, which can simplify the network input data analysis. Of course the psychological anticipation of expected economic fundamentals changes (e.g. interest rate changes) is another matter.

4.13.2 Multistage Networks

Once a neural network has been trained to forecast a time series, a time series of *forecasts* over the same time period can be created and then used as part of the input to a second network. The first set of forecasts provide an initial estimate which the second network builds on.

The input variable composition and network structure need not be the same as for the first network. Furthermore, a set of forecast inputs may be used from a range of first stage networks. For example, in forecasting a currency futures price series, a range of key currencies may be included in the input, together with their own forecasts from first stage networks.

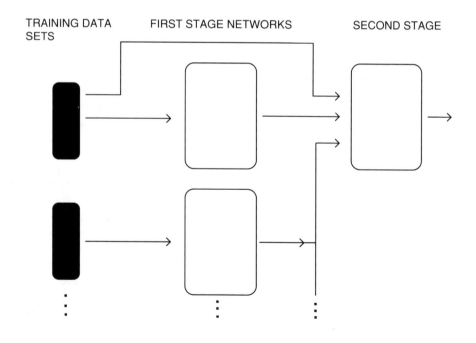

Figure 4.6 Combining neural networks in a two-stage forecasting system

Many possibilities are open for experimentation, the multistage approach provides an iterative refinement procedure for the forecasts. Figure 4.6 shows a possible system configuration.

4.13.3 Postprocessing

Postprocessing the forecasts of a trained neural network may provide clues to the performance characteristics of the network. For example, in the case of forecasting the rise or fall of a price time series, it may emerge that the network has a greater accuracy for large forecast price movements than for predictions which hover near to the last price in the series and which may indicate an uncertainty in the network as to which way the price will swing. (A rise/fall, or trend, forecast for a projected time $t + 1$ is defined by $O_{t+1} - T_t$, with the zero line defined by $O_{t+1} - T_t = 0$, i.e. time series moves horizontally.) Such a case may occur for input patterns with a large measure of noise. Even for the case where all trend forecasts have equal uncertainty, small move forecasts have a greater proximity to forecasts in the opposite direction, a clustering of errors is therefore expected for price movement forecasts close to the zero line.

In order to facilitate the analysis, which is performed once the network has converged, plot the trend forecast, for all the training input vectors, (distinguish between those forecasts that are correct from the wrong), an example is given in the sunspot benchmark. It is useful to perform a number of trials with different random weight initialisations and build up a dense plot, superimposing all the forecast moves.

If the wrong forecasts appear concentrated around the zero movement level then there is scope for error banding. Evaluate the mean and the standard deviation of just the *wrong* forecast moves. A suitable banding scheme is then to filter the forecasts, acting only on those which lie outside the one standard deviation bands $\overline{(O_{t+1} - T_t)}\,|_{wrong} \pm \sigma$. Support the visual inspection of the plot with quantitative accuracy percentage figures for the error bands.

5
Random Time Series and Market Prices

Properties of pure random time series are of interest in providing a theoretical framework for time series in general, as well as serving the purposes of control examples for comparison with financial market time series. A time series may be expressed in the form

$$p_t = p_{t-1} + u_t \tag{5.1}$$

where u is a stochastic variable, which for a purely random process would be what statisticians call 'independently and identically distributed' (IID), such as a Gaussian with zero mean and constant variance. Such a purely random series is also known as white Gaussian noise. Discretisation of a continuous time series is assumed to be performed in equal time intervals.

The first section provides an overview of random walk theory, illustrating some non-intuitive aspects of such a time series. It is also instructive to consider the series made up of u_t, the differences of the original series. Correlations between time series are discussed in the second section and the final sections introduce a novel analysis technique, the *median forecast method*, which leads to expectation bounds on the p_t time series.

5.1 THE RANDOM WALK

The random walk hypothesis was first applied to stock market analysis by Louis Bachelier[10]; this lead, through the work of Kolmogorov[87], to a more formal development of a mathematical theory known as Markov chains. There is also a link with the physics of diffusion, through what is known as Brownian motion, or the Wiener process, which occurs in the limit when the small individual steps of the random path occur so rapidly that the motion appears continuous. Study of the random walk provides a useful background to the question of the nature of financial market time series. The one-dimensional random walk can be considered as a purely random price time series. In investigating the properties of the random walk it is instructive to perform some simple numerical experiments, and I urge the reader to try the following tests for themselves on a PC.

In order to create a 1D random walk it is immaterial what length of steps are chosen, they can take on values 1 and -1, which can be compared to a coin tossing experiment, or they can be distributed according to some known distribution function. Since financial market time series steps resemble a Gaussian-like distribution, let us generate steps according to a Gaussian. First generate uniformly distributed random numbers, x, in the range (0,1); below I use the Numerical Recipes RAN2 generator[128], however a computer language compiler's generator will be adequate for these experiments. A Gaussian with unit variance and zero mean is defined by

$$p(y) = \frac{1}{\sqrt{2\pi}} e^{-y^2/2} \qquad (5.2)$$

To transform the uniform deviates, x, to Gaussian deviates y, use the Box-Muller method

$$y_1 = \sqrt{-2\ln x_1} \cos(2\pi x_2) \qquad (5.3)$$

$$y_2 = \sqrt{-2\ln x_1} \sin(2\pi x_2) \qquad (5.4)$$

where x_1, x_2 are any two uniform deviates and y_1, y_2 are their transformed Gaussian counterparts. Any desired Gaussian deviate, z, with standard deviation σ and mean μ, can now be obtained using the transformation

$$z = \sigma y + \mu \qquad (5.5)$$

Now generate 90 000 samples of z with $\sigma = 0.7$ and zero mean, and construct the random walk whose position, or price, r_t, is given by

$$r_t = r_{t-1} + z_t \qquad (5.6)$$

starting at $r_0 = 0$. The first 2 000 steps of the walk are traced out in Figure 5.1 for my generated series. Notice that the return to the start position at $r = 0$ occurs relatively few times in relation to the overall path — more on this below.

The time origin can be shifted to any point in the walk, so the question will be addressed, what is the subsequent average position of r_t as time progresses? Two distance measures will be calculated. Create a zero initialised storage on your PC named RDISTANCE(1...1000), (i.e. with dimension 1000), and using each point in the walk as a new origin r_0, evaluate the square distance $[r_{N\Delta t} - r_0]^2$ for all the N time steps Δt, given by $N = 1, \ldots, 1000$ and with unit time steps $\Delta t = 1$. Continue rolling forward the new origin $r_{t=0}$ along the 90 000 length walk, and

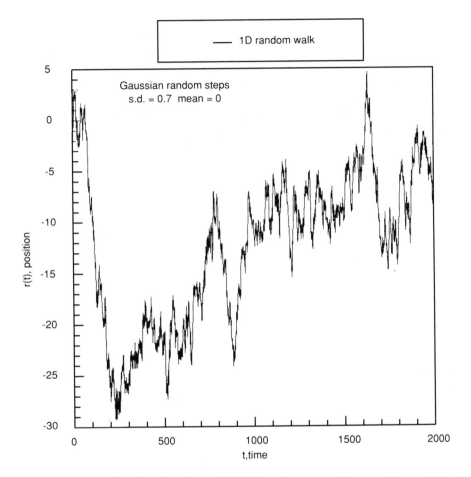

Figure 5.1 One dimensional random walk for Gaussian generated steps, with $\sigma = 0.7$ and $\mu = 0$, showing first 2000 steps

evaluate the square distances, *adding* these quantities to the appropriate element in the store RDISTANCE for each look-ahead N value. Keep a count of the number of entries performed in each element in RDISTANCE in another store TALLY(1...N). Whilst the above is being calculated, similarly calculate the distance $r_{N \Delta t} - r_0$, and *accumulate* these values in another store ADISTANCE(1...N).

Once the rolling forward sweep is accomplished, calculate the average in each entry in RDISTANCE and ADISTANCE by dividing each element by the corresponding count total in TALLY. Next take the square root of each entry in RDISTANCE, the result will be the evaluation of the RMS distances for 1 to 1000 time steps look-back (from the perspective of the end of the walk). Now divide each entry in RDISTANCE by the square root of N and in ADISTANCE divide each entry by N. Plot the entries in RDISTANCE and ADISTANCE against number of time steps N, shown for my experiment in Figures 5.2 and 5.3.

You should find that, as in Figure 5.2, all the RDISTANCE entries produce an approximate value of the selected standard deviation for the Gaussian steps, which was 0.7. Since RDISTANCE was divided by the square root of the time, there appears to be a relation here between RMS distance, σ and $\sqrt{t}$.

At this point it is worth examining some of the theory behind the random walk. Brownian motion is technically defined by three properties[11,75]:

1.   For $t_1 < t_2 < \ldots < t_k$: the steps $r(t_2) - r(t_1), r(t_3) - r(t_2), \ldots, r(t_k) - r(t_{k-1})$

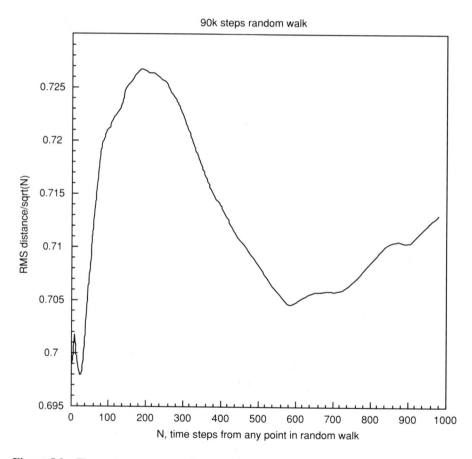

Figure 5.2   The root mean square distance of random walk from start position, divided by the square root of number of time steps lapsed, plotted against varying time periods. Data evaluated from sampling a 90 000 point random walk

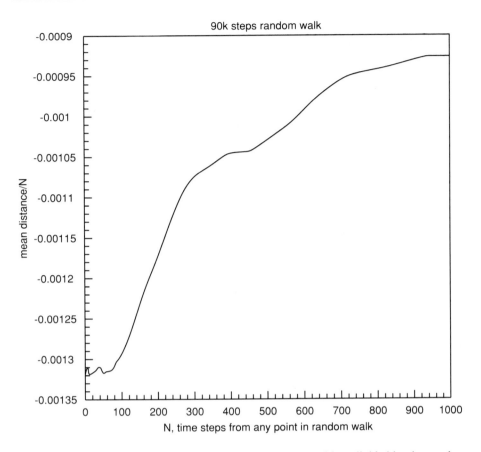

Figure 5.3 The mean distance of random walk from start position, divided by the number of time steps lapsed, plotted against varying time periods. Data evaluated from sampling a 90 000 point random walk

are independent random variables. *This states that each step is independent of previous steps.*

2. $r(t + \tau) - r(t)$ does not depend on time, t, for any interval $\tau = n\Delta t$. *This states that the steps are identically distributed.*

3.
$$\lim_{\tau \to 0} \frac{Prob(|r(t + \tau) - r(t)| \geq \Delta)}{\tau} = 0 \qquad (5.7)$$

for all $\Delta > 0$.
This guarantees that the path traced by $r(t)$ is a continuous function of time. For discrete financial time series, where r_t is sampled from $r(t)$, the condition stands down to the intrinsic limit, e.g. tick time periods for futures time series.

The combination of the first two properties defines an IID time series, (as noted, this is another term for a pure random series). The last property ensures that there are no gaps in the series, but the path will not be smooth enough for it to be differentiable (there is no reason for that in a random motion).

Irrespective of the distribution of random step lengths, the random walk results in $r_t - r_0$ following a Gaussian distribution. The mean step length and step standard deviation fully characterise the path traced by the walk: let the mean distance a be defined by

$$a_{t+\tau} = \overline{r_{t+\tau} - r_0} \tag{5.8}$$

$$= \overline{r_{t+\tau} - r_\tau} + \overline{r_\tau - r_0} \tag{5.9}$$

$$= \overline{r_t - r_0} + \overline{r_\tau - r_0} \tag{5.10}$$

$$= a_t + a_\tau \tag{5.11}$$

where the bar signifies the averaging operation. Now the final relation shows that a is linear in time: $a_t = \mu t + $ constant, where μ is a constant. But $a_0 = 0$, therefore

$$\overline{r_t - r_0} = \mu t \tag{5.12}$$

where μ is associated with the mean step length, seen when $t = 1$. It is also seen that when the step deviates are selected with a nonzero mean then the subsequent path traced over time will result in the superposition of a drift term. Hence the mean is known as the drift constant in physical processes of diffusion where an external drift force is imposed.

Considering the mean *square* distance, assume random steps z with zero mean

$$r_1 = r_0 + z \tag{5.13}$$

$$\overline{r_1^2} = \overline{r_0^2} + \overline{z^2} + 2\overline{r_0 z} \tag{5.14}$$

$$\sigma^2 = \overline{z^2} \tag{5.15}$$

$$\overline{r_1^2} = \overline{r_0^2} + \sigma^2 \tag{5.16}$$

$$\overline{r_2^2} = \overline{r_1^2} + \sigma^2 \tag{5.17}$$

$$\cdots = \cdots$$

$$\overline{r_t^2} = \overline{r_{t-1}^2} + \sigma^2 \tag{5.18}$$

where $\overline{z} = 0$ above, then summing terms over time t yields

$$\overline{r_t^2} = \overline{r_0^2} + \sigma^2 t \tag{5.19}$$

$$\sqrt{\overline{r_t^2} - \overline{r_0^2}} = \sigma\sqrt{t} \tag{5.20}$$

$$R_{rms}(t) = \sigma\sqrt{t} \tag{5.21}$$

where $R_{rms}(t)$ is the random walk RMS distance from an origin after time t has elapsed.

The standard deviation σ of the step deviates z, equation (5.15), written in expanded form is as follows

$$\sigma = \sqrt{\frac{\sum\limits_{i=1}^{N}(z_i - \mu)^2}{N}} \qquad (5.22)$$

In the above example z was drawn from a Gaussian distribution with $\mu = 0$ and $\sigma = 0.7$. Thus the quantities calculated in RDISTANCE for varying periods and plotted in Figure 5.2, confirm the theoretical relation (5.21). RDISTANCE(1) gave σ by definition, and dividing the other entries in RDISTANCE by $\sqrt{t}$ yielded approximate values for σ.

The mean distance, calculated, in ADISTANCE(1), should be zero, since the steps (or deviates) were selected from a zero mean Gaussian. In fact there appears to be a slight bias, which from the graph of ADISTANCE in Figure 5.3 is seen to be around -0.0011. A plot of the difference between the number of positive steps and negative steps (or up minus down steps) for the whole series is shown in Figure 5.4. Apart from the initial positive bias, there is a steady negative bias in the first 90 000 steps of the series, with 261 excess negative steps at the end of the series. The result of this randomly occurring bias is a chance effective mean given by $\mu = -261/90\,000 = -0.0029$. This stems from the relation:

$$(p - q)N = \mu t \qquad (5.23)$$

where p is the probability of a positive step, q is the probability of a negative step, and N is the number of steps taken. For the symmetric case here $p = q = 0.5$, however despite the theoretical zero mean expected, chance fluctuations over some finite period can give rise to a nonzero difference. Thus the discrepancy between the observed 0.0011 and 0.0029 values is due to the fact that there was no actual mean in the Gaussian deviates. Quite by chance there appeared a bias, which would alter given sufficient time (but see the comments at the end of this section). However, note that due to the existence of chance biases, the entries in ADISTANCE had to be divided by the time, t, as in the relation above, in order to verify the nonexistence of any significant mean.

Consider now the case of zero mean random deviates, as in the example. Whilst the mean distance from the origin traced by the walk is theoretically zero over an infinite number of steps, the occurrence of temporary biases due to chance over some finite period, as seen in the 90 000 steps, will take the path some distance from the original startpoint. In fact, return to the origin occurred relatively rarely, see Figure 5.1, for the first 2000 steps.

A more accurate estimate of the likely spread of the path from the origin over some finite period is the step length standard deviation. If σ is very small, distance

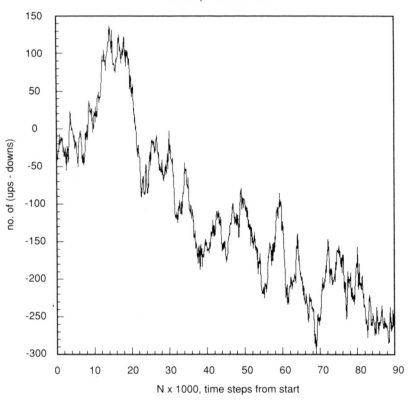

Figure 5.4   The difference between the number of increasing and decreasing steps in the 90 000 step random walk series, against elapsed time

from the origin for any given period will be less than for large variance steps which can take the walk over further distances. The actual distance from the start is given by the vector addition of the steps taken, the probable distance however is given by the RMS distance, which was derived to be the standard deviation times the square root of the time interval traveled.

To illustrate the RMS paths, 50 random walks were generated, of length 200 time steps, and plotted together with the $\pm\sigma\sqrt{t}$ paths, shown in Figure 5.5. It is seen that the RMS paths characterise the general spread of the random walks.

The 1D random walk describes purely random financial time series, the 2D random walk describes the path traced by the proverbial drunk, or pollen suspended on the surface of water—the action of the water molecules striking the pollen particle results in the continuous series of random steps first observed by Robert Brown in 1827. In 1D and 2D there is unit probability, (that is certainty), that the

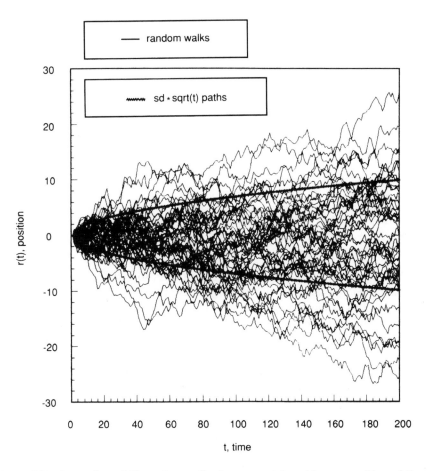

Figure 5.5   Generation of 50 random walks from an origin, with superposition of the $\pm$
RMS distance paths, where sd is the step length standard deviation

path will return to the origin, for a symmetric random walk with $p - q = \mu = 0$.
(In 3D the probability is approximately 0.35^{49}.)

The concept of diffusion linking the random walk is the result of the physicists
picture of a point peak of a large number of particles at the origin which then
spread out by the process of diffusion as each particle is governed by a random
walk. The diffusion constant can be shown to equal the variance — see Feller[49] for
a detailed treatment.

To round up this discussion of the random walk, consider some observations
on the probability of the walk returning to the origin, or equivalently, recrossing
any particular threshold previously met. The results are surprising and counterintuitive, and show the pitfalls that exist in interpreting purely random time series

as possessing nonrandom properties. Again, see Feller for proofs, only aspects of the results will be noted here.

First of all, it was seen above that some bias existed in the 90 000 steps example, with $(p - q)N = -261$ at the end of the period. In fact for most of the time over this test, there was a preponderance of negative steps to positive ones. This was no accident, there is a theorem that shows that for a pure random walk over a large number of steps, the walk will be biased on one side of some origin to the other side (note that a single example of a random walk is being considered and not the case of many random walks). This property is known as the *arc sine law:* given any *one particular* pure random walk (pure means the Brownian motion with zero mean in the deviates) then:

> For a symmetric random walk, started at $r_0 = 0$, and with $p = q = 0.5$, let λ be some fraction $0 < \lambda < 1$. Then the probability that less than or equal to $N\lambda$ time units are spent on the positive side (and hence greater than $(1 - \lambda)N$ on the negative side) tends to $2/\pi \arcsin(\sqrt{\lambda})$ for large N.

The arcsin function is U shaped over the λ range, so given a long random walk, the *most probable* case is for the majority of the time the path to be either wholly above or wholly below the origin, and is least likely to spend equal times on both sides; i.e. λ is most likely to be 0 or 1 and least likely 0.5. This result is no doubt surprising for anyone relying on some intuitive notion of an averaging process. Further analysis shows that the number of times that the walk recrosses a given threshold, after passing it N time units ago, is $\sqrt{N}$ (for large N).

The law of large numbers also has some bearing on these results: it states that the chance discrepancy between the number of positive and negative steps can *increase* in time, but in a *decreasing* proportion as time progresses. For large time t, the chance discrepancy of the position of the walk from the mean $|r_t - \mu t|$ will be small in comparison to t. However large fluctuations can still occur, but the law implies that large values of $|r_t - \mu t|/t$ will occur less frequently in time.

In theoretical analyses of stock and commodity markets, a generalised form of the random walk has been used as a model basis for price behaviour. These are stochastic models based on the Ito process, a nonstationary model with nonzero drift (mean) and standard deviation that can vary in time and with price level[69].

5.2 MARKET CORRELATIONS

Examining the correlation between two time series, p_t^x and p_t^y, can provide a number of benefits. The correlation is usually evaluated according to a linear or a nonparametric coefficient, r, that can lie within the range $[-1,1]$. A near-zero value implying noncorrelation. Before proceeding, a cautionary note on the assessment of the correlation coefficient is necessary.

Whilst it is a fact that if p_t^x and p_t^y are independent then $r(p^x, p^y) = 0$, a nonzero value for r does not imply that p_t^x and p_t^y are dependent. It is possible to find curious examples from the real-world (of some time series related to cheese, and another to chalk, so to speak) which show highly statistically significant values for r, but which are physically meaningless. To confound matters further, there are at least theoretical mathematical examples where p^y is a known function of p^x, but yet $r = 0$, although this is unlikely to occur for financial time series. The usefulness of a correlation measure is a matter of the extent to which a physically meaningful interpretation exists for possible dependency. The correlation measure then provides just one statistic within an overall view.

The benefits of analysing correlations are realised when there are plausible reasons for there being an inter-dependency between two time series. One example is between the spot price and the futures price for some financial index or commodity. The problem of constructing a continuous time series for limited-lifetime futures contracts can be alleviated if there is a high enough correlation between these prices. The forecasting analysis can then be performed on the spot time series and the results applied to the futures market. To illustrate this point, consider the British pound against the US dollar market closing prices over the period 851125 to 930203 (yymmdd), as traded at the International Money Market, Chicago.

Two time series were assembled, the spot price and the nearest futures contract by month. The roll-over dates were chosen to be the first day in the delivery month, and were ignored when calculating correlations; these amounted to 28 total omitted days over the period considered. Three correlation measures were calculated:

- *Linear Correlation, r_l*: Given two time series: p_t^x, p_t^y, $t = 1, \ldots, N$, the linear, or Pearson's, correlation coefficient is defined by

$$r_l = \frac{(N-1)^2 \sum_t (p_t^x - \overline{p^x})(p_t^y - \overline{p^y})}{N^2 \sigma_x^n \sigma_y^n} \tag{5.24}$$

  where $\overline{p^x}$ is the mean of the x-series and σ_x is the sample standard deviation; similarly for the y-series.

- *Nonparametric Correlation, r_s*: The nonparametric, or rank correlation trades off a slightly lower accuracy against an improved reliability in detecting correlations. The approach involves first replacing each element in the series p_t^x by the value of its rank among all the other elements in the series. The resulting new series comprises integers corresponding to the rank order of the original elements. (Some suitable midrank averaging is performed for any repeated occurrences of an element value.) The ranked series R^x and R^y can then be processed by a variety of statistics, here the Spearman coefficient was evaluated, defined by

$$r_s = \frac{(N-1)^2 \sum_t (R_t^x - \overline{R^x})(R_t^y - \overline{R^y})}{N^2 \sigma_x^n \sigma_y^n} \tag{5.25}$$

which is the rank equivalent of the linear coefficient. As in the linear case, the coefficient r_s takes values in the range $[-1,1]$.

- *Movement Symmetry Probability, p_{sym}*: In many forecasting applications the sole requirement is foreknowledge of the rise or fall of a time series. The movement symmetry probability for a pair of time series is a direct measure of the extent to which rises and falls move in tandem, or are symmetrical, (being a probability its range is $[0,1]$). It is calculated by counting the occurrences for which

$$(p_t^x - p_{t-1}^x)(p_t^y - p_{t-1}^y) > 0 \tag{5.26}$$

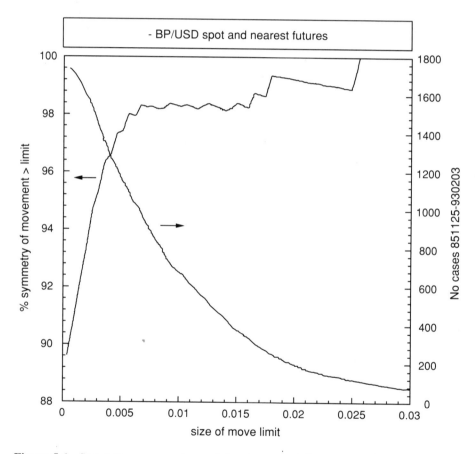

Figure 5.6 Symmetry movement correlation between daily spot and futures price time series for the British P/USD currency rate, over period 851125 to 930203. Correlations for filtering out small price moves, given by upper bound a, are plotted against a. Also shown is the number of trading days left after filtering operation has removed small movement days

and also occurrences for which both series make zero movements. It is expressed out of the total number of cases. Roll-over dates are removed where futures series are concerned, as noted above.

The values for the BP/USD case were: $r_l = .9986$, $r_s = .9986$, and $p_{sym} = .9038$. A further analysis was performed to determine the extent to which the small movements constitute noise and thereby deteriorate the p_{sym} result. The p_{sym} probability was evaluated for various size of move limits; thus the counting was performed only for $|p_t^x - p_{t-1}^x| > a$ (the principal series), where the move size limit a ranged from the minimum tick size of 0.0005 to a multiple of 60 times the

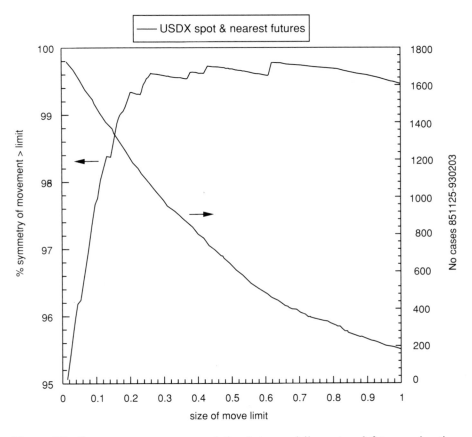

Figure 5.7 Symmetry movement correlation between daily spot and futures price time series for the FINEX US dollar index, covering period 851125 to 930203. Correlations for filtering out small price moves, given by upper bound a, are plotted against a. Also shown is the number of trading days left after filtering operation has removed small movement days

minimum. This calculation filters out small moves. Figure 5.6 shows a plot of p_{sym} against the limit a, with the number of cases involved superimposed, the principal series was BP/USD futures, and the secondary series, p_t^y, BP/USD spot prices. The plots show that $p_{sym} = 97.5\%$ by filtering out moves less than six ticks, which constitutes filtering out 22% of the days.

The imposition of such a noise filter would entail that the spot time series is a useful substitute for the futures series. Further examples are given in Figures 5.7 and 5.8; the former shows a similar filter calculation for the US dollar index traded at the FINEX market, New York, and the latter the relation between the British

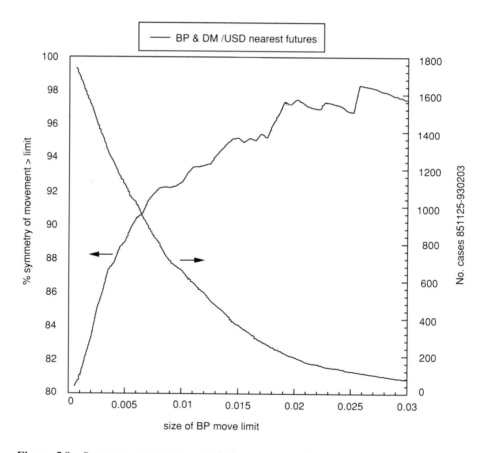

Figure 5.8 Symmetry movement correlation between daily futures price time series of British P/USD and Deutsche mark/USD IMM currency rates. Correlations for filtering out small price moves, given by upper bound a, are plotted against a. Also shown is the number of trading days left over period 851125 to 930203, after filtering operation has removed small movement days

Table 5.1 Correlation calculations for various spot and nearest-by-month futures contracts closing prices. Period covered: 851125 to 930203. Currencies are against the US dollar. Notation: ! spot price; ? futures price

p_t^x	p_t^y	$r_l(p^x, p^y)$	$r_s(p^x, p^y)$	p_{sym} %
British pound!	British pound?	0.9986	0.9986	90.4
US dollar index?	British pound?	−0.8531	−0.8811	16.2
Deutsche mark?	British pound?	0.8037	0.7737	80.1
Japanese yen?	British pound?	0.7063	0.6896	69.4
Swiss franc?	British pound?	0.8325	0.8176	78.8
Eurodollar?	British pound?	0.0116	−0.0222	50.9
S&P 500?	British pound?	0.3303	0.3145	48.1
COMEX gold!	British pound?	0.1577	0.1623	53.0
NY light crude oil!	British pound?	0.4118	0.3070	49.2
US dollar index!	US dollar index?	0.9990	0.9981	95.0
COMEX gold!	S&P 500?	−0.4830	−0.4615	49.1
CRB index?	S&P 500?	−0.3366	−0.3000	47.5
US treasury bills?	Eurodollar?	0.9878	0.9841	80.7
US treasury bonds?	Eurodollar?	0.7457	0.7222	71.2
US treasury bonds?	US treasury bills?	0.7061	0.6943	68.1

pound and the Deutsche mark futures series (IMM prices) — this being an example of inter-market effects.

Finally, a round up of correlation calculations to indicate the type of correlations that exist in the markets, shown in Table 5.1.

5.3 MEDIAN FORECAST METHOD

The characteristics of price time series differences, u_t, will now be considered. Unlike the accumulative time series, p_t, with its tendency to diffuse outwards, the price step sizes in financial time series are bounded to a large extent, and can be approximated by a Gaussian. Investigation of steps in a random walk led to a novel analysis technique, the *median forecast method*. Exploiting the boundedness of the steps provides an above even reliability in predicting the rise and fall of a time series, s, constructed from the *steps u* of a random walk, $s_t = u_t$.

Numerical trials were performed with the objective of forecasting the rise or fall of two example s series, one time step ahead, relative to the current point. One was for Gaussian steps with mean 0.5 and standard deviation 0.1, the other was for uniformly distributed steps in the range [0,1]; each series comprised 50 000 steps. The forecast value was predetermined, and fixed at that value, at each time step, as the whole course of the series was run through the analysis. A trend accuracy figure was then calculated and the trial repeated for a new fixed forecast value. The fixed forecasts were systematically chosen from the range [0,1] in increments

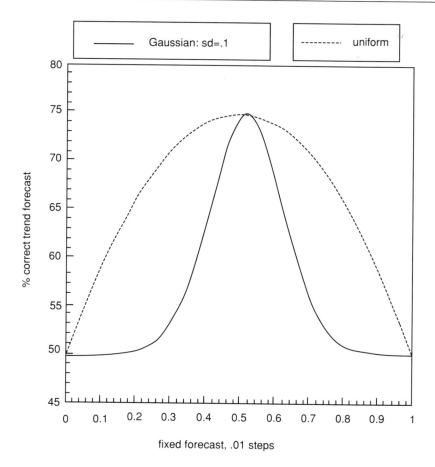

Figure 5.9 Forecasting the trend in step series s_t, using the median forecast method. Two examples shown, a Gaussian and a uniformly distributed step series, 50 000 steps long. Trend accuracy is plotted against the fixed forecast parameter a

of 0.01, resulting in 101 trials for each random time series. The plots of the trend accuracy are shown in Figure 5.9.

The trend accuracy results are rather surprising at first: for a random series bounded within some range, it is possible to predict whether the next point will be a rise or fall with an accuracy of 75% by always predicting that point to be the median of the distribution. The explanation for this result is as follows.

Downward predictions are more likely to be correct when the current point is above the median, since there is a greater than 50% chance that the next point will fall below the current point. The converse argument for forecasting rises also holds when the current point is below the median point. Thus choosing the forecast to be the median optimises the strategy for predicting both rises and falls. This argument can be formalised in an analytical proof for the uniform random time series case.

Let x be the current point, a the *fixed* forecast of the next point, and y the next actual point. The probability for correct forecasts is given in two parts: first, sum over the range $a < x \leq 1$ the probability that the next point will fall below x; second, sum over the range $0 \leq x \leq a$ the probability that y will occur above x:

$$P_{tot}(a) = \int_a^1 P(y \leq x)dx + \int_0^a P(y > x)dx \qquad (5.27)$$

$$= \int_a^1 P(y \leq x)dx + \int_0^a [1 - P(y \leq x)]dx \qquad (5.28)$$

where the property $P(y \leq x) + P(y > x) = 1$ is used. The probability density function of y, $f(y)$, is unity over the range $[0,1]$ and zero elsewhere, so

$$P(y \leq x) = \int_{-\infty}^x f(y)dy \qquad (5.29)$$

$$= x \qquad (5.30)$$

Thus, the total correct forecasts probability is given by

$$P_{tot}(a) = \int_a^1 x\,dx + \int_0^a (1 - x)dx \qquad (5.31)$$

$$= 0.5 + a - a^2 \qquad (5.32)$$

$$P_{max}(a = 0.5) = 0.75 \qquad (5.33)$$

An alternative analysis[119] covers the case where x and y have the same distribution and are independent, but where the distribution may be general. Let a be the median, the prediction is unsuccessful if either (i) or (ii) is true:

(i) $y > a$, $x > y$
(ii) $y < a$, $x < y$

If the median is half-way in the bounded range, then in the (x,y) plane, each of these regions is one-eighth of the plane, comprising half of one of four quadrants formed by the lines $x = a$ and $y = a$, with symmetry around $x = y$. The probabilities are given by the region areas, so the probability of unsuccessful prediction is 25% for *any* symmetrical distribution. For the case where the distribution is skewed, it is clear that the unsuccessful prediction total area increases to a maximum of 50% when the median falls on the boundary points.

In the general case, the possibility of forecasting the rise or fall of s_t beyond 50% can be ascertained by numerically testing the historical series for the fixed value, a, that yields a maximum accuracy: this is the median forecast method.

Note that in real-world time series, the underlying assumption that the future points y are independent of x is unlikely, while the above analysis is strictly valid only in the pure random limit. In the case of financial time series, where if any dependence between past and future prices exist, they will be hidden, so the above method should prove to be useful when applied to u_t, as will be shown in the next section.

5.4 MARKET TIME SERIES

Turning now to actual market data, the S&P 500 stock index, provides a financial series example. A histogram distribution of the differences u_t for the daily S&P 500 nearest contract by month futures series is shown in Figure 5.10. Note that the data

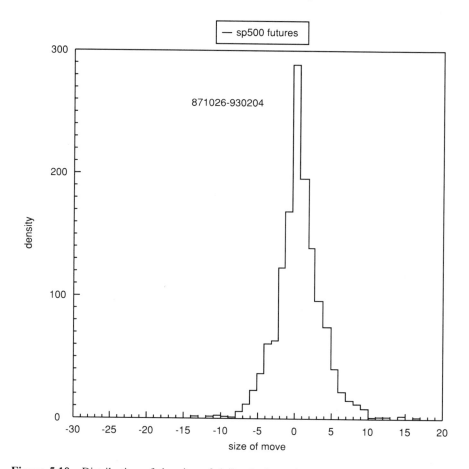

Figure 5.10 Distribution of the size of daily closing price movements for the S&P 500 IMM futures series (nearest contract by month), covering period 871026–930204

is unnormalised, the differences are measured in index points and the series covers the period 871026 to 930204, 1377 data points in total.

Applying the median forecast method to this series, over the range $[-10,10]$ in steps of 0.05, the result of the numerical experiment is shown in Figure 5.11. The figure resembles the result for the random Gaussian example; selecting the median value for the fixed forecast ($a = 0$), provides a probability of forecasting whether u_t will rise or fall to an accuracy around 75%.

The median forecast method produces an above even trend forecast accuracy due to the bounded nature of the step series s_t. In the case of the underlying time series,

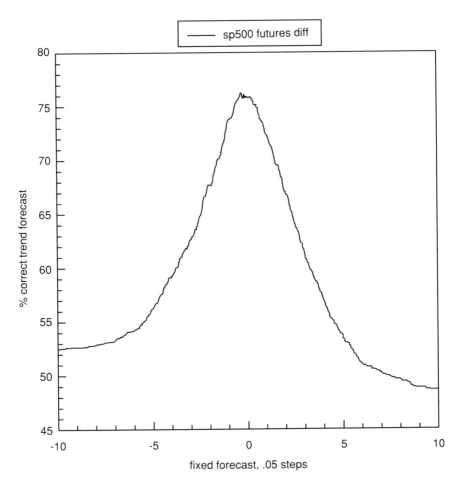

Figure 5.11 Applying the median forecast method to the S&P 500 futures series of daily price *differences*. The trend accuracy is plotted against the fixed forecast parameter a, in increments of 0.05 over the range $[-10,10]$

the path traced is unbounded as was seen in the previous section, with a general tendency to diffuse away from a given point. Thus if the same analysis is applied to the S&P 500 price time series then the characteristics change, since the size of moves are very small with respect to the overall range of the series, the median forecast method is not expected to improve on random chance trend prediction. This was confirmed, with the best a value not achieving better than approximately 50% accuracy.

The median forecast method is therefore inappropriate for time series involving an accumulative process, it is best applied to the differences of the financial market data, u_t. Now, it was established that for some given u_t series, taking the median value for the fixed parameter, a, allows the trend of u_t to be ascertained to within 75% accuracy. Such a trend is in effect a double difference with respect to the underlying series p_t. The question is whether knowing the movement of these differences can be used to determine the movement of the underlying series. To help the analysis, a sketch of the two possible cases for the p_t series movement is shown in Figure 5.12. (precise horizontal movements have been ignored to simplify

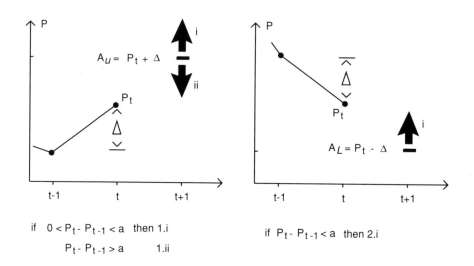

Figure 5.12 Median forecast method result, assuming $a > 0$, for price differences applied to underlying price time series, showing two cases: [1] last price move was a rise, next price will rise or fall with respect to level A_U, depending on conditions (i) and (ii). Case [2]: last price move was fall, next price will rise above A_L if condition (i) is satisfied

the analysis). The analysis below should be followed with reference to the sketch (the *i,ii* cases are defined below).

Formally, there is some value *a* for which the expression below has 75% probability of being true (considering a positive *a* value)

$$[(p_{t+1} - p_t) - (p_t - p_{t-1})][a - (p_t - p_{t-1})] > 0 \qquad (5.34)$$

This expression encapsulates the median forecast method, and is the condition for *a* to be such as to enable correct forecast of the next move. This expression gives rise to two possibilities:

> (*i*) if $a > p_t - p_{t-1}$ then $p_{t+1} - p_t > p_t - p_{t-1}$
> and $p_{t+1} > A$
> (*ii*) if $a < p_t - p_{t-1}$ then $p_{t+1} - p_t < p_t - p_{t-1}$
> and $p_{t+1} < A$

where $A = 2p_t - p_{t-1}$. Considering the two possible movements in turn:

$$\text{Condition (1): } p_{t-1} < p_t$$

Here the series is moving upwards. The bound A will be at its higher possible value due to the condition (1), $A = A_U$, and will therefore lie above the current

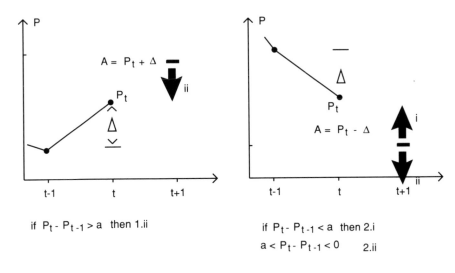

Bounds on P_{t+1} : $a < 0$

1. Last move P_t was rise

$A = P_t + \Delta$

P_t

ii

if $P_t - P_{t-1} > a$ then 1.ii

2. Last move was fall

Δ

P_t

$A = P_t - \Delta$

i

ii

if $P_t - P_{t-1} < a$ then 2.i

$a < P_t - P_{t-1} < 0$ 2.ii

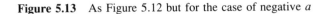

Figure 5.13 As Figure 5.12 but for the case of negative *a*

point p_t. Considering first condition (i), noting that a is positive, and including condition (1), yields:

$$0 < p_t - p_{t-1} < a$$

If the last move satisfies this expression then $p_{t+1} > A_U$, which implies a rise in the time series, (to an accuracy of 75% at best).

The second condition (ii) will also be satisfied under condition (1) for a large enough previous move. In this case $p_{t+1} < A_U$, however since p_t is already below the bound A_U then this circumstance only provides an upper limit for the next step in the series.

Condition (2): $p_{t-1} > p_t$

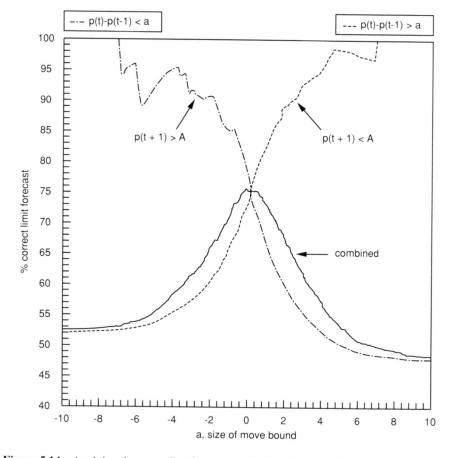

Figure 5.14 Applying the u_t median forecast method results to the time series p_t: example of S&P 500 futures prices. The bound A is defined by $A = 2p_t - p_{t-1}$. Plots given for price moves satisfying limit conditions against varying a

In this case the series is falling and the bound A will be at its lower possible value $A = A_L$, and A_L will lie below the current point p_t. Condition (i) can be satisfied with consequence $p_{t+1} > A_L$, and this provides a lower limit for the forecast point. Condition (ii) cannot be physically satisfied for condition (2).

Summarising: As a result of the fact that the median forecast method was applied to differences of a time series, the trend probability obtained in the method did not provide certainty as to the rise or fall of the time series itself, only to the forecast point p_{t+1} being bounded by limits. These limits are set above and below the current point by an amount equal to the previous size of move. If the series had been rising then the upper bound would be operative; if the series had been decreasing then the lower bound would be operative.

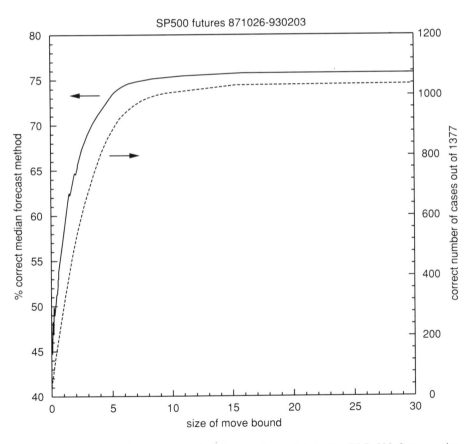

Figure 5.15 Median forecast method with $a = 0$, applied to the S&P 500 futures price time series. Reliability of method plotted against size of actual forecast price movements less than move bound. Also shown is the number of correct cases corresponding to the move bound

These limits can be applied in trading; if, as in the example here, the series comprises prices at daily close of market, then intraday fluctuations that drive the series beyond these limits are likely to reverse. Thus for the S&P 500 case, selecting from Figure 5.11 the maximum small value for a that ensures reasonably high s_t trend accuracy, provides the basis for a practical trading strategy.

The analysis above can be applied to zero and negative values of a. The case of negative a is sketched out in Figure 5.13. The zero case has only two conditions operative: (1.ii) $p_t - p_{t-1} > 0$ resulting in $p_{t+1} < A_U$ and (2.i) $p_t - p_{t-1} < 0$ with $p_{t+1} > A_L$.

The S&P 500 futures price series of daily closes was tested with this method. Figure 5.14 shows the accuracy of forecasting the next price to be above or below the bound $A = 2p_t - p_{t-1}$, considering only those days when the previous daily price move satisfied being below or above the bound a respectively. Also shown is the combined accuracy for forecasting either side of a, these combined boundary forecasts match the trend accuracy curve obtained for u_t, which is as expected.

In order to gauge how the accuracy of this method depends on the size of actual price move, the value $a = 0$ was chosen for the median forecast method, and the accuracy of the method plotted as a function of those size of moves falling below a limit b, that is $|p_t - p_{t-1}| < b$, where the abscissa is the size of move bound b, shown in Figure 5.15. The figure shows that reliability of the method increases the larger the forecast movement actually turns out to be.

The median forecast method should be compared with the common practice of setting standard deviation bounds around the current price, which entails that the next move is most likely to fall within the standard deviation bands. With the median forecast method the bounds are dynamic (being defined by the size of the last move) and are one-sided, depending on whether the last move was a rise or fall. Naturally both methods may be combined.

6
Benchmarks

Benchmarks serve two main purposes; first, they may define the state-of-the-art in performance, such as computation efficiency and speed, for some specific problem. Second, they serve to define a standard solution for the benefit of anyone wishing to gauge their results, for comparison with novel enhancements and alternative techniques, as well as for debugging purposes. The primary purpose for providing benchmarks here is the latter motivation, although the performance results quoted are near to the best, and in some cases superior to, published results.

The author's neural network simulator provided the means for implementing the various strategies and techniques discussed in the book, run on an IBM compatible 33MHz 486 PC. Computation times for all the problems were of the same order for each of the three backpropagation solvers and are therefore not quoted. To give an indication of the times, typical XOR problem runs took a few minutes for a batch of 10 random initialisation runs. Rather, the primary performance measure is the number of epochs required to achieve a given convergence criterion. Where relevant other indicators of performance are given, such as percentage accuracy of trend forecast.

Reviewing previous discussion, a number of forecast schemes are possible:

- *Single-stepping:* The network is trained over a given train set, test vectors are made up of target (actual) time series data, the network predicts one time step ahead.
- *Multistepping:* As single-stepping, except that the look-ahead interval may be greater than one time step.
- *Iterated single-stepping:* Here again the train set is fixed, the test input vectors now include forecast data in order to look-ahead further than one time step, by forecasting a series of single time steps.
- *Auto-single-stepping:* In practical use it is often the case that the train set is updated with the most recent data and the network continually re-trained.

Auto-single-stepping reflects this procedure by testing the test vectors one at a time and adding them to the training pool.

For benchmarking the single-stepping scheme is chosen throughout here. The initial selection of problems will be familiar to practitioners in the field of neuro-computing, since these problems are often cited for benchmark purposes. Of particular interest here will be the financial time series tests that complete the benchmarking suite.

Weights for the optimum performing neural networks in the benchmarks are tabulated in Appendix B. A FORTRAN program for reading the weights and producing a recall mode MLP output is listed in Appendix C.

6.1 EXCLUSIVE OR

The exclusive OR problem, XOR, served to illustrate the basic functioning of the MLP network in the tutorial — a definition of the problem will therefore not be repeated here. The bare minimum neural network design for solving this problem is the 2-1-1 multiconnectivity structure: two input nodes, one hidden neuron and one output neuron, with the input nodes also linked to the output. This structure was used throughout the tests, which compared three backpropagation solvers: steepest descent — always with weights updated immediately following a pattern presentation, Shanno's version of the conjugate gradient method and the quasi-Newton method BFGS, which are both batch weight update methods (see Appendix A for detailed descriptions of the solvers). The options tested were as follows:

- *tran:* Transfer functions: tanh (tnh) and sigmoid (sig) — brackets define the table entries. All functions had gain 1.5 in the hidden layer and 1.0 in the output layer.

- *nrm:* Input data normalisation by *external norm* method: [0,1] and [−1,1].

- *rb:* Robustness option, infinite-variance density (see Section 4.10): 0 — off, 1 — enabled.

- *a-stp:* Adaptive learning coefficient, relevant to steepest descent only: the Hertz rules (Section 4.8).

The steepest descent learning coefficient was either fixed, or initialised for *a-stp*, at 0.5 for the hidden and output layers, and the momentum coefficient similarly set at 0.9. These values were optimised, through manual trial and error, for the sigmoid transfer function. The tanh transfer function case was not tested for this solver. For Shanno and BFGS these settings are inapplicable as the learning coefficient is automatically optimally calculated.

The quadratic cost function was used throughout. Two error measures were applied, the normalised RMS error and the threshold error, table entries under *error* being *n-rms* and *thr* respectively. In the RMS case a stringent criterion of

0.05 was set. The threshold metric was applied in the case of tanh output functions, which have output in the range $[-1,1]$, so the threshold level was set to 0; this measure provides the most lax solution since the problem is considered solved as soon as outputs are on the correct side of the 0 divide.

The output linear correlation coefficient, also tabulated under *corr*, provides a measure of how well the observed outputs match the targets. The target settings for the problem, 0 and 1, were defined as 0.1 and 0.9 for the sigmoid, and -0.9 and 0.9 for the tanh neuron.

Each entry in Table 6.1 averages the results over 10 runs, for different random number generator seeds used to initialise weights. The weights were initialised from the range $[-0.1, 0.1]$. The entry under *cnvg* is the ratio of converged solutions to the total. A converged solution was defined as satisfying less than the maximum number of 400 epochs set for steepest descent, and 100 maximum restarts for Shanno and BFGS. Performance figures for the best and worst case from the converged solutions is also tabulated. The *its* entry is the number of major cycles, and *res* is the number of restarts: both only applicable to Shanno and BFGS.

The steepest descent solver always guaranteed a solution, but note that this required the initial selection of suitable learning and momentum coefficients — not a task to be lightly dismissed since the method can be highly sensitive to these parameters. The adaptive coefficient option provided the better results — but the starting point was the suitable parameter settings already found.

The main advantage of the other two solvers is that the coefficient selection is automated. The best results were obtained for the sig transfer function with inputs normalised to the range [0,1] and with the robust function operative. The

Table 6.1   XOR benchmarks. See text for definitions

solver	cvg /10	tran	err	nrm	rb	min epoch case				max epoch case			
						epch	its	res	corr	epch	its	res	corr
steep	10	sig	rms	[0,1]	1	134	—	—	1.00	220	—	—	1.00
a-stp	10	sig	rms	[0,1]	0	198	—	—	1.00	261	—	—	1.00
	10	sig	rms	[0,1]	1	123	—	—	1.00	189	—	—	1.00
	10	sig	thr	[0,1]	1	44	—	—	0.85	120	—	—	0.88
BFGS	10	sig	rms	[0,1]	1	44	38	5	1.00	337	265	37	1.00
	9	sig	rms	[0,1]	0	62	54	7	1.00	279	242	34	1.00
	4	tnh	rms	[−1,1]	1	266	29	11	1.00	506	58	23	1.00
	7	tnh	rms	[0,1]	1	94	23	4	1.00	849	181	29	1.00
	7	tnh	thr	[0,1]	1	90	20	3	0.98	845	177	29	0.95
Shann	10	sig	rms	[0,1]	1	53	36	5	1.00	189	119	16	1.00
	9	sig	rms	[0,1]	0	84	56	8	1.00	411	243	36	1.00
	7	tnh	rms	[−1,1]	1	94	23	5	1.00	150	19	6	1.00
	8	tnh	rms	[0,1]	1	56	21	3	1.00	1063	193	43	1.00
	9	tnh	thr	[0,1]	1	43	13	2	0.94	1036	178	41	0.85

Shanno and BFGS solvers proved equally efficient. The RMS criterion proved highly stringent, with the correlation results near perfect. In a few cases the Shanno and BFGS solvers provided acceptable solutions but saturated above the set error level. Although the quality of the Shanno and BFGS solutions were preferable to the steepest descent for the threshold error measure, as reflected in the correlation figures, a few further epochs would have improved the performance of the steepest descent.

6.2   PROBLEMS IN CHAOS

Chaos theory is a recent development in the analysis of complex problems, with origins in computer studies of nonlinear dynamical systems. Such systems, which are generated by deterministic equations, can show random-like behaviour under specific conditions. For our purposes, these systems serve to generate time series with random appearance, but which should be amenable to prediction (at least for short look-ahead time spans) on theoretical grounds, due to the deterministic generator. Chaotic time series are therefore ideal benchmark problems, and two cases are investigated.

The neural network model for predicting the time series may be written in terms of a mapping function f, for predicting P time units ahead:

$$x(t + P) = f[x(t), x(t - \tau), x(t - 2\tau), \ldots, x(t - m\tau)] \qquad (6.1)$$

where τ is the input sampling, or delay, time and the number of neural network inputs, $m + 1$, is known as the *embedding dimension* in chaos terminology: $d_E = m + 1$. Theoretical work[157] has shown that in order to achieve the desired mapping/prediction, the choice of embedding dimension is important and should lie in the range:

$$d_A \leq d_E \leq 2d_A + 1 \qquad (6.2)$$

where d_A is the chaotic attractor's information dimension.

6.2.1   Henon Map

Chaotic behaviour may be seen in a number of different types of deterministic systems. Here an algebraically defined two-dimensional mapping will be examined:

$$x(t) = 1 - ax^2(t - 1) + y(t - 1) \qquad (6.3)$$

$$y(t) = bx(t - 1) \qquad (6.4)$$

This is the Henon map[63,153,159], a two-dimensional system, which can be formulated to generate a one-dimensional time series $x(t)$ as follows

$$x(t) = 1 - ax^2(t - 1) + bx(t - 2) \qquad (6.5)$$

A chaotic regime occurs for $a = 1.4$ and $b = 0.3$, with information dimension $d_A = 1.25$. In the time series generated for the benchmark, the embedding dimension was taken as $d_E = 2$, and the time step, Δt, sampling time, τ and look-ahead time, P, were all set to 1. A second example with embedding dimension of $d_E = 5$ was also tested.

The training and test set sample sizes were both 500, generated after the first 1000 iterations, sufficient to allow the decay of initialisation transients. Input and output normalisation was set to the range $[-1,1]$, using the *external norm* method. The standard deviation of the pattern targets were as follows: train set 0.7180, test set 0.7103. A convergence limit of 0.05 for the normalised RMS error was preset, with a 500 epoch limit also imposed. Certain design features were kept constant throughout; the quadratic cost function, no robust feature, and multiconnectivity enabled. The adaptive steepest descent solver learning coefficients were initialised to 0.2 and 0.1 for the hidden and output layers, momentum was 0. The benchmark results are tabulated in Table 6.2, and include the following information:

- *solver:* Three variants: a-stp d is the Hertz rules adaptive steepest descent with weight update per pattern. Shanno is an inexact search variant of the conjugate gradient method. BFGS is the quasi-Newton method with inexact line search.
- *net:* Three layer nets in all cases, giving number of cells per layer. Transfer functions in hidden neurons were all tanh, with gain 1.5. The special ACE neuron for the steepest descent solver was enabled, and is in addition to the number of neurons shown in the table. The output neuron was always piecewise linear with gradient 0.5 and the linear part extended ± 2.5 on the input axis.
- *TWR:* The training patterns to weights ratio, see Section 4.13. This figure includes ACE neuron weights.

Table 6.2 Henon benchmarks. See text for definitions

solver	net	TWR	epochs	$\overline{trn_\varepsilon}$	$\overline{tst_\varepsilon}$	$\overline{trn}\%$	$\overline{tst}\%$
a-stp d	2-3-1	26.3	550	0.557	0.534	97.2	97.1
	5-3-1	14.7	509	0.308	0.299	97.9	97.7
	2-6-1	16.1	512	0.380	0.364	97.4	97.0
	5-6-1	9.1	460	0.084	0.090	99.4	99.1
BFGS	2-3-1	33.3	222	0.049	0.050	99.6	99.3
	5-3-1	18.5	277	0.049	0.052	99.5	99.4
	2-6-1	18.5	180	0.049	0.050	99.6	99.3
	5-6-1	10.4	255	0.049	0.053	99.5	99.1
Shanno	2-3-1	33.3	343	0.303	0.309	91.9	92.2
	5-3-1	18.5	500	0.710	0.736	87.4	87.4
	2-6-1	18.5	282	0.056	0.056	99.6	99.2
	5-6-1	10.4	448	0.193	0.210	96.9	96.8

- $\overline{epochs}$: The average number of epochs to the convergence limit.
- $\overline{trn_\varepsilon}$: The average train set normalised RMS error.
- $\overline{tst_\varepsilon}$: The average test set normalised RMS error.
- $\overline{trn\%}$: The trend forecast accuracy for the train set.
- $\overline{tst\%}$: The trend forecast accuracy for the test set.

The runs were repeated 10 times in each case with different random number generator seeds, used to initialise the weights, and averaged accordingly (see Table 6.2).

In these tests, the BFGS solver produced the most consistently good convergence performance. Figure 6.1 shows a comparison of the neural network forecast and the target series values for one of the BFGS solutions.

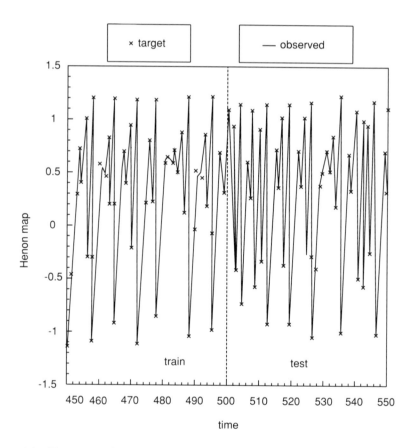

Figure 6.1 Henon map forecasts from BFGS solved neural network, compared with target time series values. Samples shown are 50 targets either side of the training/test set divide

Table 6.3 Henon map: input sensitivity analysis ranking

rank	test		control	
	input node	s value	input node	s value
6	3	6.3	1	8.2
5	1	17.2	2	23.8
4	2	24.8	3	32.7
3	4	26.8	B	34.2
2	B	36.2	4	35.0
1	5	47.6	5	44.3

Note inclusion of the bias node B in the input nodes.

In order to illustrate the use of the weight sensitivity analysis method, described in Section 4.12, a further case was examined. A network with structure 5-6-1 as above was designed, but with the third input node assigned random numbers from the range $[-1,1]$; the input nodes were therefore presented with the following window of values:

node-1	node-2	node-3	node-4	node-5
$x(t-5)$	$x(t-4)$	(random)	$x(t-2)$	$x(t-1)$

The weight sensitivity results are compiled in Table 6.3, which shows the BFGS solver result for 10 runs with different weight initialisations, and also as control comparison, the case where the third node is assigned value $x(t-3)$. The *s value* entry is the sensitivity analysis weight summation factor. The ranking starts with the weakest node. Note that the bias node is also included, designated B, and hence there are six entries.

The sensitivity analysis ranks the third node in the test case as weakest, reflecting the randomised nature of the input. All the other inputs are ranked according to their position in time, whilst the bias node occupies typical positions of importance.

6.2.2 Mackey-Glass Equation

The Mackey-Glass (MG) equation was originally developed for modelling white blood cell production. It is a time delay ordinary differential equation:

$$\frac{dx}{dt} = \frac{ax(t-\tau)}{1 + x^c(t-\tau)} - bx(t) \tag{6.6}$$

Integrating the equation over the range $[t, t + \Delta t]$ by the trapezoidal rule yields, after re-arranging terms

$$x(t + \Delta t) = \frac{2 - b\Delta t}{2 + b\Delta t}x(t) + \frac{a\Delta t}{2 + b\Delta t}\left[\frac{x(t + \Delta t - \tau)}{1 + x^c(t + \Delta t - \tau)} + \frac{x(t-\tau)}{1 + x^c(t-\tau)}\right] \tag{6.7}$$

Note that the approximation resulting from the numerical integration will introduce some noise into the time series.

Under a suitable choice for the parameters, the time series will be governed by a chaotic regime. The most extensively studied case[29,92,111,153] is also selected here: $a = 0.2$, $b = 0.1$ and $c = 10$. The time delay parameter, τ, controls the nature of the chaotic behaviour. The value chosen here, $\tau = 30$, results in a time series with a low dimensional chaotic attractor, of information dimension $d_A = 3.6$. The embedding dimension should therefore satisfy

$$3.6 \le d_E \le 8.2 \tag{6.8}$$

The problem benchmarked here corresponds to generating the time series with $\Delta t = 1$, under the initial condition $x(t) = 0.9$ for $0 \le t \le \tau$, with the initial 3000 data points discarded, allowing for the initialisation transients to decay. The time series was then *sampled* every six points, $\tau = 6$, and a rolling window of input vectors generated for six inputs, $d_E = 6$. The target was selected to be six time units ahead, $P = 6$.

In keeping with previous published work on this equation, 500 training patterns were used, selected from a continuous sequence of data, with the test set comprising the subsequent 500 patterns. The results reported in Table 6.4 include the following options:

Table 6.4   MG benchmarks. See text for definitions

solver	cf	net	m	TWR	input	rb	cvg /10	min ep	$\overline{trn}_\varepsilon$	$\overline{tst}_\varepsilon$	max % acc trn	tst
a-stp	e	6-5-1	1	10.6	[−1,1]	0	9	35	0.0477	0.0441	99.2	98.6
	e	6-5-1	1	10.6	[−1,1]	1	9	75	0.0497	0.0468	99.4	99.2
	e	6-5-1	1	10.6	[0,1]	0	9	201	0.0499	0.0449	99.0	98.8
	n	6-5-1	1	10.6	[−1,1]	0	2	213	0.0685	0.0681	99.0	99.2
	e	6-5-1	0	12.2	[−1,1]	0	5	116	0.0529	0.0512	99.4	98.2
	e	6-10-1	1	5.8	[−1,1]	0	10	34	0.0458	0.0417	99.0	99.4
BFGS	e	6-5-1	1	10.6	[−1,1]	0	10	65	0.0482	0.0457	99.6	98.4
	e	6-5-1	1	10.6	[0,1]	0	9	74	0.3449	0.3318	99.2	98.8
	n	6-5-1	1	10.6	[−1,1]	0	8	104	0.0517	0.0505	99.6	98.4
	e	6-5-1	0	12.2	[−1,1]	1	10	84	0.0491	0.0493	99.2	98.6
	n	6-5-1	0	12.2	[−1,1]	1	10	105	0.0488	0.0489	99.4	98.2
	e	6-10-1	0	6.2	[−1,1]	0	7	70	0.0646	0.0639	99.2	98.4
Shann	e	6-7-1	0	8.8	[−1,1]	0	6	267	0.1461	0.1410	99.0	98.8
	e	6-8-1	0	7.7	[−1,1]	0	8	229	0.0608	0.0606	99.4	98.2
	e	6-8-1	0	7.7	[0,1]	0	0	—	0.5844	0.5712	96.8	97.4
	e	6-8-1	1	7.0	[−1,1]	0	8	293	0.1662	0.1641	98.8	98.8
	n	6-8-1	0	7.7	[−1,1]	1	7	229	0.0608	0.0606	99.4	98.2
	e	6-10-1	0	6.2	[−1,1]	0	9	247	0.1107	0.1052	99.2	98.0

- *solver:* Three variants: *a-stp* is the Hertz rules adaptive steepest descent with weight update per pattern. *Shann* is the Shanno variant of conjugate gradients with inexact line search. *BFGS* is the quasi-Newton method with inexact line search.

- *cf:* Cost function, either quadratic (Euclidean), *e*, or nonEuclidean with $p = 1.5$, *n*.

- *net:* Three layer nets in all cases, giving number of cells per layer. Transfer functions in hidden neurons for *a-stp*; *net 6-5-1*: 3 tanh, 1 cos and ACE, *net 6-10-1*: 4 tanh, 3 cos, 2 piece-wise linear and ACE. For *BFGS*; *net 6-5-1*: 4 tanh, 1 pw-lin; *net 6-10-1*: 5 tanh, 3 cos and 2 pw-lin. For *Shanno*: all tanh. The output neuron was always piece-wise linear. All p-w linear functions had gradient 0.5 and the linear part extended ±2.5 on the input axis. All tanh functions had gain 1.5.

- *m:* multiconnectivity option: 0 — off, 1 — on.

- *TWR:* The training patterns to weights ratio, see Section 4.13. This figure includes ACE neuron weights for *a-stp*.

- *input:* The input range *external* normalised, either to [0,1] or [−1,1].

- *rb:* Robustness option, infinite-variance density (see Section 4.10): 0 — off, 1 — on.

- *cvg:* The number of converged cases, out of 10 random weight initialisation runs. The convergence criterion was 0.05 for the standard deviation normalised RMS error. For the BFGS solver, a cutoff was imposed of five restarts or 200 epochs, whichever came first. Similarly with the Shanno solver, but the epoch limit was raised to 500. For the steepest descent there was a limit of 200 epochs in the first phase and 50 epochs for the ACE neuron phase.

- *min ep:* The number of epochs to convergence for the best train run.

- $\overline{trn}_\varepsilon$: The average train set normalised RMS error.

- $\overline{tst}_\varepsilon$: The average test set normalised RMS error.

- *max % acc:* Percentage figures for the train and test sets of rise and fall trend prediction accuracy, given for the best train case, with its corresponding test set figure.

In all cases the error metric was the s.d. normalised RMS error: the standard deviations of the targets for the train set was 0.2656 and for the test set was 0.2847. The learning coefficient, applicable to steepest descent only, was 0.2 and 0.1, in the hidden and output layers respectively and the momentum coefficient was always 0. The ACE neuron was trained by the same solver as the first stage. The minimum number of epochs entry in Table 6.4 includes both ACE stages in the steepest descent case.

For the case of the last entry of the adaptive steepest descent method, a further run was performed with no error convergence limit but epoch limits of 100 and

50, for first stage and ACE stage respectively. The average norm RMS error over the 10 random restarts was, train set: 0.0345, test set: 0.0369. The average trend accuracy was, train set: 99.4%, test set 99.0%. A plot of the target and forecast for the last 100 patterns in the test set is shown in Figure 6.2 for this case.

The convergence rates for train and test sets are plotted for the adaptive steepest descent solver in Figures 6.3 and 6.4 respectively, with the epochs extended to 200. Note the reduction in error once the ACE neuron becomes operative in second stage training.

A control test was also performed: the *differences* of the Mackay-Glass series (for the *every sixth point sampled* series) were re-ordered according to a uniform randomisation of the original sequence of steps. The series ranged over $[-0.5, 2.0]$

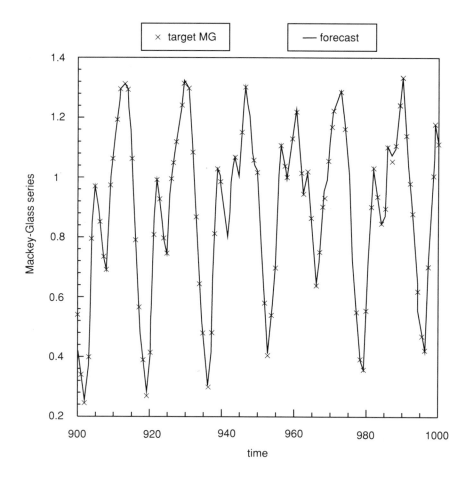

Figure 6.2 Mackey-Glass equation forecasts compared with target values, for adaptive steepest descent solution. Last 100 samples in the test set shown

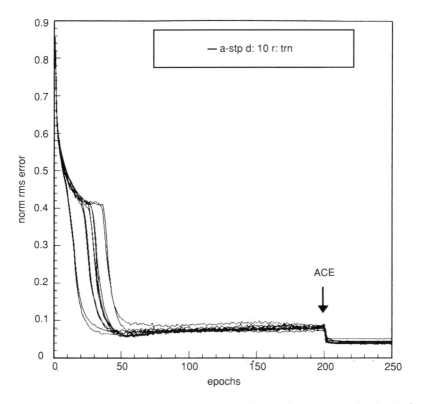

Figure 6.3 Learning the Mackey-Glass equation with adaptive steepest solved neural network: Convergence rate for *train* set, 10 runs superimposed for different random starting weights. ACE neuron operative after 200 epochs

with steps distributed close to a Gaussian over the step sizes $[-0.2, 0.25]$. A new time series was then constructed from these differences, starting at the original point of the Mackay-Glass series. In all other respects the numerical experimental conditions were as above, with the adaptive steepest descent solver chosen and multiconnectivity on, robust function off, quadratic cost function and *external* normalisation performed to the range $[-1, 1]$. The average training and test normalised RMS errors were 0.099 and 0.131 respectively. The average trend forecast accuracies were 54.1% and 53.2% for train and test sets respectively. Standard deviation band noise filtering improved the trend accuracy to: train $90/149 = 60.4\%$; test $111/182 = 61.0\%$.

One conclusion from these tests is that *external* normalising the input data to the range $[-1, 1]$ has an edge over $[0, 1]$, for learning the Mackey-Glass equation. Selecting a suitable initial learning coefficient for the steepest descent solver posed

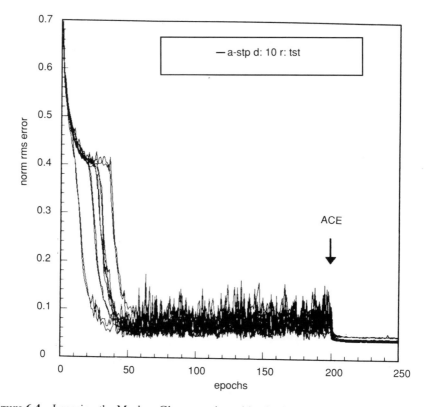

Figure 6.4 Learning the Mackey-Glass equation with adaptive steepest descent solved neural network: Normalised RMS error for *test* set monitored during training, 10 runs superimposed for different random starting weights. ACE neuron operative after 200 epochs

no problems, and this solver provided the fastest training within the defined convergence criterion of norm RMS error 0.05, with 34 epochs. The Shanno solver required more epochs to reach performance figures similar to the other two solvers. The use of the robust function, multiconnectivity and Euclidean or nonEuclidean cost function remains a matter for experimentation, although there is indication that the Euclidean without the robustness option is more satisfactory.

6.3 SUNSPOT NUMBER SERIES

Sunspots are regions of subdued luminous activity on the solar surface, which viewed from a telescope appear as dark spots, usually clustered in groups. The dark hole appearance is a contrast effect, the spots do emit visible radiation, but substantially less than adjacent regions. The spots correspond to regions of unusually high magnetic fields and have some influence on the ionic solar wind which reaches Earth. Astronomers have kept records of the sunspot numbers from around 1700. An arbitrarily defined quantity, the international (previously Zurich) relative sunspot number R_I is the accepted standard for characterising sunspot abundance:

$$R_I = k(10g + f) \tag{6.9}$$

where g is the number of sunspot groups, f is the number of individual sunspots and k is a factor for aligning different telescopic readings to the same scale.

The R_I numbers are reported by the Sunspot Index Data Center[84]. A cycle of approximately 11–15 years is observed, corresponding to polarity reversals of the sun's rotating solar magnetic fields. No physical law has been found that predicts the sunspot numbers, so they remain of empirical interest, and form a classic benchmark problem in statistical forecasting methodology, see for example Priestley[129], Tong and Lim[163] and Gabr and Rao[131]. Recent nonlinear models applied to the series include neural networks by Weigend et al[170] and weighted maps by Stokbro[154].

The yearly means are tabulated in Tables 6.5 and 6.6, calculated from the monthly data quoted in Marple[103] up to 1981, and the Sunspot Index Data Center's figures thereafter. Marple notes that data prior to 1835 is of a lesser reliability than subsequent measurements. Due to the limited length of the series all the data is used here, from 1700 onwards. In any case, it is noted[103] that yearly means are more stable figures. Three input embedding schemes were considered here:

- *A:* An input window of length six elements representing adjacent points, with the seventh point as target. This corresponds to $P = 1$, $\tau = 1$ and $m = 5$ in the chaos embedding terminology.

- *B:* A window of length eight elements comprised seven points sampled one in two points ($\tau = 2$), the eighth point is the next adjacent and the target similarly the next one along ($\tau = 1$, $P = 1$). This input window thus spans 14 adjacent points of the sunspot series.

- *C:* An averaging scheme in a similar vein to Jurik's[73]. An input window or vector, v, of dimension eight covering a block of 15 sunspot series points, x, as follows:

$$v(1) = \frac{1}{5}\sum_{i=1}^{5} x_i$$

$$v(2) = \frac{1}{5}\sum_{i=5}^{9} x_i$$

$$v(3) = \frac{1}{3}\sum_{i=8}^{10} x_i$$

Table 6.5 Yearly mean R_I sunspot numbers: years 1700–1849

Year	$\overline{R}_I$	Year	$\overline{R}_I$	Year	$\overline{R}_I$	Year	$\overline{R}_I$	Year	$\overline{R}_I$	Year	$\overline{R}_I$
1700	6.0	1725	38.0	1750	83.4	1775	7.0	1800	14.6	1825	16.6
1701	11.0	1726	74.0	1751	47.8	1776	19.9	1801	34.0	1826	36.5
1702	17.0	1727	113.0	1752	48.0	1777	92.8	1802	45.0	1827	49.7
1703	23.0	1728	98.0	1753	30.7	1778	154.7	1803	43.0	1828	62.6
1704	35.0	1729	67.0	1754	12.3	1779	125.7	1804	47.6	1829	67.1
1705	54.0	1730	44.0	1755	9.6	1780	85.0	1805	42.2	1830	70.9
1706	29.0	1731	28.0	1756	10.2	1781	68.0	1806	28.1	1831	47.8
1707	21.0	1732	11.0	1757	32.5	1782	38.5	1807	10.0	1832	27.5
1708	11.0	1733	6.0	1758	47.5	1783	22.7	1808	8.1	1833	8.5
1709	8.0	1734	17.0	1759	54.0	1784	10.2	1809	2.5	1834	13.2
1710	3.0	1735	33.0	1760	63.1	1785	24.2	1810	0.0	1835	56.9
1711	0.0	1736	64.0	1761	85.8	1786	83.0	1811	1.4	1836	121.9
1712	0.0	1737	77.0	1762	60.9	1787	132.2	1812	5.0	1837	138.1
1713	2.0	1738	106.0	1763	45.2	1788	131.3	1813	12.2	1838	103.4
1714	11.0	1739	96.0	1764	36.4	1789	118.0	1814	13.9	1839	85.7
1715	27.0	1740	67.0	1765	20.9	1790	89.6	1815	35.4	1840	63.3
1716	44.0	1741	39.0	1766	11.5	1791	66.6	1816	45.8	1841	36.8
1717	58.0	1742	20.0	1767	37.9	1792	60.2	1817	41.0	1842	24.2
1718	56.0	1743	16.0	1768	70.0	1793	46.9	1818	30.5	1843	10.7
1719	38.0	1744	6.0	1769	106.3	1794	41.0	1819	24.0	1844	15.1
1720	28.0	1745	11.0	1770	100.5	1795	21.1	1820	15.7	1845	40.0
1721	26.0	1746	22.0	1771	81.7	1796	16.0	1821	6.6	1846	61.4
1722	22.0	1747	39.0	1772	66.6	1797	6.4	1822	4.0	1847	98.8
1723	11.0	1748	56.0	1773	34.8	1798	4.1	1823	1.8	1848	124.9
1724	22.0	1749	80.9	1774	30.4	1799	6.7	1824	8.5	1849	95.6

$$v(4) = \frac{1}{3} \sum_{i=10}^{12} x_i$$

$$v(5) = x(12)$$

$$v(6) = x(13)$$

$$v(7) = x(14)$$

$$v(8) = x(15)$$

The target is the 16th point.

As before, the whole series was *external* normalised; benchmark results are tabulated for [0,1], which was found to have a marginal edge over [−1,1] for this series. The error measure was the standard deviation normalised RMS error, which as noted before, is invariant to scaling and has the convenient interpretation that

Table 6.6 Yearly mean R_I sunspot numbers: years 1850–1992

Year	$\overline{R_I}$	Year	$\overline{R_I}$	Year	$\overline{R_I}$	Year	$\overline{R_I}$	Year	$\overline{R_I}$	Year	$\overline{R_I}$
1850	66.4	1875	17.0	1900	9.4	1925	44.4	1950	83.9	1975	15.5
1851	64.2	1876	11.4	1901	2.7	1926	63.9	1951	69.4	1976	12.6
1852	54.3	1877	12.3	1902	5.1	1927	68.8	1952	31.6	1977	27.5
1853	39.0	1878	3.3	1903	24.4	1928	78.0	1953	13.9	1978	92.5
1854	20.5	1879	6.0	1904	42.2	1929	65.0	1954	4.5	1979	155.4
1855	6.7	1880	32.3	1905	63.3	1930	35.6	1955	38.0	1980	155.1
1856	4.3	1881	54.2	1906	54.0	1931	21.0	1956	142.1	1981	140.5
1857	22.9	1882	59.4	1907	61.7	1932	11.2	1957	190.2	1982	115.9
1858	55.0	1883	63.7	1908	48.6	1933	5.5	1958	184.8	1983	66.6
1859	93.9	1884	63.6	1909	43.9	1934	8.7	1959	159.0	1984	45.9
1860	96.0	1885	52.0	1910	18.5	1935	36.1	1960	112.6	1985	17.9
1861	77.1	1886	25.4	1911	5.7	1936	79.9	1961	53.9	1986	13.4
1862	59.0	1887	13.1	1912	3.6	1937	114.4	1962	37.5	1987	29.2
1863	44.0	1888	6.8	1913	1.4	1938	109.5	1963	27.9	1988	100.2
1864	47.1	1889	6.3	1914	9.6	1939	88.7	1964	10.2	1989	157.6
1865	30.4	1890	7.1	1915	47.4	1940	68.0	1965	15.1	1990	142.6
1866	16.2	1891	35.7	1916	57.2	1941	47.5	1966	47.0	1991	145.7
1867	7.3	1892	73.2	1917	104.2	1942	30.4	1967	93.9	1992	94.3
1868	37.5	1893	85.1	1918	80.8	1943	16.3	1968	106.2		
1869	74.0	1894	78.0	1919	63.5	1944	9.7	1969	105.5		
1870	139.2	1895	63.9	1920	37.7	1945	33.2	1970	104.5		
1871	111.1	1896	41.7	1921	26.1	1946	92.6	1971	66.6		
1872	101.8	1897	26.2	1922	14.2	1947	151.6	1972	69.1		
1873	66.1	1898	26.6	1923	5.8	1948	136.7	1973	38.0		
1874	44.6	1899	12.1	1924	16.8	1949	134.7	1974	34.5		

Table 6.7 Neural network data input schemes for sunspot benchmarks

input scheme	train set			test set		
	sd	years	size	sd	years	size
A	34.23	1706–1914	209	48.10	1915–1992	78
B	33.97	1714–1922	209	51.60	1923–1992	70
C	34.00	1715–1923	209	51.07	1924–1992	69

a value of 1 signifies forecasts no better than the mean target value. The standard deviation was calculated separately for the train and test sets. In order to translate the table norm RMS error values to absolute unscaled RMS error, the values should be multiplied by the standard deviation figures in Table 6.7. Also shown is the range of target sunspot years used under each scheme and the number of vectors.

All the runs were repeated 10 times for different random weight initialisations, averages are over these reruns. In all cases, the robust function and multiconnectivity were not used, and the quadratic error cost function was selected. All the

Table 6.8   Sunspot R_I Benchmarks. See text for definitions

solver	net	ACE	η	TWR	epo lim	$\overline{trn}_\varepsilon$	$\overline{tst}_\varepsilon$	$\overline{trn}\%$	$\overline{tst}\%$
a−stp d	A:6-5-1	1	0.2,0.1	5.1	300,50	0.377	0.446	84.6	95.0
	C:8-3-1	1	0.2,0.1	6.7	170,30	0.362	0.428	85.9	92.8
BFGS	A:6-5-1	0	—	5.1	300	0.282	0.505	85.2	93.2
	B:8-6-1	1	—	3.4	200,50	0.283	0.551	88.1	85.6
	C:8-6-1	1	—	3.4	200,50	0.271	0.513	87.2	90.9
	C:8-3-1	1	—	6.7	200,50	0.344	0.427	85.8	94.2
Shann	A:6-5-1	0	—	5.1	300	0.993	0.815	70.1	78.6
	C:8-4-1	0	—	5.1	300	0.373	0.415	83.2	92.0

hidden neuron transfer functions were tanh with gain 1.5 in all cases. The output layer neuron was always piece-wise linear and had gradient 0.5 with the linear part extended ± 2.5 on the input axis. No convergence limit was set, rather a fixed number of epochs was preset for training cessation. The results reported in Table 6.8 include the following options:

- *solver:* Three variants: *a-stp* is the Hertz rules adaptive steepest descent with weight update per pattern. *Shann* is the Shanno variant of conjugate gradients with inexact line search. *BFGS* is the quasi-Newton method with inexact line search.

- *net:* Three layer nets in all cases, giving number of cells per layer. Prefix letter corresponds to the data input scheme. The hidden number includes the ACE neuron, when selected.

- *ACE:* The ACE neuron option: 0 — off, 1 — on. Note that the *a-stp d* solver is used to train the ACE neuron in these benchmarks, irrespective of the first stage solver choice.

- η: The learning coefficient, applicable to steepest descent only: given as pair (hidden layer, output layer). Also, the momentum coefficient was always set to 0.

- *TWR:* The training patterns to weights ratio, see Section 4.13. This figure includes ACE neuron weights.

- *epo lim:* The epoch training limits. Given as pair where ACE neuron was used.

- $\overline{trn}_\varepsilon$: The average train set normalised RMS error.

- $\overline{tst}_\varepsilon$: The average test set normalised RMS error.

- $\overline{trn}\%$: The forecast change accuracy for the train set.

- $\overline{tst}\%$: The forecast change accuracy for the test set.

Convergence rate examples for the steepest descent solver are shown in Figures 6.5 and 6.6, which plot the training and test set errors respectively, for 10 runs with epochs fixed at 450 and 50 for the two stages.

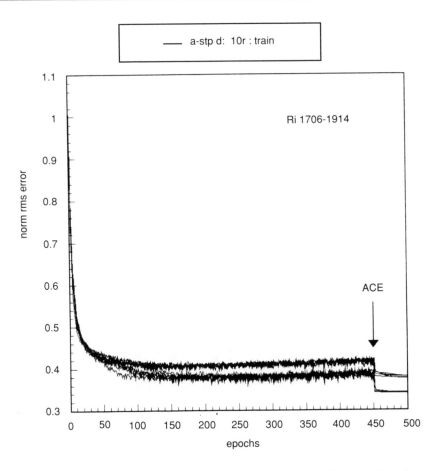

Figure 6.5 Sunspot time series: Normalised RMS error train set performance for adaptive steepest descent solver. R_I years 1706 to 1914, with 10 runs superimposed for different weight initialisations. ACE neuron operative after 450 epochs

In order to provide a basis for determining the network training cessation point and also have available an independent means of evaluating performance, the test data can be split into a validation set, $vTST$, and a prediction set, $pTST$. In subsequent sunspot benchmarks the data was divided into three sets: the training set, TRN, comprised target years 1706 to 1914, 209 vectors, with standard deviation (unnormalised) 34.23; $vTST$ target years 1915–1949 (35 vectors); $pTST$ target years 1950 to 1992 (43 vectors). The target standard deviation of the combined test sets was 40.59. These sd figures will allow the normalised RMS errors reported below to be transformed into absolute RMS figures. As above, 10 runs were performed for different random weight initialisations and the performance figures were averaged over these runs. The data input scheme A, using a rolling window of six adjacent

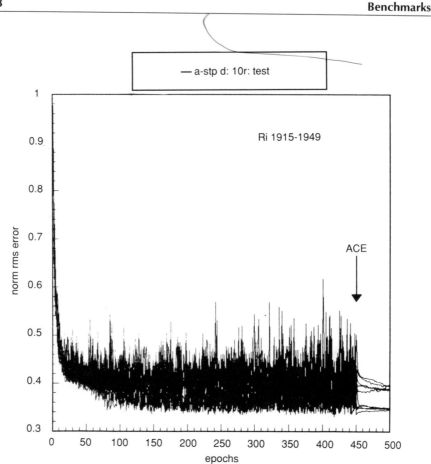

Figure 6.6 Sunspot time series: Test set performance, monitored during training phase shown in Figure 6.5

time series points, was used throughout. The network multiconnectivity was operative, and the ACE neuron was operative. However the ACE neuron only improved the steepest descent solver solution, in the case of the batch weight update methods the RMS error remained horizontal with no further reduction.

Training cessation was determined by two methods: a fixed limit on the number of epochs, with 380 for the first stage and 20 for the second stage in the steepest descent case, and 450 epochs for BFGS and Shanno; a normalised RMS error criterion of 0.335, established by analysing the *vTST* set performance. Results are tabulated in Table 6.9 (ACE is only included in the steepest descent results).

The pre-ACE performance figures for the steepest descent case, at 380 epochs, was $\epsilon_{trn} = 0.394$, $\epsilon_{vtst} = 0.403$, resulting in a 10% improvement after 20 epochs with the ACE neuron.

Table 6.9 Sunspot R_I benchmarks, second set

solver	net	TWR	norm rms error			ave trend %		
			TRN	vTST	pTST	TRN	vTST	pTST
a−stp d	6,3,1	6.7	0.356	0.360	0.404	82.5	94.6	90.2
BFGS	6,2,1	9.1	0.336	0.352	0.418	82.1	94.6	89.5
	6,3,1	6.7	0.335	0.342	0.368	82.3	94.9	93.0
	6,4,1	5.4	0.334	0.341	0.374	82.7	95.4	94.2
Shanno	6,2,1	9.1	0.375	0.401	0.463	80.1	96.0	91.6
	6,3,1	6.7	0.351	0.355	0.377	81.2	93.1	91.9
	6,4,1	5.4	0.407	0.396	0.414	79.8	92.0	90.5

The lowest prediction set error was given by the BFGS solver for a network with three hidden neurons. A plot of the forecasts and sunspot series targets is shown in Figure 6.7 for this case. The converged solution weights for this network is listed in Table E.4, with the best case from the 10 runs selected, corresponding to normalised RMS errors: $\epsilon_{trn} = 0.33$, $\epsilon_{vtst} = 0.34$, and $\epsilon_{ptst} = 0.33$.

A conclusion that can be drawn from the above examples is that at a certain threshold, lower train set error can be achieved at the expense of higher prediction set error, but not necessarily with higher validation set error. Since the test sets were split according to years, the validation set being nearest in time to the train set, some advantage in lower error may be expected for target years closest to the training years. One way round this is to select the validation and prediction test vectors randomly from within the available test data.

There is further scope for optimising the sunspot series forecasts, however this is not the main concern here. In so far as comparison is made with previous reported results, of interest is the fact that a lag, or input dimension, of six was found satisfactory here, where others[162,172] used 12 dimensional inputs. Tong and Lim[163] produced a normalised RMS error, for prediction set target years 1956–1979, of 0.53, whilst Weigend et al[169] quote 0.59. The best figure here for prediction set years 1950–1992 was 0.33. All cases had a similar number of intervening years used for the validation set, and similar target years used for training. The lower training and validation set errors quoted by Tong and Lim and Weigend et al may therefore imply some over-training in their models.

Next, a standard deviation band error analysis, as discussed in Section 4.13.3, was performed for one of the above examples. Postprocessing the forecasts can help to reduce the effects of noise in the data. Forecasts can be classed according to four permutations, depending on the correctness of the trend and size of move. A forecast move is defined as $O_{t+1} - T_t$, i.e. the forecast with respect to the current known value. Seen from the viewpoint that trend prediction is more important than knowing the size of the move, the forecasts can be analysed as a

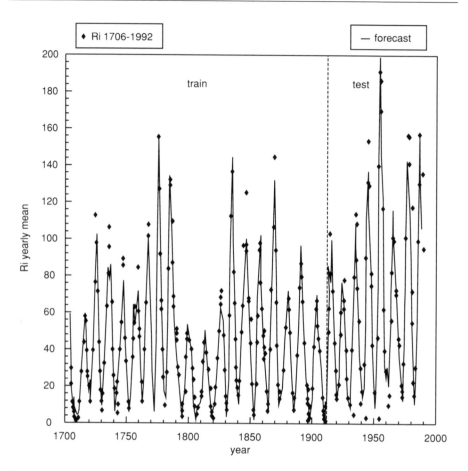

Figure 6.7 Sunspot time series: Forecasts for the best BFGS solver neural network. Test set forecasts include validation and prediction set periods. Target values indicated

problem of whether the forecast sizes are a measure of the network's confidence in the trend.

Thus an examination of the correct and wrong forecast moves, plotted for the *TRN* and *vTST* data at the end of training, as shown in Figure 6.8 (which also includes *pTST* data), can reveal whether small size forecasts are prone to error, either due to an indeterminacy in the network, or simply as a result of their proximity to the zero line if all forecasts have equal uncertainty. Uncertainty in the network may be due to noise having an overwhelming influence in the particular input pattern. A plot, not shown, of all the forecasts for 10 runs superimposed, revealed that the majority of wrong forecasts were indeed banded close around the zero line. Evaluating the mean wrong forecast and constructing one standard

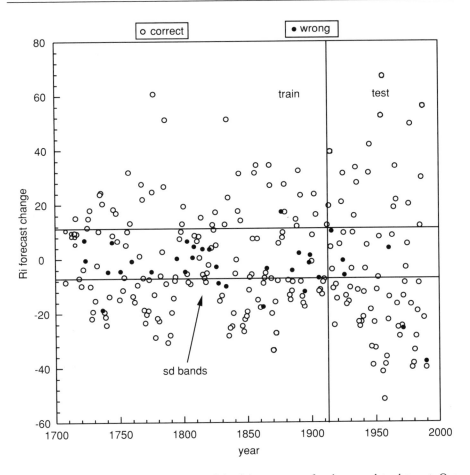

Figure 6.8 Sunspot time series: Plots of the forecast move for the complete data set. One standard deviation bands about the mean also shown, evaluated exclusively from *wrong* forecast movements

deviation bands for the wrong forecasts, provided a straightforward method for filtering out the noisy forecasts, with these figures calculated from the training set only. Figure 6.8 shows the forecasts for all target years 1706 to 1992, for one of the BFGS solved networks, with the 1 sd bands evaluated over the 10 runs of different weight initialisations.

The corresponding trend figures were broken down into those forecasts that fell within the sd bands (< sd in Table 6.10) and those greater than the bands (> sd). Table 6.10 reports the analysis, where the *vTST* and *pTST* set figures were combined. Figures correspond to one network result, these being similar over the 10 runs. The '> sd sz' data corresponds to the case where correct size of forecast matters, measured relative to the bands. The same trend data was re-analysed

Table 6.10 Sunspot trend forecasts analysis for BFGS solved network. Validation and prediction test figures combined. Notation: Hits are correct forecast moves. *sd* refers to ±1 standard deviation bands calculated for wrong forecast moves. *sd sz* refers to hits requiring correct size of move (relative to sd bands) being taken into account

bands	train set			test set		
	sample	hits	%	sample	hits	%
≤ sd	61	30	49.2	12	9	75.0
≤ sd sz	61	15	24.6	12	2	16.7
> sd	148	141	95.3	66	64	97.0
> sd sz	148	117	79.1	66	53	80.3
Total	209	171	81.8	78	73	93.6

Table 6.11 Sunspots train set trend analysis for BFGS solved network based on falls and rises breakdown. Notation as Table 6.10

bands	falls			rises		
	sample	hits	%	sample	hits	%
≤ sd	31	19	61.3	30	11	36.7
> sd	86	81	94.2	62	60	96.8

according to falls and rises, with Table 6.11 providing the breakdown for the train set, and Table 6.12 for the combined test sets.

The sd bands filter out a significant number of wrong forecasts, with a resultant increase in the '> sd' trend accuracy, with about one third of the total sample size filtered out. The breakdown according to size (> sd sz) reveals that forecast moves greater than the bands are also likely to be so in reality. The breakdown according to falls and rises shows that the network is equally good in either case when the forecast moves are greater than the bands, with performance above 90%. To select one figure of merit for the noise filter, the train set trend accuracy improved from 81.8% to 95.3% and the combined test set trend from 93.6% to 97%.

Table 6.12 Sunspots test set trend analysis for BFGS solved network based on falls and rises breakdown. Notation as Table 6.10

bands	falls			rises		
	sample	hits	%	sample	hits	%
≤ sd	6	5	83.3	6	4	66.7
> sd	43	41	95.3	23	23	100.0

6.4 S&P 500 FUTURES

The Standard and Poor's 500 market index is a value-weighted arithmetic mean of the market value of its 500 components. These consist of 400 industrial, 20 transportation, 40 utilities and 40 financial issues traded in the USA. The index is continually updated and provides a measure of the market as a whole, with respect to the launch in April 1982 when the index started at 100. The futures contract in the index was launched simultaneously, traded at the Chicago Mercantile Exchange's Index and Options Market, and is one of the most actively traded in the futures market.

The S&P 500 futures contract is available for delivery (cash settled, being an index) on the third Friday in March, June, September and December. The time series analysed here is constructed from an unadjusted concatenation of the nearest active contract daily prices, with roll-over to the next nearest contract in the delivery month. For example, in August the series will follow the September futures prices, on 1 September the series switches to tracking the December contract. The series will incur glitches on the roll-over dates, in the benchmark tests the only compensation for this is the removal of input vectors with targets that fall on these dates. A plot of the concatenated S&P 500 futures prices by nearest month time series is shown in Figure 6.9.

A particular point to note in the data presentation is that actual S&P 500 futures price values are used for the target. This differs from the standard practice in econometrics and quantitative finance of using natural logarithm ratios, $ln(p_{t+1}/p_t)$. There is a possibility that some underlying information may be distorted by such manipulations, a view attracting increasing support[35,126], hence the resort to the original series.

The following data structure for the network target and input patterns, p, was used, where $c(0)$ is the target daily closing price, $c(-x)$ is the close x days prior to the target day, s is the spot or cash closing price, v is the volatility indicator (see Section 3.2.2) and $r(-1)$ is the random walk indicator over a one day look-back period (see Section 3.2.1)—the average RWI and volatility values used in their calculation were 2.32 and 16.79 respectively:

$$p(1) = v(-2)$$
$$p(2) = v(-1)$$
$$p(3) = r(-1)$$
$$p(4) = [v(-6) + v(-5) + v(-4)]/3$$
$$p(5) = [v(-5) + v(-4) + v(-3)]/3$$
$$p(6) = [v(-4) + v(-3) + v(-2)]/3$$
$$p(7) = [v(-3) + v(-2) + v(-1)]/3$$

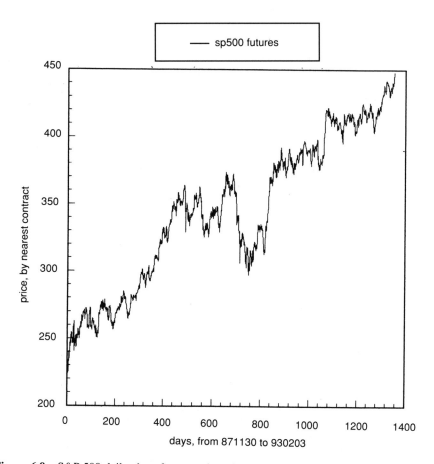

Figure 6.9 S&P 500 daily close futures prices time series, by nearest contract month, used in the benchmarks

$$p(8) = c(-15)$$
$$p(9) = c(-10)$$
$$p(10) = s(-3)$$
$$p(11) = s(-2)$$
$$p(12) = s(-1)$$
$$p(13) = c(-5)$$
$$p(14) = c(-4)$$
$$p(15) = c(-3)$$

$$p(16) = c(-2)$$
$$p(17) = c(-1)$$
$$p(18) = c(0)$$

The vector channels were split into two groups for the purpose of normalisation: channels 1–7 contain variables with sign information, so *along norm 0-offset* channel normalisation was selected. The remaining input channels 8–17 were grouped together for along channel normalisation to the range [−1,1].

Apart from the above original (or forward) series, named *ori* below, two further data structures were constructed for control purposes; *rev* a time reversal of the series, and *ran* a randomisation of the time series over the same period. The random series r was constructed by first taking differences of the S&P 500 futures series $u_t = p_t - p_{t-1}$ and then randomising the order of u. The random control time series was then constructed: $r_t = r_{t-1} + u_t$ with $r_0 = p_0$. The series r thus had the same distribuion of size of moves as the original series. The random and reverse control series used only close of day prices as network inputs. In the case of the reverse control series, a strict reversal would use the forward time open prices as the new closing prices and the close as the new openings, however this approach was not used, it was preferred to deal with the same target prices used in the original forward time series.

The error measure was the standard deviation normalised RMS error. The standard deviation was calculated separately for the train and test sets and is tabulated below. The unscaled absolute RMS error is obtained by multiplying the norm RMS figures by the sd, given in Table 6.13. Note that the contract roll-over date target removal was not performed for the random series, hence the larger sample size.

All the runs were repeated 10 times for different random weight initialisation, averages are over these reruns. In all cases, the robust function was off, multiconnectivity on and the quadratic cost function used. The output neuron was always piece-wise linear and had a gradient 0.5 with the linear part extended ±2.5 on the input axis. No convergence limit was set, rather a fixed number of epochs was preset for training cessation: Adaptive steepest descent had 500 epochs for the first stage (pre-ACE) and 50 epochs for the ACE neuron; Shanno had 500 epochs

Table 6.13 S&P 500 benchmark time series data

input scheme	train set			test set		
	sd	dates	size	sd	dates	size
ori	44.44	871130–911206	1033	11.89	911209–930204	300
rev	40.43	921230–881223	1033	12.65	881222–871026	300
ran	33.06	random	1054	35.10	random	300

Table 6.14 S&P 500 benchmarks. Average results shown, with best performance in brackets

solver	data	TWR	$\overline{trn}_\varepsilon$	$\overline{tst}_\varepsilon$	$\overline{trn}\%$	$\overline{tst}\%$
a-stp d	ori	6.1	0.074 (0.074)	0.393 (0.391)	53.9 (55.8)	54.5 (57.6)
	ori	7.8	0.074 (0.074)	0.393 (0.391)	53.9 (55.8)	54.5 (57.7)
	rev	6.1	0.077 (0.076)	0.378 (0.378)	55.3 (55.8)	49.4 (52.7)
	ran	6.1	0.097 (0.097)	0.181 (0.180)	53.2 (54.9)	49.7 (50.7)
BFGS	ori	6.8	0.074 (0.072)	0.414 (0.391)	56.5 (58.5)	54.5 (56.0)
	rev	6.8	0.279 (0.072)	0.922 (0.542)	56.6 (60.1)	53.2 (55.2)
	ran	6.8	0.265 (0.094)	1.703 (3.611)	56.0 (58.4)	49.8 (52.0)
Shanno	ori	6.8	0.325 (0.073)	1.209 (0.407)	53.5 (55.3)	52.4 (52.7)
	rev	6.8	0.130 (0.077)	0.652 (0.373)	52.6 (54.6)	50.3 (50.3)
	ran	6.8	0.378 (0.098)	0.466 (0.184)	52.3 (55.1)	48.5 (49.3)

for first stage with no ACE and BFGS had 180 epochs with no ACE. The network structure was the same in all cases: three cell layers 17-7-1, and hidden neuron transfer functions, 4 tanh, 2 piece-wise linear, 1 cosine. The steepest descent case had an additional ACE neuron in the hidden layer, and the second *ori* case had two fewer tanh neurons ($TWR = 7.8$). The results reported in Table 6.14 include the following options:

- *solver:* Three variants: *a-stp* is the Hertz rules adaptive steepest descent with weight update per pattern. The learning coefficient starting values were 0.2 and 0.1 for the hidden and output layers. *BFGS* is the quasi-Newton method with inexact line search. *Shanno* is the Shanno variant of the conjugate gradient method with inexact line search.

- *Data:* *ori* is the original time series of S&P 500 futures by nearest month contract. *rev* is the reversal in time of the series. *ran* is a randomised scrambling of the price differences.

- *TWR:* The training patterns to weights ratio, see Section 4.13. This figure includes ACE neuron weights.

- $\overline{trn}_\varepsilon$: The average train set normalised RMS error.

- $\overline{tst}_\varepsilon$: The average test set normalised RMS error.

- $\overline{trn}\%$: The forecast change accuracy for the train set.

- $\overline{tst}\%$: The forecast change accuracy for the test set.

The performance figures given in brackets are for the run with the best training performance.

Note that in the Shanno *ori* and *rev* cases some of the runs diverged, so that the best run figures (in brackets) provide more suitable figures for comparison.

The results in Table 6.14 show that the Shanno solutions are the most inconclusive, whilst the steepest descent and BFGS solutions reveal a hint of structure in the original and reverse data. Note that there is a good case for arguing that if nonrandom structure exists in the market then the reversal of the time series should also reveal that future data can predict the past. A plot of a steepest descent solution, comparing forecasts with targets, is shown in Figure 6.10. As will be discussed in the next chapter, the important aspect of a solution is its quality of correctly timing the large swings in the market, an overall percentage accuracy figure alone does not reflect that. There are many possibilities for further development. The next benchmark also provides ideas that can be applied to the S&P 500.

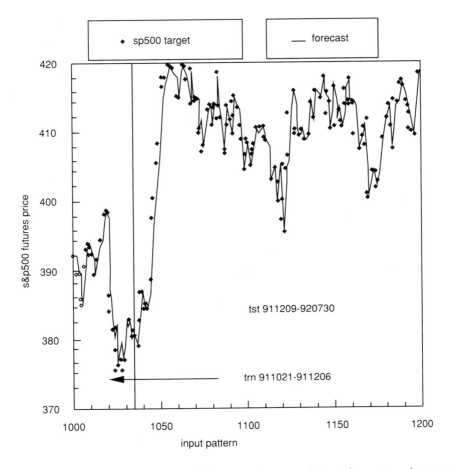

Figure 6.10 S&P 500 neural network (steepest descent solution) forecasts and targets, with plotted train (trn) and test (tst) periods indicated. Graph plotted against input pattern (or target number), covering examples either side of the train/test set divide

6.5   BP/USD CURRENCY FUTURES

The global foreign exchange turnover is, using recent estimates, about $1000bn per day. A large measure of this trading is taken up by the arbitrage operations of banks in the forward and futures markets. Futures in foreign exchange were first launched by the innovative Chicago Mercantile Exchange at the International Money Market (IMM) in 1972. Since launching their own contracts in 1982, the London International Financial Futures Exchange has risen to rank first by market share, followed by the IMM and Tokyo.

The IMM's British Pound against US dollar contract will be taken as the currency rate futures example. Like the S&P 500 futures, it has delivery months March, June, September and December, with delivery on the third Wednesday. The price quoted is in cents per pound. The historical prices here were constructed by concatenating the prices for the nearest futures contract, with roll-over to the next nearest contract on the first day of each delivery month. Those neural network input vectors whose targets fell on the roll-over date were removed from the training and test sets. This was the only provision against the artificial glitch that occurs in the time series at roll-over. A plot of the British pound/dollar daily close futures prices used in the benchmark is shown in Figure 6.11.

The following data structure was used for the network target and input patterns, p, where $c(0)$ is the target closing price, $c(-x)$ is the close x days prior to the target day, s is the spot or cash closing price and $r(-x)$ is the random walk indicator over a x days look-back period (see Section 3.2.1). Again, note that the target $p(12)$ is the actual (normalised) closing price and not a price difference:

$$p(1) = [c(-3)+c(-2)+c(-1)]/3$$
$$p(2) = s(-2)$$
$$p(3) = s(-1)$$
$$p(4) = c(-5)$$
$$p(5) = c(-4)$$
$$p(6) = c(-3)$$
$$p(7) = c(-2)$$
$$p(8) = c(-1)$$
$$p(9) = r(-3)$$
$$p(10) = r(-2)$$
$$p(11) = r(-1)$$
$$p(12) = c(0)$$

The vector channels were split into two groups for the purpose of normalisation: channels 9–11 contain variables with sign information, so *along norm 0-offset*

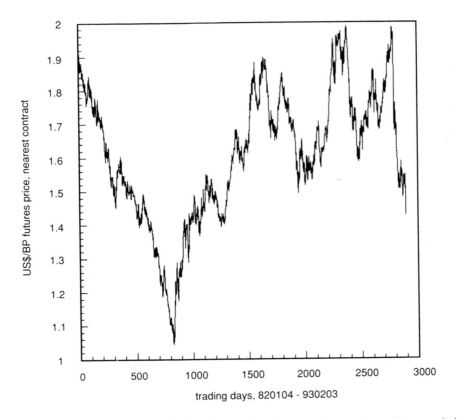

Figure 6.11 British P/USD daily close futures prices by nearest contract month over period 820104 to 930203

channel normalisation was selected. The other input channels were *along channel* normalised to the range [−1,1].

For control purposes, in addition to the original time series, named *ori* below, two further data structures were constructed; *rev* a time reversal of the series, and *ran* a randomisation of the time series over the same period, constructed as in the S&P 500 benchmark. The neural network inputs for *rev* and *ran* comprised a mix of random walk indices for various look-back periods and historical values of the close prices; again these series only comprised close prices (the random walk index being a function of the close prices only).

The error measure was the standard deviation normalised RMS error, with the sd calculated separately for the train and test sets, tabulated below. The unscaled absolute RMS error is obtained by multiplying the norm RMS figures by the sd, given in Table 6.15. Note that the contract roll-over date target removal was not performed for the random series, hence the larger sample size.

Table 6.15 BP/USD benchmark time series data

input scheme	train set			test set		
	sd	dates	set size	sd	dates	set size
ori	0.2054	840109–911206	2033	0.1394	911209–930204	300
rev	0.1857	921230–850201	2033	0.1070	850131–831205	300
ran	0.2030	random	2069	0.1176	random	300

All the runs were repeated 10 times for different random weight initialisations, quoted averages are over these reruns. In all cases the robust function was off, multiconnectivity on, and the cost function was quadratic. The output neuron was always piece-wise linear and had gradient 0.5 with the linear part extended ± 2.5 on the input axis. Training was stopped after a fixed number of epochs, given in the results table. The network structure was the same in all cases: three layers with cells 11-5-1 and hidden neuron transfer functions; 3 tanh, 1 piece-wise linear, 1 cosine. The steepest descent case had an additional ACE neuron in the hidden layer. The results reported in Table 6.16 include the following options:

- *solver a-stp* is the Hertz rules adaptive steepest descent with weight update per pattern. The learning coefficient starting values were 0.2 and 0.1 for the hidden and output layers. *BFGS* is the quasi-Newton method with inexact line search.
- *Data ori* is the original time series of S&P 500 futures by nearest month contract. *rev* is the reversal in time of the series. *ran* is a randomised scrambling of the price differences.
- *TWR:* The training patterns to weights ratio, see Section 4.13. This figure includes ACE neuron weights for the steepest descent solver.
- *epochs:* The fixed limit of training epochs applied. For the steepest descent case the second figure is for the ACE neuron.
- $\overline{trn_\varepsilon}$ The average train set normalised RMS error.
- $\overline{tst_\varepsilon}$: The average test set normalised RMS error.
- $\overline{trn\%}$: The forecast change accuracy for the train set.
- $\overline{tst\%}$: The forecast change accuracy for the test set.

Table 6.16 BP/USD benchmarks. Average results shown, with best performance in brackets

solver	data	TWR	epochs	$\overline{trn_\varepsilon}$	$\overline{tst_\varepsilon}$	$\overline{trn\%}$	$\overline{tst\%}$
a-stp d	ori	22.6	100/30	0.055 (0.055)	0.232 (0.232)	52.9 (53.7)	48.3 (49.2)
	rev	22.6	200/50	0.087 (0.087)	0.109 (0.108)	49.0 (50.0)	45.6 (44.4)
	ran	23.0	200/50	0.068 (0.068)	0.170 (0.170)	47.6 (50.0)	45.3 (44.8)
BFGS	ori	26.4	180	0.263 (0.054)	0.550 (0.235)	53.2 (55.3)	48.6 (50.8)
	rev	26.4	180	0.070 (0.070)	0.201 (0.202)	50.2 (52.4)	44.0 (43.0)
	ran	26.9	180	0.072 (0.063)	0.183 (0.171)	47.5 (49.8)	46.8 (47.0)

The performance figures given in brackets are for the run with the best training performance.

The performance figures reveal that the original series can be trained to a lower RMS error than the control series, so again this is a hint of an underlying structure. However, the RMS error for the original series test set is much higher than the control series figures, although the percentage accuracy is better. Whilst the above figures are inconclusive, they should be useful in further model development.

One alternative approach is to select targets according to the day of the week. Thus a second series of benchmarks was produced for each day of the week using just the BFGS solver at a fixed 200 epochs, covering the same period. Table 6.17 provides details of the time series.

The same 11-5-1 neural network structure and parameter settings, as described above for the BFGS solver, was used again, however two stages were deployed. The forecasts from the first stage were used to construct another set of training and test vector sets, with the forecast as another input. The best performing run out of 10 different weight initialisations was selected from the first stage, based on

Table 6.17 BP/USD days of the week benchmarks data

day	train set			test set		
	sd	dates	set size	sd	dates	set size
Mon	0.1938	820222–910128	453	0.1244	910204–930201	100
Tue	0.1965	820223–910219	465	0.1121	910226–930202	100
Wed	0.1971	820224–910306	457	0.1126	910313–930203	100
Thu	0.1980	820225–910307	465	0.1134	910314–930204	100
Fri	0.1958	820226–910222	465	0.1141	910308–930129	100

Table 6.18 BP/USD days of the week, two stage input formats, where $O(0)$ is the stage 1 forecast

input	stage 1	stage 2
p(1)	JY(−1)	stage 1 O(0)
p(2)	DM(−1)	c(−3)
p(3)	s(−1)	c(−2)
p(4)	[v(−3)+v(−2)+v(−1)]/3	c(−1)
p(5)	v(−1)	s(−2)
p(6)	c(−6)	s(−1)
p(7)	c(−5)	v(−1)
p(8)	c(−4)	[v(−3)+v(−2)+v(−1)]/3
p(9)	c(−3)	r(−1)
p(10)	c(−2)	r(−2)
p(11)	c(−1)	r(−3)
target	c(0)	c(0)

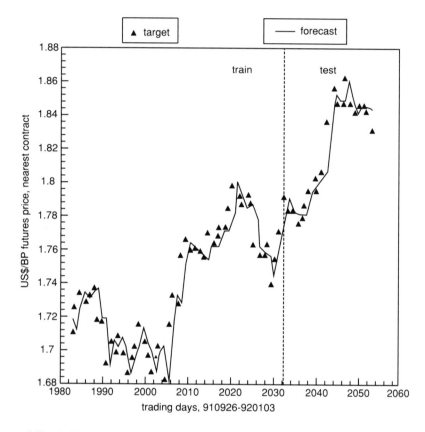

Figure 6.12 British P/USD futures prices: BFGS neural network forecasts and target prices plotted for trading days either side of train and test set divide (days counted from 820104)

training performance, and used to construct the second stage inputs. The second stage runs were then also repeated for 10 different weight initialisations. Table 6.18 summarises the input structure; the RWI and volatility indicators involve calculating average values over the historical period, these were 0.009271 and 0.000141 respectively.

Note the use of Japanese yen (JY) and Deutsche mark (DM) futures data in stage 1. The same notation as before is used for the other variables, with $O(0)$ being the network output layer output. *Along channel* normalisation was performed, and with the sign sensitive method where appropriate (channels 3–5 in stage 1 and 7–11 in stage 2). The TWR figure for each of the networks was 5.9. The following benchmark performance figures relate to the final second stage results.

Table 6.19 BP/USD days of the week benchmarks. The last columns are sd band filtered percentages. Average results shown, with best performance in brackets

day	$\overline{trn}_\varepsilon$	$\overline{tst}_\varepsilon$	$\overline{trn}\%$	$\overline{tst}\%$	> bnd trn	> bnd tst
Mon	0.060 (0.059)	0.409 (0.408)	57.8 (58.3)	55.4 (54.0)	$\frac{124}{188} = 65.9$	$\frac{40}{66} = 60.6$
Tue	0.053 (0.052)	0.442 (0.445)	62.1 (61.3)	47.6 (50.0)	$\frac{136}{179} = 76.0$	$\frac{30}{55} = 54.5$
Wed	0.046 (0.045)	0.405 (0.405)	58.8 (57.8)	52.0 (53.0)	$\frac{144}{226} = 63.7$	$\frac{26}{44} = 59.1$
Thu	0.050 (0.049)	0.417 (0.421)	59.5 (59.6)	46.7 (49.0)	$\frac{50}{73} = 68.2$	$\frac{25}{48} = 52.1$
Fri	0.059 (0.056)	0.400 (0.389)	56.2 (57.8)	54.7 (59.0)	$\frac{60}{82} = 73.2$	$\frac{24}{35} = 68.6$

Also given in Table 6.19 are the trend percentage accuracies for forecasts occurring beyond the ± 1 standard deviation bands (as calculated from wrong train set forecast movements only).

The day of the week results look more promising, in particular the sd band filter provides a significant boost in accuracy. Combining the results for the days of the week, Figure 6.12 shows the forecasts and target prices for a representative sample of trading days either side of the training and test data sets. The question of quality of timing is paramount when evaluating trend accuracy, so percentage accuracy alone is not a sufficient indicator of profitability. This aspect will be further discussed in the next chapter.

7

Futures Forecasts Implementation

Acting on forecasts in finance is often a task for the derivatives specialist, who may exploit the forecasts in the futures and options markets. The implementation process is thus a question of constructing a trading system, and also the risk management of the capital funds available for trading. The first section may be skipped by readers familiar with the mechanics of futures markets and trading; it provides a brief introduction to futures, sufficient for following subsequent material in this chapter.

7.1 OVERVIEW OF COMMODITY AND FINANCIAL FUTURES

The global commodity and financial instruments trading is a multibillion dollar activity that today has a role in the financial health of every trading nation. The capital markets facilitate the financing requirements of existing and emerging enterprises, as well as preserving wealth through investments. The futures markets have become a key part in financial strategic thinking, providing a means of hedging against unforeseen events and thereby providing stability. The logical force of these markets is one of their strongest assets, since in a free market they are governed by the best impression of the nature of world events that can be ascertained.

The application of forecasting techniques to futures markets is one element within futures trading, but from the viewpoint of forecasting, futures is a key area for implementing financial time series forecasts. For this reason, futures provide the principal financial examples in this book, and this chapter in particular treats the subject in greater detail. Note that terminology for futures and options contracts include the generic terms *derivatives* and *financial instruments* (options are closely related to futures, but will not be discussed here, see Chapter 8 for further reading).

To provide a historical perspective[54], the earliest example of a futures market was created in 17th century Japan, for hedging against the seasonal variations in the cost of rice. In the West, the formation of the Chicago Board of Trade, in 1848, saw the launch of the first organised trading in grain forward contracts, later standardised into futures. Chicago, through its geographical location and the growth of rail links emanating from the city, arose as the commercial centre of the US midwest. The Chicago Board of Trade and the Chicago Mercantile Exchange (relaunched in 1919 as a transformation of the Chicago Produce Exchange), were responsible for the development of the modern era in futures trading beyond the needs of solely agricultural concerns. This was achieved with the gradual introduction of novel financial trading instruments in the 1970s and '80s, that met the needs of banks, insurance companies, pension and other investment funds, and treasury departments of multinational companies. The rapid rise in the size of trading turnover has been largely due to the trading in securities, foreign exchange and other financials such as stock indices. The launch of the London International Financial Futures Exchange, in 1982, strengthened the cross-border nature of futures trading, which today is a 24 hour global activity. London was home to the first joint stock company in 1553 and the first trading club to bear the name Stock Exchange, in 1773; in futures it lagged behind the innovative Chicago markets, but London is now on par with Chicago in futures trading turnover. Tokyo and New York are the other major futures market centres.

The concept of futures contracts is markedly different from tangible assets such as stock shares. The majority of trading in commodities is transacted in the physicals markets, the principal function of futures markets is in risk management, that is reducing or controlling risk, with the majority of contracts closed out before delivery results. In the case of financial futures there is no underlying commodity as such, contracts still active at delivery time are cash settled against an index. The problem of the customer forgetting to close out a position and being landed with the proverbial pork bellies is safeguarded by instructing the broker to act on his behalf and close out expiring contracts. Thus considering the main usage of futures trading, the contract involves only price differentials, and it is due to this practice that it is possible to trade a commodity in quantities far above world production capacity.

A futures contract is foremost a standard for trading in the underlying item, and specifies the following articles: the unit size, the delivery date, the currency in which the price is quoted and the unit for which the price is quoted (usually not the same as the contract unit size), the minimum fluctuation allowable in the price (called tick size), and in the case of commodities the grade (or quality) and delivery location. Contracts are usually active for about nine months prior to the delivery date and in many cases delivery dates are spaced at three month intervals, so a choice of contracts exists at any given time. A futures contract involves taking a long or a short position in the market: if the market price is expected to rise the trader takes a net bought position, called going *long*, while a net sold position, called *short*, becomes profitable if the market price drops. Once the contract is closed out (also called *squaring*, whereby a second trade is transacted that cancels the trader's position) the resultant price differential entails either a profit or loss, which is credited or debited to the trader's account with his broker. Also positions which are still active at the close of a trading day are compared to the prevailing settlement price and accounts accordingly updated, this procedure being known as *marking to market*.

Commission for executing the trade is payable to the broker only on completion of a *round turn* — the opening and closing of a contract. However in order to participate in the trade the futures exchange stipulates the depositing of a minimum cover with the broker (who may require a greater amount) in the eventuality of a loss, known as the *initial margin*. This is a guarantee against default, and is valued at around 2% to 20% of the underlying value of the contract, depending on the volatility of the particular market, and is deposited per contract traded. Volatility is a measure of the average historical daily movement of the market price. For example, the S&P 500 contract is valued at $500 times the index, which at 430 (Autumn 1992) equals $215 000; the initial margin is $20 000 per contract.

Although the deposit is returnable, it forms the main capital tied down by the trader, and is thus the basis for calculating the leverage factor of a futures contract, which may vary from 5 to 50. It is this leverage that makes futures trading risky (and attractive) for speculators, since gains and losses are in excess of the margin requirements. While an active contract remains in the market, it may encounter unfavourable prices that will erode the initial margin, so a topping up will be necessary, known as *maintenance*, or *variation* margin, which is enforced at the close of day account reckoning. Most exchanges set maintenance calls at 75% of the original margin requirements, that is when the trading account equity falls below 75% of the required margin a topping up is called for to bring the amount back to 100%. Note that since the margin is a deposit there is no reason why it should not earn interest, exchanges permit securities as margins, such as treasury bills; brokers can make the arrangements and pay interest directly into the account.

There are two main types of trader, those who deal in the physicals (commodities, stocks) and the speculator. For the speculator futures is a high risk venture due to the leverage exposure, for the physicals trader participating in futures trading is part of his low risk strategy. Some comments on this aspect will reveal the method of hedging with futures. Physicals traders divide into producers and consumers (both camps involve retail traders, whether in supplying, distributing, adding value etc); as a terminology the producer enters the market from the viewpoint of having physicals to sell, while the consumer has a view to buy physicals — some traders may need to both buy and sell the physicals.

Consider a producer who would be happy to sell at the *current* spot price x at a time in the future when his produce becomes available on the physicals market. To hedge the price against adverse price falls the producer takes a short position in the futures market, at price y. Just before the delivery date the producer closes out his futures position by going long at price y' and sells his produce on the physical market at the prevailing price x'. The net income will therefore be $x' + y - y'$. Now assume that the futures price tracked the spot price exactly, then $y - y' = x - x'$. Therefore substituting for the ys, the net income becomes just x, which was the producer's required strategic pricing level for his produce. Thus regardless of whether the futures and physicals price rose or fell during the period, the net income was assured at a constant.

Of course had the physicals price x' risen with respect to x, the producer would have stood better without trading in the futures — the point of hedging though is to reduce risk by locking in today's price for tomorrow's trade. Perhaps the producer may also have had good reason to expect the price to fall, such as for seasonal reasons.

A similar calculation applies for the consumer trader who would enter the futures market with a long position, in contrast to the producer's short. The speculator trading over the same period would not have the cover of the physical market, so his net balance would be $y - y'$ on a short followed by a long, and $y' - y$ on a long followed by a short.

The central assumption in the above calculations was that the futures price exactly tracked the spot price. In practice this tracking is only approximate (we have seen in Chapter 6 that the trend correlation can be very high, however what is concerned here is also the actual size of the price moves, not just the direction symmetry). The difference between the physicals and futures price is known as the basis, and basis hedging strategies can be devised that further secure the low risk policy. Thus narrowing and widening of the basis can be accounted for with appropriate trading methods[15].

The point of the physicals trader's risk management strategy is that futures market losses are anticipated and form part of the strategy, while the speculator invariably aims to profit on all futures trades. Speculators play an important role in the market in maintaining high liquidity, since the opposite position to the long or short hedger may very likely be taken up by a speculator. In a highly liquid market there will always be the availability of a trader to take an opposite position.

The sequence of action in a trade is as follows: The trader conveys to his broker an order; professionals make use of about 20 recognised abbreviated terms. The newcomer may use plain English but should become familiar with the wide variety of executions available — sophisticated traders make full use of the flexibility of orders (Battley[15] provides a comprehensive description of trading orders). The broker then relays the order to the firm's representative at the market, who then passes the information to his floor trader, who finally executes the trade by open outcry in a trading pit or ring. Alternative arrangements through electronic trading systems are increasingly encroaching on floor trading, with brokers executing trades directly through a computerised futures exchange.

The cost of trading so far mentioned is the broker's commission fees, these depend on the nature of the client-broker relationship: a discretionary service that makes decisions on the client's behalf naturally charges the highest rate, whilst a discount service, which only executes orders, is the cheapest. Rates vary depending on number of contracts traded (additional volume discounts operative) and whether round turns are inter-day or intra-day (half-price commissions). The additional costs in trading may be termed hidden costs, since their occurrence is a function of the particular market behaviour, they are nevertheless important aspects that should be properly accounted in costing a trading exercise. Thus these costs are explicitly estimated as additional losses in historical testing; in real-time actual performance figures, the hidden costs will be implicitly reflected in the final profit and loss balance. These hidden costs are slippage and spread.

Slippage is the price difference between the desired market entry price and the actual executed entry, the difference is a consequence of the delay between making the order and the order reaching the trading floor; in a fast moving market slippage may be so serious that orders are issued with limits which specify entry on condition that price is below (for a long) or above (for a short) the limit level — unless these limits are satisfied entry is not initiated, but the use of limit orders also risks being left out of a favourable market move. Unless you utilise a contrary entry strategy (buy long when prices are falling, or sell short when prices are rising), slippage will invariably work against you and therefore must be considered as an additional cost. Slippage may also occur when a position is closed out. In testing computerised trading systems slippage should be assumed to take place with every trade.

The bid-ask spread is the prevailing difference between the buyer's price (bid) and seller's price (ask); since prices can change only in small fixed increments known as ticks, the smallest spread is one tick and is naturally the most favourable circumstance for traders. One tick spreads characterise highly liquid markets — liquidity is measured by the number of active contracts, known as open interest. In futures trading most positions are eventually closed out before delivery, so open interest is a clear indicator of the *future* trading to be performed, a high liquidity ensures that any new entrant to the market is sure to fulfil his order. Furthermore, high liquidity also ensures that large trades may be entered without the market noticing — secrecy is an important element in trading — and also minimises slippage.

At any given time, a number of delivery months will be available in a particular contract, however the nearest contract by month tends to be the most liquid — contracts expiring in the current month are usually too near the delivery date to be of interest to new entrants, so there tends to be a roll-over of trading into the next nearest month, the practice is usually to perform the switch the day prior to, or on the first day of the delivery month. All the examples of futures time series discussed in this book concatenate the futures prices on this nearest-month roll-over basis in order to produce a long time scale historical series.

The bid-ask spread therefore contributes an additional cost in trading, it is reasonable to assume in historical data testing $100 loss per trade, which includes commission, slippage and spread. The effects of trading costs depends on the adopted trading strategy, frequent trading on a short-time scale results in higher costs with the need for greater profits to cover the overheads. However, the long term trader will also incur additional costs due to roll-over transactions. Anther point to note is that volatility is smaller on the short-time scale, making the establishment of profits that much harder. On the other hand, trading on a medium to long term may involve greater risk. Short-term trading, and especially intra-day trading, tends to be the preserve of professionals, as opposed to small traders.

During the opening and end-of-market (also closing or settlement) sessions of the trading day, the spread may be as high as six ticks where one tick is the norm, and slippage may also be high, this is due to hectic trading activity. The closing session is marked by floor traders closing out their own positions for fear of remaining vulnerable overnight, or weekend, to unfavourable price moves. The opening session is similarly marked by a build up of day-time entry requirements. Prices quoted by the exchanges for these sessions vary, but it is common practice to quote the very first trade as the opening price, and the mid-range price at the closing session. The mid-range price is a better representative of the opening session, and is quoted by the data vendor Commodity Systems Inc (see Chapter 8).

There are four prices commonly quoted during the day and, as a final summary, at the day's close. These are the open and current/close prices and the highest and lowest prices reached since the open. However there is no indication of which of the high and low came first; one estimate is to take the smallest range from $|O-H|$, $|O-L|$, $|C-H|$ and $|C-L|$, and treat the two prices as having occurred nearest in time.

Note that with the introduction of evening floor trading sessions and night-time electronic trading, it is important to ascertain the exact timing of the quoted prices. Many data vendors split the day-time and night-time data histories. However, anomalies can still crop up, as with the US Treasury Bond futures whose day-time open price quote corresponds to the opening price of the previous evening session. Contact the exchange's information service for the necessary details.

After a one day delay the trading volume and open interest are also posted by the exchange (estimates are provided at the close of the same day). Volume is a count of the number of contracts involved in a trade, whilst, as mentioned, open interest counts the number of outstanding contracts. The volume and open interest figures are available separately for each delivery month or as totals for all the contracts combined.

7.2 FUTURES TIME SERIES

There are a number of considerations in forecasting futures price series. The target in training the neural network, which is the time series to be forecast, should correspond to the futures contract that is actually traded. As previously noted, the limited contract lifetime poses problems when long historical time series are required. One possibility is to use the spot price as a substitute time series. This would only be advisable if the correlation between the two was sufficiently high, the movement symmetry probability is a good indicator for this purpose (see Section 5.2) since positions are entered in the market on the basis of whether a price will rise or fall. Every commodity and financial futures has an underlying spot value, whether it is a price or index. Now, if for example the movement symmetry correlation was 80%, and a spot price trained neural network accuracy was 70%, then the transformed accuracy for the futures series would be 56%. Thus some serious erosion of the performance can result unless the symmetry correlation is above 90%; as was seen in Section 5.2 this could be achieved with the use of a small movement filter.

Concatenation of different delivery months' price histories is the only other alternative. The usual recourse is to construct a time series of high *open interest* contracts, such as the nearest active contract, or next nearest in the delivery month, with roll-over performed at the start of the delivery month. An alternative here is to perform switches precisely in keeping with the delivery month that has the highest open interest. However, the nearest-by-month will normally be a close enough approximation to that.

Nevertheless, the concatenated time series will reflect the lifecycle of the futures prices since, at roll-over, an abrupt price change may occur due to any disparity between the two delivery month series. Neural network input vectors whose target coincides with the roll-over date should be removed. Those input vectors immediately following this date will contain the artifact price change in the input field, for whatever the duration of the field. Removing these vectors could seriously hamper the training, not least due to a reduction of available vectors, so they are best left in. One possibility is to dampen any occurring glitch.

Certain commodity price data vendors create interpolated price time series with varying weights for individual contracts. As a particular contract nears expiration its weight approaches zero, to be replaced by another contract (the weights are calculated on the basis of a fixed period ahead, say 90 days). These artificial price series are variously known as 'constant-forward' and 'perpetual' series, their main disadvantage being that they do not correspond to any real tradeable contracts, nor do they reflect the natural lifecycle price variation of real contracts. These issues have been raised in the trading literature[25,146], suggestions have included the creation of back-adjusted nearest contract series, where the difference at roll-over between the current contract's price and the new contract's price is removed by adding the difference to all of the past data. This however is also an artificial price series that will not only corrupt long term trends in the data but may create spurious new ones. A deceptive pitfall is that applying back-adjusted data to neural networks may not only result in excellent training performance, but also excellent test set results, with the danger that the system will bear no relation to actual events.

Unadjusted nearest-by-month contract price constructs are probably the safest time series to use. Note that the contract life-cycle pattern will be learned by the neural network, so that in itself poses no problem. With the removal of targets falling on the roll-over dates, trading can be suspended on those days.

The look-ahead forecast period also has a bearing on the selection of input variables. For example, volume of trading and open interest figures are given for a day's trade and are usually available only after a one day delay, (estimates are provided at the end of day, but historical inspection shows these not to be reliable enough). Thus if a look-ahead period of two days or greater is selected for the target, then these important items of market information may be exploited for use in the input data.

7.3   TRADING SYSTEMS

The neural network provides forecasts of market moves, these can then form the basis for trading the market within an automated system. A pre-trained network is the natural choice for real-time trading, having been trained overnight, over the previous weekend, or much further in the past; whichever, the computation speed of the pre-trained network is rapid enough to make such a system practicable for instantly downloading real-time market data and producing an immediate response.

The implementation of the forecasts requires a strategy for dealing with adverse market moves; the question of when to enter and exit the market is largely governed by the forecasts. *Stops* and *limits* provide safety facilities for controlling risk, the best values to use may be found through an optimisation process over a historical training period. Some guidelines may be mentioned.

The purpose of a stop is to pre-set an exit from the market, the order having been left with the floor trader to execute the exit as soon as the price hits the level. Stops are an important element in the strategy of cutting losses short. A large stop level will result in large losses incurred when they are hit, although they also give time for a recovery to take place. Narrow stops will be hit more frequently, but the losses will be relatively smaller. One approach is to measure the historical volatility of the market and set the stop at some function of the standard deviation of daily moves. Various strategies exist for re-positioning the stop level as time progresses. For example, the stop level may be re-set to the break-even point or it may be allowed to dynamically track the latest price.

When calculating the effect of a stop in historical testing, include the consequence of a large overnight close–open gap bypassing the stop level, by entering the trade at the open price and not the stop level. Currency futures are especially prone to this problem due to the active global round the clock trading. This is a type of slippage which should be accounted for separately to the standard practice of allowing a $100 cost per trade in historical testing.

The limit is similar to the stop but applies to the entry rather than exit. Thus an order to enter the market may be made with the provision that should the price have changed in *favour* of the prospective position, due to slippage, by an amount greater than the limit, then entry is delayed until (and if) the market reverses. Limits add the risk that favourable market prices are missed out altogether, however they do ensure that entries are executed in accordance with the trading system signals.

The evaluation of the overall system, forecasts plus stop/limit strategy, should be performed over a test period set aside and neither previously used in training the network, nor in optimising stops and limits. The system should generate at least 30 trades over the test period in order to provide a minimum sample size to measure performance.

Performance measures are important in evaluating whether targets have been met and for comparing various alternative strategies in a trading system. Criteria in setting up a trading strategy will vary according to the degree of risk exposure permitted, so the assessment criteria selected are a matter of choice, depending on priorities.

A benchmark that should be included as a matter of course is a buy and hold strategy over the historical period tested, calculated on a per contract basis. Another useful benchmark is in calculating the return of investing the total amount of required margin in a stock market index linked account, over the same period.

The following list describes suitable performance measures:

- *Balance*: A balance of the account at the end of the test period: broken into total gain, total loss, and profit and loss balance. Any remaining open interest should be closed out at the last settlement price and included in the assessment. Further breakdown may also prove useful, such as separate balances for longs and shorts, and a separate balance for the open interest.

- *Number of trades and cost*: The number of closed trades plus the open interest, and the cost of trading, given by a reasonable factor of around $100 times the total number of trades. The cost should be included in the loss part of the balance statement. Also provide the separate number of profitable and losing trades, useful when stated as a percentage.

- *Averages*: Open interest is probably best left out of these calculations. The average profit per closed trade (after costs are included) — a low figure indicates a narrow margin of error. The average profit over only the profitable trades — a high figure indicates good exploitation of winning trends. The average loss over only the losing trades — a low figure indicates losses cut short.

- *Maximi*: The maximum drawdown with and without open interest — both figures provide useful information. Drawdown is a valuation of the profit and loss balance over the least favourable period in the historical test. On a chart of the balance it is the measure of the biggest overall drop, which may include interludes of profit, and is equivalent to the balance achieved upon initiating trading at the worst possible time (historical maximum balance preceding minimum balance) and ceasing trading at the worst time (historical minimum balance). The maximum consecutive loss and the maximum consecutive win also provide useful monitors, as well as the maximum profit and maximum loss on a single trade.

- *Return Ratios*: These ratios may be evaluated over the test period for comparing against each other, for example where parameters in the trading system are varied. In comparing against other published performance figures, rates of return should be calculated by dividing the return with the period covered (in the same time units used to produce the return figure). The rate of return can then be used to provide a return for any period required, T, by suitable multiplication with T (yielding a simple interest return).

The holding period return[140] (without compounding), expressed as a percentage, is defined by

$$R = 100 \frac{I + B - M}{C + M} \tag{7.1}$$

where I is the interest earned on margin deposits, B is the total balance including costs, C is the cost (which comprises commission and hidden costs in historical testing), and M is the total sum of lost margin over the test period. This may also be called the return on margin. Note that exchanges vary margin levels depending on prevailing market volatility, although this is only done during periods of extremely rapid price changes. See Balsara[12] for a more precise treatment that also accounts for variation margin and interest rates.

Two ratios which include a measure of the risk, through the standard deviation, are the Sharpe ratio[140] and a variation due to Kaufman[77]: The Sharpe ratio is defined by

$$R_s = \frac{R - R_I}{\sigma} \tag{7.2}$$

where σ is the standard deviation of the profit and loss balance over the test period, R is the holding period return and R_I the interest rate on treasury bills, or other risk free security, adjusted over the holding period. The annualised Sharpe Ratio may be calculated by evaluating the ratio over weekly periods and averaging accordingly. Low risk entails small standard deviation, so the Sharpe ratio will be relatively high for the same return.

Kaufman[77] introduced the Equity Drop Ratio: $EDR = R/\sigma_d$, where σ_d is the standard deviation of only the equity drops, where an equity drop is the profit and loss balance measured from all lows to previous highs (and including open interest).

Schwager[145] developed the Average Maximum Retracement ratio, as follows

$$AMR = \frac{1}{N} \sum_{i=1}^{N} pos(MCE_i - TE_i) \tag{7.3}$$

where the function pos equals the argument when it is positive, and is zero otherwise. MCE is the closed trade equity (profit and loss balance) prior to day i, TE is the total equity (closed trades and open interest) only for day i.

The Risk-Reward Ratio is defined as the net profit over the test period divided by the maximum drawdown. The Performance Ratio is defined as the ratio of average profit per trade divided by the standard deviation of the average profit.

The degree of portability should also be estimated, where sufficient historical data permits this, by measuring performance over more than one test period. Also useful is a sensitivity test whereby the stop and limit levels are perturbed up and down to see what effect this has on the performance. Babcock[9] has suggested evaluating pessimistic variations of the above returns, where 1 standard deviation less winners and 1 standard deviation more losers are included.

Since nonrandom behaviour is based on the premise of recurrent patterns in market movement, there are different schools of thought as to whether a trading system needs to be retrained/optimised. It is probably a good policy to periodically review stop and limit levels as a function of market volatility.

Other aspects to consider include whether to trade a diverse range of futures, taking on board modern portfolio theory thinking on spreading risk. Also, with a large number of markets traded simultaneously, entries may be more selective with only particularly promising trends traded.

The question of how many contracts to trade depends on the level of risk exposure allowed. The next section discusses the optimal f method for allocating capital, which in turn determines the number of contracts to trade. Here, one direct method will be mentioned that stood up well in Babcock's[9] comparative analysis of various rule-based approaches. This was the anti-martingale: start with one contract, double the number after each win and restart with one after each loss. The decisions on number of contracts to place are made at the end of a closed position, or round turn trade.

Another consideration is whether to pyramid contracts in a profitable position in order to build on strength during the lifetime of a contract. In the next section the question of risk will be quantified. Given that unrealised profits exist in a particular position, the number of active contracts may be built up without increasing the risk exposure. Should the market reverse, various strategies may be applied in closing out positions, but the risk exposure should never be violated by holding on to positions beyond the initial risk strategy.

A final consideration concerns quality of timing. Trading systems that are based on technical analysis rules are either tuned to be profitable during periods of trend or during periods of sideways price movements, since no single rule-based system can be profitable in both (of course one can combine systems, but one will always be losing when the other is winning). Trend following systems are the most popular, and characterised by having the majority of trades as losers, with losses cut short, while the minority winning trades are typically much larger in size (profits allowed to run), thereby providing an overall profit. This brings to light the property of timing quality, since a few good trades, yielding large profits, are more important than many small losses. Thus the percentage accuracy of trades is not a useful performance measure when taken in isolation, (unless, of course, it is very much higher than 50%).

The timing aspect has also a bearing on neural network based systems. Whilst very high accuracies will undoubtedly result in profitable results, there is no reason to assume that a low forecast accuracy is necessarily unprofitable, until the forecasts are implemented in a trading system and the capability to exploit large moves is gauged.

7.4   RISK MANAGEMENT

The subject of risk management will only be briefly discussed to provide the reader with a feel for the part that risk and monetary control have in relation to trading as a whole. The main items of concern here are the following:

- Risk of ruin
- Allocating the risk capital in an optimal way
- Diversification: applying stock market modern portfolio theory to futures

7.4.1   Risk of Ruin

The two parameters that play a central role in risk calculations are the probability of winning, p (and the corresponding probability of losing $q = 1 - p$), and the payoff ratio, R_p. In lieu of unknown future performance of a trading system, the expected winning probability is estimated over historical performance, as is the payoff ratio, which is defined by

$$R_p = \frac{\overline{W}}{\overline{L}} \tag{7.4}$$

where $\overline{W}$ is the average of just the winning trade amounts, and similarly $\overline{L}$ is the size of the average losing trade.

The risk of ruin calculation, and the associated duration (in number of trades to reach either ruin or success), provide an estimate of whether the given primary parameters of a trading system will lead, over many trades, to a favourable outcome. In addition to p and R_p, these parameters are the initial capital z, the size of capital at which the trader will quit altogether a, the amount k staked in each trade, assumed fixed throughout a trial, and with each trade closed out on either a win of kR_p or loss of amount k.

The risk of ruin problem for payoff ratio $R_p = 1$ is also known as *the classical ruin problem*, and is treated in Feller[49]. Assuming that costs are negligible, then the formulae for probability of ultimate ruin q_z, expected gain $E[G]$, and duration of game D_z, are given as follows for $p \neq q$.

$$q_z = \frac{(q/p)^{a/k} - (q/p)^{z/k}}{(q/p)^{a/k} - 1} \tag{7.5}$$

$$E[G] = a(1 - q_z) - z \tag{7.6}$$

$$D_z = \frac{1}{k(q-p)}\left[z - a\frac{1-(q/p)^{z/k}}{1-(q/p)^{a/k}}\right] \qquad (7.7)$$

where trading ceases with either loss of z or gain $a - z$. At $p = q = 0.5$ the formulae breakdown and need to be replaced by

$$q_z = 1 - \frac{z}{a} \qquad (7.8)$$

$$E[G] = 0 \qquad (7.9)$$

$$D_z = \frac{z(a-z)}{k^2} \qquad (7.10)$$

note that q_z is now independent of the stake, but the duration is still dependent on k.

If the ratio a/k is very large (e.g. $a \to \infty$) then the formulae may be simplified as follows (the expected gain is meaningless now)

$$\begin{aligned} q_z &= 1 && \text{if } p \le q \\ &= \left(\frac{q}{p}\right)^{z/k} && \text{if } p > q \\ D_z &= \frac{z}{(q-p)k} && \text{if } p < q \\ &= \infty && \text{if } p \ge q \end{aligned}$$

Feller's method for deriving the $R_p = 1$ formulae can also be extended to the $R_p = 2$ case, where a winning trade earns $2k$ and a losing trade loses amount k. The formulae are now, for $2p \ne q$

$$q_z = \frac{\lambda^{a/k} - \lambda^{z/k}}{\lambda^{a/k} - 1} \qquad (7.11)$$

$$E[G] = a(1 - q_z) - z \qquad (7.12)$$

$$D_z = \frac{1}{k(q-2p)}\left[z - a\frac{\lambda^{z/k} - 1}{\lambda^{a/k} - 1}\right] \qquad (7.13)$$

where

$$\lambda = \sqrt{\frac{1}{4} + \frac{q}{p}} - \frac{1}{2} \qquad (7.14)$$

When $\lambda = 1$ the expressions breakdown, this occurs for $2p = q$, ($p = \frac{1}{3}$ and $q = \frac{2}{3}$), then the formulae need to be replaced by

$$q_z = 1 - \frac{z}{a} \qquad (7.15)$$

$$E[G] = 0 \qquad (7.16)$$

note there is no simple analytical formula for D_z in this circumstance. The limiting case of $a/k \to \infty$ is given by

$$q_z = 1 \qquad \text{if } 2p \le q$$
$$= \lambda^{z/k} \qquad \text{if } 2p > q$$
$$D_z = \frac{z}{(q-2p)k} \qquad \text{if } 2p < q$$
$$= \infty \qquad \text{if } 2p \ge q$$

where strictly the duration is meaningless for $2p \ge q$, in achieving an infinite target.

The strategy for optimising the success probability, as a function of the stake for given initial start fund and a target amount, depends on the governing probabilities p and q. Tables 7.1 and 7.2 illustrate the characteristics of the ruin problem by selecting key examples, all for an initial start fund $z = 5000$.

The characteristic patterns which emerge from the examples in the tables reveal that when $p > q$ for $R_p = 1$ and $2p > q$ for $R_p = 2$, the best strategy is to play small stakes. When $p < q$ for $R_p = 1$ and $2p < q$ for $R_p = 2$, the target is best achieved by playing large stakes per trade, and aiming for a modest gain. The payoff ratio $R_p = 2$ enables a successful strategy to be played for p down to just above $1/3$, with positive expected gains.

The last entries in each table show examples where the risk of ruin is below average, and yet the expected gain is negative. The reason for this is that whilst in an above average number of trials, the modest gain is achieved, when a ruin does occur it involves a much larger loss, hence the overall expectation is negative.

Table 7.1   Selected cases of the $R_p = 1$ ruin problem, for initial capital $z = 5000$. Trading ceases with loss z (ruin) or gain $a - z$ (capital a)

probabilities		aim	stake	probabilities		expectations	
win p	lose q	a	k	ruin	success	gain	duration
0.55	0.45	10^6	100	0.000	1.000	10^6	10^5
			500	0.134	0.866	$8.6\,10^5$	$1.7\,10^4$
			1000	0.367	0.633	$6.3\,10^5$	6284
			2500	0.669	0.331	$3.3\,10^5$	1302
0.50	0.50	5500	1	0.091	0.909	0	$2.5\,10^6$
		5500	100	0.091	0.909		250
		10^4	1000	0.500	0.500		25
		10^6	1000	0.995	0.005		4975
0.45	0.55	10^4	100	1.000	0.000	-5000	500.0
			1000	0.732	0.268	-2317	23.2
			2500	0.599	0.401	-990	4.0
		7500	2500	0.402	0.598	-515	2.1

Table 7.2 Payoff ratio $R_p = 2$ ruin problem examples, for initial capital $z = 5000$. Trading ceases with loss z (ruin) or gain $a - z$ (capital a)

probabilities		aim	stake	probabilities		expectations	
win p	lose q	a	k	ruin	success	gain	duration
0.50	0.50	10^6	1000	0.090	0.910	$9.1\,10^5$	1809.7
0.40	0.60	10^6	10	0.000	1.000	10^5	$5.0\,10^5$
			500	0.142	0.858	$8.5\,10^5$	8526.6
			1000	0.377	0.623	$6.2\,10^5$	3088.6
			2500	0.677	0.323	$3.2\,10^5$	635.8
$\frac{1}{3}$	$\frac{2}{3}$	5500	1	0.091	0.909	0	—
		5500	100	0.091	0.909		—
		10^4	1000	0.500	0.500		—
		10^6	1000	0.995	0.005		—
0.28	0.72	7500	100	0.984	0.016	−4879	305.0
			500	0.614	0.386	−2104	26.3
			1000	0.476	0.524	−1073	6.7
			2500	0.390	0.610	−423	1.1

7.4.2   Capital Allocation

Since each trade involves a risk of loss, the problem of how to maximise gains given a finite capital base is one of ascertaining the fraction, f, of risk capital to expose at each trade. If simplifying assumptions are made then it is possible to produce an analytical formula for f, known as the optimal f value.

As in the classical ruin problem, assume that all wins are in fixed amount kR_p and all losses in amount k. The Thorp[160] or Kelly[79] system evaluates the fraction f, as the difference between the probable amount expected to win, pkR_p and the amount expected to lose $(1 - p)k$, divided by the former, yielding

$$f = \frac{(1 + R_p)p - 1}{R_p} \qquad (7.17)$$

which is independent of k.

Modifications of the Kelly system have been suggested[177]; Vince[165] has recently proposed a development in optimal f, first by introducing an empirical method for calculating f, and later developing a parametric version of the method[166]. The former relies on historical trades to calculate f, while the parametric model assumes that the distribution of wins and losses are known, dispensing with the need for historical data.

The empirical method is well-suited to trading systems, since f can be tuned to the characteristics of the particular system. The method is based on optimising a compounded, or geometric series, of weighted relative returns, R_w, defined by

$$R_{wi} = 1 + f\frac{R_i}{|\hat{R}_L|} \qquad (7.18)$$

where R_i is the return for the ith trade, and $|\hat{R}_L|$ is the absolute value of the return for the maximum losing trade (the historical test period must contain at least one losing trade for this method to be valid). The geometric series of R_{wi} for n historical trades yields a compounded gain

$$G_c = \prod_{i=1}^{n} R_{wi} \qquad (7.19)$$

($\prod$ is notation for multiplication) which is then optimised by numerically solving for the optimal f that maximises G_c. A straightforward search method may be used since f lies in the range $[0,1]$. Vince has found the resulting optimal fraction f to yield superior returns.

The number of contracts, N_c, to trade in a commodity is now just a matter of deciding on a maximum permissible risk for that trade, as set by the positioning of the stop level — let this be amount S, then

$$N_c = \frac{fT}{S} \qquad (7.20)$$

where T is the total capital available.

7.4.3   Diversification

The fundamental concept of modern portfolio theory is that risk reduction may be achieved through investment diversification in securities, stocks, and commodities, whose individual risk factors are independent of each other, or are highly anti-correlated. Risk is measured by the standard deviation, or its square the variance, of the expected returns; Markowitz[102] showed that pooling can have the effect of reducing the overall standard deviation. This is possible where the constituent investments in the pool have mutual return correlation coefficients less than 1.

Consider the example of two commodities A and B, combined within a portfolio P in quantities N_A and N_B, such that a total of $N = N_A + N_B$ futures contracts are active simultaneously. The proportions of A and B in the portfolio may be written, $W_A = N_A/N$ and $W_B = N_B/N$.

Consider the history of trading each commodity individually: let there be available n annualised (or other suitable period) returns data, the returns variance will be given by

$$V_A = \frac{1}{n-1}\sum_{i=1}^{n}(R_{Ai} - \overline{R_A})^2 \qquad (7.21)$$

and similarly for B, the portfolio variance can be written (note R_p is the portfolio return)

$$V_p = \frac{1}{n-1} \sum_{i=1}^{n} (R_{pi} - \overline{R_p})^2 \tag{7.22}$$

and using $R_p = W_A R_A + W_B R_B$ and $\overline{R_p} = W_A \overline{R_A} + W_B \overline{R_B}$, yields

$$V_p = \frac{1}{n-1} \sum_{i=1}^{n} [W_A(R_{Ai} - \overline{R_A}) + W_B(R_{Bi} - \overline{R_B})]^2 \tag{7.23}$$

$$= W_A^2 S_A^2 + W_B^2 S_B^2 + 2W_A W_B S_A S_B C_{AB} \tag{7.24}$$

where the standard deviation of the returns for the individual commodities are S_A and S_B, and C_{AB} is their linear correlation coefficient, defined by

$$C_{AB} = \frac{\sum_{i=1}^{n} (R_{Ai} - \overline{R_A})(R_{Bi} - \overline{R_B})}{S_A S_B} \tag{7.25}$$

The role of the linear correlation coefficient in reducing the overall variance is now clear: if $C_{AB} = 1$ (high positive correlation) then the variance, and hence the risk, would be a maximum. If $C_{AB} = 0$ (minimum correlation, or noncorrelation) then some reduction in risk would ensue. For example if the individual standard deviations were the same and so were the proportions traded, then the portfolio standard deviation would be reduced by the square root of the number of contracts traded in each commodity:

$$S_p = \frac{S}{\sqrt{N}} \tag{7.26}$$

In the case of high anti-correlation $C_{AB} = -1$ the ideal reduction in risk would result, the portfolio standard deviation could then be written

$$S_p = |W_A S_A - W_B S_B| \tag{7.27}$$

and the proportions to be traded could then be calculated so as to yield $S_p = 0$.

In practice combining risky commodities may at best yield mutual correlation coefficients between 0 and 0.5, due to similar forces influencing such commodities, however this is still a better strategy than trading just one high-risk commodity. High-risk markets are usually favoured by speculating traders, since the volatility is equated with opportunities for profits, so a portfolio approach provides a certain degree of built-in safety.

The optimal f method applied in calculating capital allocation for each individual commodity may also be applied in optimising the proportion of commodity holdings in a portfolio[12,166].

Increasing the number of different commodities in a portfolio suffers from a law of diminishing benefit. The portfolio variance for M different commodities is given by

$$V_p = \sum_{j=1}^{M} W_j^2 S_j^2 + \sum_{\substack{j=1 \\ j \neq k}}^{M} \sum_{k=1}^{M} W_j W_k S_j S_k C_{jk} \tag{7.28}$$

Now as M increases the second term tends to dominate, and in the limit will equal the variance of the market as a whole, thus establishing a minimum risk level. The portfolio variance tends to fall rapidly as the portfolio is built up, and levels off to the saturation value with around 10 commodities[140].

8
Further Reading and Information

In addition to works already mentioned, further reading material that may be of interest is noted here, these being a sample of books available.

A number of books deal with the question of nonrandom behaviour in financial time series, for informal discussions see Johnson[71] and Casti[31]. Recent academic works include Dimson[38], Schiller[143], Dwyer and Hafer[42], Lorenz[97] and Brock et al[24].

An up to date text on traditional statistical approaches to time series analysis, as well as modern model building, can be found in Kendall and Ord[80], and with an emphasis on financial time series in Taylor[157a]. Other recent developments in time series forecasting see Priestley[130] and Tong[162].

An informal introduction to the various paradigms in current neural network architectures is given in Caudill and Butler[32]. Wasserman[168] and Dayhoff[37] also provide introductory material but at a more advanced level. Turning to academic material, the recent new wave of interest in neural networks was sparked by the publication in 1986 of two volumes on parallel distributed processing[139,106]. A later third volume[107] provided a thorough tutorial on many aspects of neural computing and came with software written in C. At a more advanced level Hertz[64] and Maren[101] provide good treatments on diverse network architectures. For detailed background material on neural networks there is no substitute for reading the original papers, collected in Neurocomputing[3], and Neurocomputing 2[4].

An introduction to quantitative investment analysis can be found in Rutterford[140], see also Elton and Gruber[46]. Introductory books on trading in futures and options include Battley[15], NYIF[118] and Kolb[86] (includes software). An academic treatment of derivative securities is given in Hull[69]. A comprehensive treatment of developing rule-based trading systems is given in Babcock[9], see also Pardo[123] and articles by Knight[83] and Burke[26]. The money management aspect of trading is covered in

Balsara[12] and Vince[166]. For a wide range of specialist books on trading see the Edward Dobson Catalogue: Traders Press Inc, PO Box 6206, Greenville, SC 29606, USA. Waters Information Services Ltd (407/408 Bedford Chambers, The Piazza, Covent Garden, London WC2E 8HA, UK) publish *The Handbook of Digital Dealing Room Systems* and *The RTFI Index* (professional reference to real-time financial information).

Newsletters and journals that contain pertinent material are as follows:

Sixth Generation Systems. Derek Stubbs, Editor and Publisher, PO Box 155, Vicksburg, MI 49097, USA. Latest news, trends, and hot topics, covering industrial and academic neurocomputing and related.

Intelligence. Edward Rosenfeld, Editor and Publisher, PO Box 20008, NY, NY 10025–1510, USA. Latest news, trends, and hot topics, covering industrial and academic neurocomputing and related.

AI Expert. Miller Freeman Inc, 600 Harrison St, San Francisco, CA 94107, USA. Broad range of AI articles, including on neurocomputing, mostly in a review/tutorial style.

Neural Computing and Applications. Springer-Verlag London Ltd, Springer House, 8 Alexandra Road, Wimbledon, London SW19 7JZ, UK. Broad range of papers with an emphasis on practical applications of neurocomputing.

Neural Networks. Pergamon Press Inc, 660 White Plains Road, Tarrytown, NY 10591–5153, USA. Broad range of papers with a bias towards the theoretical.

Neural Computation. The MIT Press, 55 Hayward St, Cambridge, MA 02142, USA. Broad range of papers with a bias towards the theoretical.

IEEE Trans. Neural Networks. IEEE Service Center, 445 Hoes Lane, PO Box 1331, Piscataway, NJ 08855–1331, USA. Neural network papers from a largely signal processing viewpoint.

NeuroVest Journal. PO Box 764, Haymarket, Virginia 22069, USA. New launch, covers neural networks in finance.

Journal of Forecasting. John Wiley & Sons, Baffins Lane, Chichester, West Sussex PO19 1UD, UK. Statistics and econometrics papers on forecasting.

Futures and Options World. Metal Bulletin plc, Park House, Park Terrace, Worcester Park, KT4 7HY, UK. Also publishes: International Futures and Options Databook. Articles on derivatives trading.

Technical Analysis of Stocks and Commodities. Technical Analysis Inc, 3517 SW Alaska St, Seattle, WA 98146–2700, USA. Articles on derivatives trading using technical analysis. Includes monthly futures liquidity table.

Futures. 219 Parkade, Cedar Falls, Iowa 50613, USA. Publishes two supplements: the *Futures Annual Source Book* — directories on brokers, computer services, international firms, organisations, exchanges and regulators; the *Annual Guide to Computerised Trading*. Articles on derivatives trading.

Financial Analysts Journal. The Association for Investment Management and Research, PO Box 3668, Charlottesville, VA 22903, USA. Papers on broad range of financial analysis subjects.

Risk Magazine. 104–112 Marylebone Lane, London W1M 5FU, UK. Articles on broad range of financial instruments and derivatives.

Journal of Futures Markets. John Wiley & Sons Inc, 605 Third Avenue, New York, New York 10158, USA. Papers on futures with theoretical bias.

Annual conferences on forecasting in financial services that focus on advanced techniques are as follows. Note that the IEEE and INNS organise major annual conferences on neural networks for research presentations, and numerous specialised conferences are regularly announced, see the calendar sections in the above neural network journals.

- Artificial Intelligence Applications on Wall Street. Conference sponsored by Division of Management, Polytechnic University, 333 Jay St, Brooklyn, New York, NY 11201, USA.
- International Business Communications organise seminars in London, past subjects covered Rocket Science, Neural Networks and Genetic Algorithms. IBC Technical Services Ltd, Gilmoora House, 57–61 Mortimer St, London W1N 7TD, UK.
- IBC also organise advanced trading technologies conferences in New York. International Business Communications USA Conferences Inc, 8 Pleasant Street, Bldg D, South Natick, MA 01760, USA.
- The Statistical Office of the European Communities (EUROSTAT) organises occasional workshop/conferences under the DOSES programme. EUROSTAT, Batiment Jean Monnet, L–2920 Luxembourg.

Associations and trading regulatory bodies:

Neural Computing Applications Forum. PO Box 62, Malvern, Worcestershire, WR14 4NU, UK. Membership includes quarterly *Neural Computing & Applications*.

International Neural Network Society. Suite 300, 1250 24th Street, NW Washington, DC 20037, USA. Membership includes *Neural Networks*, published eight per annum.

European Neural Network Society. (Linked with INNS) Technical University of Denmark, Division of Molecular Biophysics, DK 2800 Lyngby, Denmark. Membership includes *Neural Networks*, published eight per annum.

Society of Technical Analysts. 28 Panton St, Cambridge CB2 1DH, UK. Also publishes quarterly *Market Technician*.

Market Technicians Association. 71 Broadway, Second Floor, New York, NY 10006, USA. Also publishes quarterly *The MTA Journal*.

American Association of Individual Investors Inc. 625 N Michigan Street, Chicago, IL 60611, USA. Also publishes *Computerized Investing* and annually: *The Individual Investor's Microcomputer Resource Guide.*

The Society of Investment Analysts. 211–213 High Street, Bromley BR1 1NY, UK.

The Institute for Quantitative Investment Research. C/o Bischoff & Co, Epworth House, 25 City Road, London EC1Y 1BY, UK.

The Institute for Quantitative Research in Finance. 4 Augustus Lane, Greenwich, CT 06830, USA.

European Managed Futures Association. International House, 1 St Katherine's Way, London E1 9UN, UK.

Securities and Futures Authority. Cottons Centre, Cottons Lane, London SE1 2QB, UK. Regulatory body for all derivatives trading and registering of traders.

National Futures Association. 200 W Madison St, Suite 1600, Chicago, IL 60606–3447, USA. Trader's regulatory body.

A selection of financial data vendors offering computer on-line services. Note that data vendors, for historical quotes, daily quotes and real-time intra-day prices are considerably cheaper in the USA. For this reason connecting via a telecommunications gateway to the USA for computer on-line downloading may be the most cost effective strategy for non-US users. Alternate means for real-time data are via satellite links. Services within the London City perimeter are also cheaper than UK nationwide. In negotiating real-time data contracts in particular, ensure that the data to be supplied is specified in the contract, and note that for futures data, some exchanges require separate licensing (arranged through the vendor) with additional cost overheads. Services categorisation: *H—historical, D—daily, R—real-time.*

Commodity Systems Inc. 200 W Palmetto Park Road, Boca Raton, Florida 33432 USA. *H,D*

Tick Data Inc. 720 Kipling Street, Suite 115, Lakewood, CO 80215, USA. *H,D*

Technical Tools. 334 State Street, Suite 201, Los Altos, CA 94022, USA. *H,D*

FINSTAT. The Financial Times Statistics Service, 2nd Floor, 126 Jermyn Street, London SW1Y 4UJ, UK. *H,D*

Data Broadcasting Corp. 1900 S Norfolk Street, PO Box 5979, San Mateo, CA 94402–0979, USA. *R*

Blomberg. City Gate House, Finsbury Square, London EC2, UK. *R*

Knight-Ridder. Commodity Research Bureau, 30 S Wacker Drive, Suite 1820, Chicago, IL 60606, USA. *H,R*

FutureSource UK. European Regional Headquarters, 1 Marble Quay, St Katharine's Way, London E1 9UL. *R*

FutureSource. A Division of Oster Communications Inc, 955 Parkview Blvd, Lombard, IL 60148, USA. *R*

ICV Limited. Real-Time Financial Data, ICV House, 72 Chertsey Road, Woking GU21 5BJ, UK. *R*

CQG International Ltd. Thames House, 18 Park Street, London SE1 9EL, UK. *R*

Dow Jones/Telerate. Harborside Financial Center, 600 Plaza Two, Jersey City, NJ 07311–3992, USA. *R*

Reuters Inc. 1700 Broadway, New York, NY 10019, USA. *R*

A selection of neural network simulation software companies, by product name follows. Categorisation is based on network paradigms available: *P — proprietary; B — backpropagation, possibly one other; C — comprehensive multi-architecture.* A number of simulators operate within established spreadsheet programs, indicated by *S* below. See also the recent review of commercial simulators by Jurik[74] and Hammerstrom[56] and academic simulators by Lutzy and Dengel[99].

DynaMind. NeuroDynamX Inc, PO Box 323, Boulder, CO 80306, USA. *B*

Brainmaker. California Scientific Software, 10024 Newtown Road, Nevada City, CA 95959, USA. *B*

NeuroShell. Ward Systems Group Inc, Executive Park West, 5 Hillcrest Drive, Frederick, MD 21702, USA. *B*

ExplorNet. HNC Inc, 5501 Oberlin Drive, San Diego, CA 92121–1718, USA. *C*

NeuralWorks. NeuralWare Inc, Penn Center West, Building IV, Pittsburgh, PA 15276, USA. *C*

Nexpert Object. Neuron Data, 156 University Avenue, Palo Alto, CA 94301, USA. *C*

HNeT. AND America Ltd, 2140 Winston Park Drive, Suite 202, Oakville, Ontario, Canada L6H 5V5. *P*

Autonet. Recognition Research Ltd, 140 Church Lane, Marple, Stockport, SK6 7LA, UK. *P*

Nestor Learning System. Nestor Inc, One Richmond Square, Providence, RI 02906, USA. *P.*

Brain. Talon Development Corp, PO Box 11069, Milwaukee, WI 53211–0069, USA. *S P.*

Braincel. Promised Land Technology, Suite 335, 900 Chapel Street, New Haven, CT 06510, USA. *S B (backpercolation)*

SNNS. A Zell, Universitat Stuttgart Fachbereich Informatik, Stuttgart, Germany. *B: available for academics.*

Newcomers to the field of neurocomputing are advised to opt for a single paradigm network simulator (*B* or *P* above), and then upgrade to a wider range of paradigms, which also allow greater user fine tuning, as required. For programmers, a number of books may be found that can get them started in C and C++, including McClelland and Rumelhart[107], Eberhart and Dobbins[43], Muller and Reinhardt[115], Blum[18] and Masters[104].

Next, a selected list of mathematical and statistical software tools by product name, including fuzzy logic and genetic algorithms. Wavelet software, for Discrete Wavelet Transform preprocessing of time series, is available in an increasing number of mathematical tools, indicated by *DWT*. Principal Component Analysis is also available as a standard feature in many statistical and mathematical software packages, indicated below by *PCA*. The IEEE publication *Spectrum* includes annually in its November issue a software guide to engineering and scientific application tools (IEEE address in journals list).

AIM. AbTech Corporation, 508 Dale Avenue, Charlottesville, VA 22903, USA. Abductive modelling tool.

CubiCalc. Hyperlogic Corp., 1855 East Valley Parkway, Suite 210, Escondido, CA 92027, USA. Fuzzy logic modelling tool.

TILSHELL. Togai InfraLogic Inc, 5 Vanderbilt, Irvine, CA 92718, USA. Fuzzy logic modelling tool.

C Darwin. ITANIS International Inc, 1737 Holly LN, Pittsburgh, PA 15216–1151, USA. Genetic algorithms development tool.

XerpertRule. Attar Software Ltd, Newlands Road, Leigh, Lancs WN7 4HN, UK. Genetic algorithms development tool.

MathCAD. MathSoft Inc, 201 Broadway, Cambridge, Mass. 02139–1901, USA. *PCA,DWT*

Mathematica. Wolfram Research, Inc, 100 Trade Center Drive, Champaign, IL 61820–7237, USA. *PCA*

MATLAB. The Math Works Inc, 24 Prime Park Way, Natick, MA 01760, USA. *PCA*, also includes neural networks toolbox.

UltraWave Explorer. Aware Inc, One Memorial Drive, Cambridge, MA 02142, USA. *DWT*

Fast Wavelet Transform. by Mac A Cody. *Dr Dobb's Journal*, pp.16–28, April 1992. *DWT*

UNISTAT. UNISTAT Ltd, PO Box 383, Highgate, London N6 5UP, UK. *PCA*

BMDP. Statistical Software, 1964 Westwood Boulevard, Suite 202, Los Angeles, CA 90025, USA. *PCA*

Numerical Recipes. Customer Services Department, Cambridge University Press, Edinburgh Building, Shaftesbury Road, Cambridge CB2 2RU, UK. *DWT* State-of-the-art, low cost, subroutine library.

NAG. Numerical Algorithms Group Ltd, Wilkinson House, Jordan Hill Road, Oxford OX2 8DR, UK. Professional subroutine library.

IMSL. IMSL Sales Division, Suite 3000, 14141 Southwest Freeway, Sugar Land, Texas 77478, USA. Professional subroutine library.

Appendix A
Backpropagation

Training weights by backpropagation is formally equivalent to function minimisation by gradient descent techniques. The function in question for neural network applications is the cost, or energy function, which is tailored by the designer to reflect the particular problem to be solved. The original backpropagation[138,139] method utilised the steepest descent method[128], however other gradient descent methods, such as conjugate gradients and the BFGS algorithm may be substituted. In conventional (non-neural) optimisation analysis, these more sophisticated methods have proven superior to steepest descent. A variant of conjugate gradients and the BFGS quasi-Newton method are discussed here; see also Battiti[14].

The conventional disadvantages of steepest descent are mitigated in the neural network context, when stochastic weight updates are used. It thus compares favourably against the other methods discussed here. This, however, presupposes a good choice for the learning and momentum coefficients (often just learning coefficient, with momentum set to zero), which are not always easily found.

The main advantage of the conjugate gradient and BFGS approaches is the automated learning step size calculation. A possible disadvantage may be their restriction as batch weight update methods. Comparisons are provided in the benchmark chapter; in the final analysis it is always useful to have available a number of solvers for trying out on a problem.

A.1 STEEPEST DESCENT METHOD

The task of minimising the cost function can be described in terms of general concepts. Each weight in the network represents a unique dimension in a multidimensional weight space. The cost function, being a function of the weights, will have the features of an undulating 'landscape' of troughs, peaks, valleys and tunnels, in this multidimensional space, with scattered localised minima but one global minimum, whose coordinates are the weight values that are sought for the problem solution.

Let there be N weights, represented as a vector, then the cost function, $E(\vec{w})$, will be N-dimensional. After one epoch of training pattern presentations the weights are updated so as to minimise E (in practice it is often preferable to update the weights after each pattern), this will be by some magnitude η along some (unit) direction in the weight space $\vec{u}$. Thus there is a two fold task, first is the choice of which direction $\vec{u}$ to take in weight space, and then selecting the magnitude η for which E is a minimum along that path. Having found appropriate values, the best value for E is now

$$\vec{w} \rightarrow \vec{w} + \eta\vec{u} \tag{A.1}$$

$$E \rightarrow E(\vec{w} + \eta\vec{u}) \tag{A.2}$$

and the procedure continues with the next epoch, starting from the latest weight vector $\vec{w}$.

In traditional problems, the most successful minimisation methods make use of the gradients of the function E, to determine the direction $\vec{u}$. The original backpropagation made use of the first vector partial derivative of E with respect to the weights, in what is known as the *method of steepest descent*. The gradient will give the direction of a tangent to the curvature of E at the position $\vec{w}$, by choosing a negative sign it is ensured that the gradient points downwards towards the local minimum of E, which it is hoped will lead to the global minimum.

$$E \rightarrow E\left(\vec{w} - \eta\frac{\partial E}{\partial w}\right) \tag{A.3}$$

Although this method is the simplest gradient descent technique, it has what turns out to be an advantage in practice, the possibility of updating the weights immediately after an input vector presentation. The disadvantage is that the selection of η will be arbitrary. This constant is called the learning coefficient in the neural literature and is the source of much debate in proposing suitable values for it. Section 4.8 discusses various strategies for selecting η, which may be varied layer by layer, neuron by neuron, and/or by epoch iteration. The more sophisticated conjugate gradient, and related, methods not only provide better choices for the direction $\vec{u}$ but also automate the procedure of selecting η after each epoch by line search techniques. The conjugate gradient and quasi-Newton, or variable metric, methods, are batch-learning techniques when applied to neural networks, since the cost function can only be evaluated with an epoch of input pattern presentations, and cost function evaluations are required as an integral part of these methods.

The steepest descent method provides a general formulation for updating the weights, the backpropagation method gives an explicit procedure for applying the updates to hidden layer weights in the network. Figure A.1 defines the notation

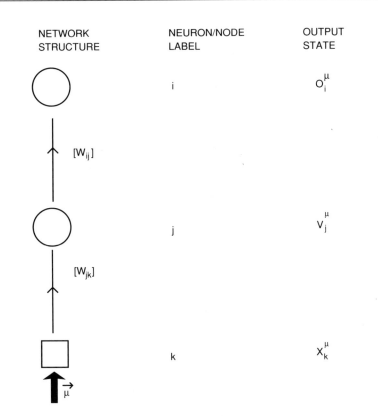

NETWORK
STRUCTURE

NEURON/NODE
LABEL

OUTPUT
STATE

i

O_i^μ

$[W_{ij}]$

j

V_j^μ

$[W_{jk}]$

k

X_k^μ

$\vec{\mu}$

Figure A.1 Notation for neural network structure in the backpropagation derivation

and structure of a three layer network. Note that the bias node is subsumed in the general notation for cells and not treated specially here. The application of the method for additional hidden layers is routine. With reference to this figure, a pattern, or input vector, $\vec{\mu}$ comprises the input variables x_k^μ. The transfer function, $f(a)$, in the first hidden layer of j neurons, will have input a_j^μ, and output V_j^μ, defined by

$$a_j^\mu = \sum_k w_{jk} x_k^\mu \tag{A.4}$$

$$V_j^\mu = f(a_j^\mu) \tag{A.5}$$

Similarly, the input to the output layer transfer functions and corresponding outputs are given by

$$a_i^\mu = \sum_j w_{ij} V_j^\mu \tag{A.6}$$

$$O_i^\mu = f(a_i^\mu) \tag{A.7}$$

$$= f^i \left[\sum_j w_{ij} f^j \left(\sum_k w_{jk} x_k^\mu \right) \right] \tag{A.8}$$

where the transfer functions f^i, f^j are distinguished since, in general, each neuron may have a unique transfer function.

The weight updates, Δw, for the weights in the hidden-output region, are obtained by applying the chain rule to the steepest descent method:

$$w_{ij} = w_{ij} + \Delta w_{ij} \tag{A.9}$$

$$\Delta w_{ij} = -\eta \frac{\partial E}{\partial w_{ij}} \tag{A.10}$$

$$= -\eta \sum_\mu \frac{\partial E}{\partial O_i^\mu} \frac{\partial O_i^\mu}{\partial a_i^\mu} \frac{\partial a_i^\mu}{\partial w_{ij}} \tag{A.11}$$

$$= -\eta \sum_\mu \frac{\partial E}{\partial O_i^\mu} f'(a_i^\mu) V_j^\mu \tag{A.12}$$

$$= \eta \sum_\mu \delta_i^\mu V_j^\mu \tag{A.13}$$

where f' is the transfer function derivative with respect to a, and δ, giving rise to the alternative name for the method, *general delta rule*, is defined by

$$\delta_i^\mu = -f'(a_i^\mu) \frac{\partial E}{\partial O_i^\mu} \tag{A.14}$$

The weights in the input-hidden region are now updated as follows:

$$w_{jk} = w_{jk} + \Delta w_{jk} \tag{A.15}$$

$$\Delta w_{jk} = -\eta \frac{\partial E}{\partial w_{jk}} \tag{A.16}$$

$$= -\eta \sum_\mu \sum_i \frac{\partial E}{\partial O_i^\mu} \frac{\partial O_i^\mu}{\partial a_i^\mu} \frac{\partial a_i^\mu}{\partial V_j^\mu} \frac{\partial V_j^\mu}{\partial a_j^\mu} \frac{\partial a_j^\mu}{\partial w_{jk}} \tag{A.17}$$

$$= \eta \sum_\mu f'(a_j^\mu) x_k^\mu \sum_i \delta_i^\mu w_{ij} \tag{A.18}$$

$$= \eta \sum_\mu \delta_j^\mu x_k^\mu \tag{A.19}$$

with

$$\delta_j^\mu = f'(a_j^\mu) \sum_i w_{ij} \delta_i^\mu \qquad \text{(A.20)}$$

The above weight update rules are expressed in terms of a general cost function E, and general transfer function f. For specific cases the expressions for δ can be simplified in terms of the error $T - O$, however this is only of historical interest. A general computer program implementing backpropagation should cater for individual neurons having different transfer functions, and for the user to define the cost function E. Chapter 4 describes suitable cost and transfer functions and their respective derivatives, $\partial E / \partial O$ and f', for substituting into the above equations.

The extension to multiconnectivity networks is straightforward. Thus, updating weights connecting the input to output layers is performed by similar equations to those for the hidden-output region with appropriate changes, e.g. V is replaced by x.

A.2   CONJUGATE GRADIENT AND QUASI-NEWTON METHODS

A.2.1   Shanno Method

Given the cost function $E(\vec{w})$, with its multidimensional landscape, the steepest descent method seeks to locate the minimum by selecting the search direction to be the local downhill gradient. These directions do not necessarily lead to the global minimum in the most efficient manner. If the search has found a minimum along some direction, it would be desirable to start a new search direction that does not spoil the minimum already located, such a direction is known as a conjugate direction. Following a series of conjugate gradient directions ensures that minima found along the way are retained.

For a cost function that has a quadratic form it is possible to construct a series of conjugate gradient searches that guarantees convergence on the minimum. In the general case, it is recommended that after N conjugate direction cycles the series of searches be restarted with the local downhill gradient, where N is the number of weights in the network. This leads to a convergence on the global minimum, at which any cost function will in fact be well approximated by a quadratic form. There are a number of possible procedures in constructing the conjugate directions, the variation used in the benchmarking is due to Shanno[148]. A general outline of conjugate gradient methods is as follows.

The Taylor expansion of the cost function around some point $\vec{w}_i$, to within the quadratic approximation, is

$$E(\vec{w}) = E(\vec{w}_i) + (\vec{w} - \vec{w}_i) \cdot \nabla E(\vec{w}_i) + \frac{1}{2}(\vec{w} - \vec{w}_i) \cdot H \cdot (\vec{w} - \vec{w}_i) \qquad \text{(A.21)}$$

where H is the Hessian matrix $[H]_{jk} \equiv \left. \frac{\partial^2 E}{\partial w_j \partial w_k} \right|_{\vec{w}_i}$

The local gradient at any point is then given by

$$\nabla E(\vec{w}) = \nabla E(\vec{w}_i) + H \cdot (\vec{w} - \vec{w}_i) \qquad (A.22)$$

Now it is desired to construct a series of gradients $\vec{g}_i$, with $i = 1 \ldots N$

$$\vec{g}_i = \nabla E(\vec{w}_i) \qquad (A.23)$$

that satisfy the conjugate condition $\vec{g}_{i+1} \cdot \vec{g}_i = 0$. This can be achieved by selecting search directions $\vec{d}$ that satisfy

$$\vec{d}_{i+1} = -\vec{g}_{i+1} + \beta_i \vec{d}_i \qquad (A.24)$$
$$\vec{d}_{i+1} \cdot H \cdot \vec{d}_i = 0 \qquad (A.25)$$

where the Polak-Ribiere conjugate gradient version has these conditions satisfied by setting β to

$$\beta_i = \frac{(\vec{g}_{i+1} - \vec{g}_i) \cdot \vec{g}_{i+1}}{\vec{g}_i \cdot \vec{g}_i} \qquad (A.26)$$

Start the minimisation procedure by selecting the steepest descent gradient for $\vec{d}$. At the ith step, starting from some point $\vec{w}_i$ along the direction $\vec{d}_i$, a new point $\vec{w}_{i+1}$ is to be found that is the minimum of E along that direction.

$$\vec{w}_{i+1} = \vec{w}_i + \tau \vec{d}_i \qquad (A.27)$$

where τ is found by a line search method. Having found this minimum the next gradient $\vec{g}_{i+1}$ is selected to be

$$\vec{g}_{i+1} = \nabla E(\vec{w}_{i+1}) \qquad (A.28)$$

This allows the new β and new search direction $\vec{d}_{i+1}$ to be calculated. This procedure continues until N steps have been performed. The procedure is then re-started with the steepest descent selected for $\vec{g}$ at the local minimum $\vec{w}_N$. The process should then converge on the global minimum of $E(\vec{w})$. Notice that the method does not require evaluation of the Hessian, only function and function gradient information is used. However, as defined above, the conjugate gradient method requires accurate line minimisation.

An alternative approach relaxes the assumption that τ is the exact line minimum and adds correction terms to the search direction $\vec{d}$. In the inexact search conjugate gradient method due to Shanno[148] the search direction is given by

$$\vec{d}_{i+1} = -\vec{g}_{i+1} - \left[\left(1 + \frac{\vec{y}_i \cdot \vec{y}_i}{\vec{p}_i \cdot \vec{y}_i} \right) \frac{\vec{p}_i \cdot \vec{g}_{i+1}}{\vec{p}_i \cdot \vec{y}_i} - \frac{\vec{y}_i \cdot \vec{g}_{i+1}}{\vec{p}_i \cdot \vec{y}_i} \right] \vec{p}_i + \frac{\vec{p}_i \cdot \vec{g}_{i+1}}{\vec{p}_i \cdot \vec{y}_i} \vec{y}_i \qquad (A.29)$$

where

$$\vec{p}_i = \vec{w}_{i+1} - \vec{w}_i \tag{A.30}$$

$$\vec{y}_i = \vec{g}_{i+1} - \vec{g}_i \tag{A.31}$$

In the implementation selected here for the benchmarks, the Shanno version of the conjugate gradient method was used with Shanno's γ scaling for the initial search direction selection as follows

$$\vec{d}_1 = -\frac{\vec{p}_0 \cdot \vec{y}_0}{\vec{y}_0 \cdot \vec{y}_0}\vec{g}_1 - \left(2\frac{\vec{p}_0 \cdot \vec{g}_1}{\vec{p}_0 \cdot \vec{y}_0} - \frac{\vec{y}_0 \cdot \vec{g}_1}{\vec{y}_0 \cdot \vec{y}_0}\right)\vec{p}_0 + \frac{\vec{p}_0 \cdot \vec{g}_1}{\vec{y}_0 \cdot \vec{y}_0}\vec{y}_0 \tag{A.32}$$

and

$$\vec{d}_0 = -\frac{\vec{g}_0}{|\vec{g}_0|} \tag{A.33}$$

The use of inexact search techniques facilitates an efficient use of computation time, since a very precise line search is unnecessary, noting that the line does not pass the global minimum until the final iteration.

A.2.2 BFGS Method

Quasi-Newton, or variable metric, methods are similar to conjugate gradient methods, however their main feature involves a series of approximations to the Hessian. We had above for the local gradient $\nabla E(\vec{w})$

$$\nabla E(\vec{w}) = \nabla E(\vec{w}_i) + H \cdot (\vec{w} - \vec{w}_i) \tag{A.34}$$

Following Newton's method, where the gradient is set to zero (this will be true at the global minimum $\vec{w}$), yields

$$\vec{w} - \vec{w}_i = -H^{-1} \cdot \nabla E(\vec{w}_i) \tag{A.35}$$

and the iterative formula is obtained by subtracting the above formula for the next point $\vec{w}_{i+1}$

$$\vec{w}_{i+1} - \vec{w}_i = H^{-1} \cdot [\nabla E(\vec{w}_{i+1}) - \nabla E(\vec{w}_i)] \tag{A.36}$$

The essence of the method involves approximating the true Hessian by positive definite matrices, which drive the search directions towards the global minimum where the positive definite property is satisfied. The method adopted here in the benchmarking is the Broyden-Fletcher-Goldfarb-Shanno (BFGS) method, as given in Numerical Recipes[128], with their inexact search routine. For further details of the Hessian constructions, refer to their text.

A.3   SECOND ORDER ANALYSIS

Optimal Brain Damage[95] (see Section 4.11) makes use of second order information on the cost function to provide an analytical expression for the local effect a weight perturbation has on the cost function. A measure, known as the *saliency*, can then be assigned to each weight, with the final ranking allowing low saliency weights to be removed from the network (in practice these weights are simply set to 0). The technique has particular importance for very large networks, not only in increasing the training to weights ratio TWR, but also in that de-scaling improves the efficiency of locating the cost function global minimum.

The weights in a neural network represent the free parameters of the model upon which the cost function is dependent. Perturbing the weights by a small amount will result in a consequent change in the cost function. Let the weights, w_{ij}, be represented by a single index parameter, $u_i \in U$, then the Taylor expansion for the cost function E perturbation is as follows.

$$\delta E = \sum_i g_i \delta u_i + \frac{1}{2}\sum_i h_{ii}\delta u_i^2 + \frac{1}{2}\sum_{i \neq j} h_{ij}\delta u_i \delta u_j + O(\|\delta U\|^3) \qquad (\text{A.37})$$

where the gradient $g_i = \partial E / \partial u_i$, and the Hessian components $h_{ij} = \partial^2 E / \partial u_i \partial u_j$.

The perturbation is performed only for a converged network, which is then either at the global or a local minimum. A general E will therefore be close to a quadratic curve and the higher order terms can be neglected. Furthermore the first term will also vanish at the minimum. Finally, make a diagonal Hessian approximation, with cross-terms assumed small, then the third term can be neglected. Thus

$$\delta E \approx \frac{1}{2}\sum_i h_{ii}\delta u_i^2 \qquad (\text{A.38})$$

where the diagonal terms h_{ii} correspond to the second derivative of each weight w_{pq}

$$h_{ii} = \frac{\partial^2 E}{\partial w_{pq}^2} \qquad (\text{A.39})$$

The change in E for any particular weight perturbation is δE_{pq}. A measure of the influence of each weight on the network output is then provided by the saliency, s, defined by

$$s_{pq} = |\delta E_{pq}|w_{pq}^2 \qquad (\text{A.40})$$

$$s_{pq} \approx |h_{ii}|w_{pq}^2 \qquad (\text{A.41})$$

In order to evaluate the Hessian components, the equations obtained in the backpropagation steepest descent derivation will be made use of here. The same three layer network will be assumed and the terms derived from the output layer downwards through the network. Thus for the hidden-output region weights, w_{ij}, the first derivative of E is given by

$$\frac{\partial E}{\partial w_{ij}} = \frac{\partial E}{\partial O_i} \frac{\partial O_i}{\partial a_i} \frac{\partial a_i}{\partial w_{ij}} \qquad (A.42)$$

$$\frac{\partial E}{\partial w_{ij}} = \frac{\partial E}{\partial O_i} f'(a_i) V_j \qquad (A.43)$$

Differentiating the first derivative once more by parts

$$\frac{\partial^2 E}{\partial w_{ij}^2} = f'(a_i) V_j \frac{\partial}{\partial w_{ij}} \left(\frac{\partial E}{\partial O_i} \right) + \frac{\partial E}{\partial O_i} V_j f''(a_i) V_j \qquad (A.44)$$

$$\frac{\partial^2 E}{\partial w_{ij}^2} = [f'(a_i) V_j]^2 \frac{\partial^2 E}{\partial O_i^2} + \frac{\partial E}{\partial O_i} V_j^2 f''(a_i) \qquad (A.45)$$

The weights in the input-hidden region are treated next. The first derivative is as follows.

$$\frac{\partial E}{\partial w_{jk}} = \sum_i \frac{\partial E}{\partial O_i} f'(a_i) w_{ij} f'(a_j) x_k \qquad (A.46)$$

Taking the second derivative yields

$$\frac{\partial^2 E}{\partial w_{jk}^2} = \sum_i f'(a_i) w_{ij} f'(a_j) x_k \frac{\partial}{\partial w_{jk}} \left(\frac{\partial E}{\partial O_i} \right) + \sum_i \frac{\partial E}{\partial O_i} w_{ij} x_k \frac{\partial}{\partial w_{jk}} [f'(a_i) f'(a_j)] \qquad (A.47)$$

$$\frac{\partial^2 E}{\partial w_{jk}^2} = f'(a_j) x_k^2 \sum_i w_{ij}^2 \frac{\partial^2 E}{\partial a_i^2} + f_j'' x_k^2 \sum_i w_{ij} f'(a_i) \frac{\partial E}{\partial O_i} \qquad (A.48)$$

where

$$\frac{\partial^2 E}{\partial a_i^2} = f'^2(a_i) \frac{\partial^2 E}{\partial O_i^2} + f''(a_i) \frac{\partial E}{\partial O_i} \qquad (A.49)$$

The second derivative can be written in a more compact form by first making the following substitution

$$\frac{\partial E}{\partial V_j} = \sum_i w_{ij} f'(a_i) \frac{\partial E}{\partial O_i} \qquad (A.50)$$

then finally

$$\frac{\partial^2 E}{\partial a_j^2} = f'(a_j) \sum_i w_{ij}^2 \frac{\partial^2 E}{\partial a_i^2} + f_j'' \frac{\partial E}{\partial V_i} \qquad (A.51)$$

$$\frac{\partial^2 E}{\partial w_{jk}^2} = x_k^2 \frac{\partial^2 E}{\partial a_j^2} \qquad (A.52)$$

Appendix B
Benchmark Weights

Weight solutions for the non-financial benchmarks are tabulated here. The financials involve larger networks and are not convenient for tabulation; their weights are listed in the files WEISP5.MAT and WEIBPX.MAT in the following appendix.

B.1 XOR FUNCTION

Table B.1 XOR function weight solution for best Shanno solved multiconnectivity network with nodal structure 2-1-1; all neurons have *tanh* transfer functions with gains 1.5 and 1.0 in the hidden and output layers, respectively. Input nodes are notated according to their time lag, and are $[-1,1]$ normalised. Network was trained to better than 0.05 norm RMS training error

	receiver	
source	hid1	output
t-2	−1.6822	−1.5420
t-1	−1.5582	−1.6319
hid1	—	−2.4719
bias	0.1867	0.7736

B.2 HENON MAP

Table B.2 Henon map series weight solution for best BFGS solved multiconnectivity network with nodal structure 2-3-1; hidden neuron transfer functions are all *tanh* with gain 1.5. Output layer neuron is piece-wise linear with slope 0.5 and cut-off 2.5. Input nodes are notated according to their time lag, and are [−1,1] normalised. Network trained to better than 0.05 norm RMS training error

| | receiving neuron | | | |
source	hid1	hid2	hid3	output
t-2	−0.0946	−0.0387	−0.4387	0.2982
t-1	−2.3656	−1.1180	−0.3755	5.3499
hid1	—	—	—	2.5770
hid2	—	—	—	4.4798
hid3	—	—	—	−1.1565
bias	2.1089	0.3516	0.4543	−2.4997

B.3 MACKEY-GLASS EQUATION

Table B.3 Mackey-Glass series weight solution for adaptive steepest descent solved multiconnectivity network with input data norm [−1,1], and nodal structure 6-5-1 (hidden transfer functions, all with gain 1.5: 2 *tanh*, 1 *cosine*, 1 piece-wise linear, 1 ACE with amplitude 0.0226; piece-wise linear output layer neuron, with slope 0.5 and cut-off 2.5). Input nodes are notated according to their time lag. Network trained to better than 0.05 norm RMS training error

| | receiving neuron | | | | | |
source	hid1	hid2	hid3	hid4	ACE	output
t-6	0.4805	−0.3894	−0.0682	−0.7712	−0.0596	0.0742
t-5	2.0721	−0.9682	−0.0078	−1.5838	0.1078	0.3600
t-4	−0.4115	−0.0252	0.0532	−0.7185	−0.0501	−0.2101
t-3	0.1423	−0.0106	0.0006	0.0975	−0.0300	0.1239
t-2	−0.1164	−0.1989	0.0396	0.5020	−0.0520	−0.3004
t-1	0.2137	0.2610	−0.1026	0.7695	0.0172	1.4933
hid1	—	—	—	—	—	−1.1541
hid2	—	—	—	—	—	−0.7274
hid3	—	—	—	—	—	−0.0466
hid4	—	—	—	—	—	0.0342
ACE	—	—	—	—	—	0.9993
bias	−0.9665	−0.7080	0.0755	0.1310	0.0630	−0.7330

B.4 SUNSPOT NUMBERS

Table B.4 Sunspot series weight solution for best BFGS solved multiconnectivity network with nodal structure 6-3-1. Hidden transfer functions all *tanh* with gain 1.5. Piece-wise linear output layer neuron with slope 0.5 and cut-off 2.5. Input nodes are notated according to their time lag, with the input [0,1] normalised. Network was trained to 200 epochs

| | receiving neuron | | | |
source	hid1	hid2	hid3	output
t-6	−0.3739	−0.1344	−0.1434	0.0447
t-5	−0.6567	−0.3335	0.1845	−0.3860
t-4	1.5402	1.0775	−0.0929	0.2716
t-3	0.4791	1.0238	−0.1741	−0.3562
t-2	2.2860	0.6956	0.7663	0.2437
t-1	−0.6170	1.2117	0.0558	1.2484
hid1	—	—	—	−1.4044
hid2	—	—	—	1.3166
hid3	—	—	—	0.2430
bias	0.1931	0.1191	0.1174	0.0897

Appendix C
Recall Mode MLP Simulator

The program reMLP.FOR is a recall mode MLP neural network simulator that sets up the benchmark solutions in the form of pre-trained neural networks. Present test patterns for the selected time series benchmark to the input nodes, according to the formats specified in Chapter 6, and the network will produce a forecast. Normalisation is performed automatically in the program. The test patterns should be filed in REMLP.TST, and for trend calculations also create file REMLP.TRE, with formats as instructed below.

The program is written in FORTRAN-77, which has the advantage of being relatively readable. A command file REMLP.COM defines the memory requirements and also acts as the input file for setting the program requirements.

The weights for the benchmarks are in the files WEI***.MAT, which also contains information for transfer functions, scaling and the standard deviation in calculating the sd norm RMS error. The XOR problem, not being a time series, is omitted. Also, only the solution for Monday is provided for the BP/USD exchange rate.

```
C--------------------------------------------------------
C reMLP.FOR
C----------
C RECALL MODE MULTICONNECTIVITY MULTILAYER PERCEPTRON
C NEURAL NETWORK SIMULATOR FOR TIME SERIES FORECASTING
C
C Copyright (c) E M Azoff 1993
C All rights reserved
C
C--------------------------------------------------------
C This program creates a pre-trained MLP network by
C reading the weights file for the benchmark
C specified by the flag BMRK. Input patterns may then
C be cycled forward through the network to produce a
C forecast. Depending on the MODE setting, the network
```

```
C output may be compared with a known target if available.
C
C Output may also be reported as a movement with respect
C to a previous element in the time series:
C set ITREND to 1 for this option and supply previous
C elements, one for each input pattern, in file REMLP.TRE.
C
C The input vectors should conform to the format specified
C in the benchmarks chapter, UNNORMALISED. Normalisation
C is performed automatically here using scaling parameters
C derived in the benchmarking.
C
C REMLP.COM is the command input file: only a few
C integer parameters need setting, as described below.
C
C*********************************************************
C USER SUPPLIED INPUT VARIABLES in REMLP.COM
C-------------------------------------------
C
C BMRK: SET ACCORDING TO THE BENCHMARK
C      1 = HENON MAP; 2 = MACKEY-GLASS;
C      3 = SUNSPOTS; 4 = S&P500; 5 = BP/USD
C MODE: SET TO 0 FOR RECALL MODE WITH TARGET AVAILABLE
C           1                          NO TARGET
C ITREND: SET TO 1 FOR EVALUATING FORECAST TREND.
C    REQUIRES DATA FILE REMLP.TRE.
C NPAT: NUMBER OF INPUT PATTERNS TO BE PROCESSED
C
C*********************************************************
C
          INCLUDE 'REMLP.COM',NOLIST
          INTEGER I
          CHARACTER*3 BNAME(5)
          CHARACTER*10 WFILE
          EXTERNAL TKEYS,READW,RDPATTS,RDSCA,RDTREND,RDSDTST
          EXTERNAL RDAAMP,RECALL1,COMBINE,RECALL
          DATA WFILE /'WEI   .MAT'/
          DATA (BNAME(I),I=1,5) /'HEN','MGE','SUN','SP5','BPX'/
C----------------------------------------------------------
C EXTERNAL FILES
C--------------
C
C USER SUPPLIED:
C
C REMLP.TST: FILE CHANNEL  7: INPUT PATTERNS FOR TESTING
C FORMAT PER LINE: NODE(1...NIN),TARGET
C where NODE is the input node value (unnormalised)
```

```
C where NIN is the number of input nodes
C where TARGET is optional (if available set MODE=0)
C BENCHMARK 5: BP/USD USES TWO STAGES OF NETWORKS
C SUPPLY SECOND INPUT PATTERN SET FOLLOWING FIRST
C ENSURE DUMMY VALUE USED FOR ELEMENT TO BE
C OVERWRITTEN BY FIRST STAGE FORECAST (POSITION
C IS FIRST INPUT NODE)
C REMLP.TRE:      CHANNEL 8: TREND DATA, OPTIONAL ON ITREND
C          LISTS THE UNNORMALISED PREVIOUS ELEMENT IN TIME SERIES
C          FOR TREND EVALUATION, EACH ELEMENT PAIRED WITH DATE
C          (DATE CAN BE ANY DUMMY INTEGER).
C          TOTAL NPAT NUMBER OF LINES IN REMLP.TRE.
C-------------------------------------------------------
C OTHER FILES
C------------
C WEI___.MAT: FILE CHANNEL 3: WEIGHTS PLUS OTHER DATA
C          LISTING OF ALL *.MAT FILES FOLLOWS PROGRAM CODE BELOW
C REMLP.LOG:      CHANNEL 11: OUTPUT INFORMATION FILE
C REMLP.PST:      CHANNEL 15: POST-PROCESSING DATA FILE
C  IF MODE=0 THEN REMLP.PST CONTAINS
C    DATE PREVIOUS TARGET OBSERVED CHNG-IN-TAR CHNG-IN-OBS
C  ELSE
C    DATE PREVIOUS OBSERVED CHNG-IN-OBSERVED
c          where OBSERVED is the network output
c          where PREVIOUS is the previous element in
C            the time series, as read from REMLP.TRE
C          where CHNG... is the change with respect to PREVIOUS
C          if ITREND=0 then PREVIOUS and CHNG-IN-OBS
c            are dummy variables
C-------------------------------------------------------
C
        WFILE(4:6)=BNAME(BMRK)
        OPEN(UNIT=3,FILE=WFILE)
        OPEN(UNIT=7,FILE='REMLP.TST')
        IF (ITREND.EQ.1) OPEN(UNIT=8,FILE='REMLP.TRE')
        OPEN(UNIT=11,FILE='REMLP.LOG')
        OPEN(UNIT=15,FILE='REMLP.PST')
C-----------------------------------------------------------
C READ NET STRUCTURE
C
        CALL TKEYS
        CALL READW
        CALL RDPATTS
        CALL RDSCA
        CALL RDTREND
        CALL RDSDTST
        if (BMRK.EQ.2) CALL RDAAMP
```

```
        IF (BMRK.EQ.5) THEN
            CALL RECALL1
            CALL TKEYS
            CALL READW
            CALL RDPATTS
            CALL COMBINE
            CALL RDSCA
            CALL RDSDTST
        ENDIF
C
C PROCESS PATTERNS
C
        CALL RECALL
C
        STOP
        END
C
C-----------------------------------------------------------
C
C       SUBROUTINES
C
C-----------------------------------------------------------
C READ NEURON TRANSFER FUNCTION KEYS
C
        SUBROUTINE TKEYS
        INCLUDE 'REMLP.COM',NOLIST
        INTEGER I,J,NKEYS,K,IST,IEND,IVAL,NNOD,NNIN(5)
C
C PRE-SET NUMBER OF INPUT NODES FOR BENCHMARKS
        DATA (NNIN(I),I=1,5) /2,6,6,17,11/
C
C READ KEY PATTERN DATA: TRANSFER FUNCTION MAP
C
        NIN=NNIN(BMRK)
        SZNET(1)=NIN+1
        DO 300 I=2,LAY
            READ(3,*) NKEYS,NNOD,GAIN(I)
            IF (I.EQ.LAY.AND.NOUT.NE.NNOD) THEN
                WRITE(6,700) I,NNOD,(SZNET(I)-1)
  700           FORMAT(10X,'WARNING: LAY-NNOD.NE.NOUT  STOPPING'
      #               /,2X,3I8)
                STOP
            ENDIF
            SZNET(I)=NNOD+1
            DO 10 K=1,NKEYS
                READ(3,*) IST,IEND,IVAL
                DO 12 J=IST,IEND
```

```
  12                      TKEY(J,I-1)=IVAL
  10              CONTINUE
                  IF (IEND.NE.(SZNET(I)-1)) THEN
                      WRITE(6,710) I,IEND,(SZNET(I)-1)
 710                  FORMAT(10X,'WARNING: IEND.NE.SIZE-1  STOP'
     #                /,2X,'LAYER  IEND  SZNET(LAYER)-1: ',3I8)
                      STOP
                  ENDIF
 300      CONTINUE
C
C SET BIAS
          DO 310 K=1,LAY
 310         O(SZNET(K),K)=1.0D0
C
          RETURN
          END
C
C READ PATTERN DATA
C
          SUBROUTINE RDPATTS
          INCLUDE 'REMLP.COM',NOLIST
          INTEGER I,J
C
          IF (MODE.EQ.0) THEN
             DO 30 I=1,NPAT
             READ(7,*) (INPTS(I,J),J=1,NIN),(OPTS(I,J),J=1,NOUT)
  30         CONTINUE
          ELSE
             DO 300 I=1,NPAT
                READ(7,*) (INPTS(I,J),J=1,NIN)
 300         CONTINUE
          ENDIF
          RETURN
          END
C
C READ SCALE DATA
C
          SUBROUTINE RDSCA
          INCLUDE 'REMLP.COM',NOLIST
          INTEGER I
C
          DO 10 I=1,NIN
              READ(3,*) SCALEI(I),OFFSETI(I)
  10      CONTINUE
          READ(3,*) SCALEO,OFFSETO
          RETURN
          END
```

```
c
c READ STANDARD DEVIATION OF TEST PATTERN TARGETS
c
        SUBROUTINE RDSDTST
        INCLUDE 'REMLP.COM',NOLIST
        READ(3,*) SDTS
        RETURN
        END
c
c READ ACE NEURON ERROR AMPLITUDE
c (for Mackey-Glass benchmark using ACE)
c
        SUBROUTINE RDAAMP
        INCLUDE 'REMLP.COM',NOLIST
        READ(3,*) ERRLVL
        RETURN
        END
c
c READ TREND ANALYSIS DATA
c
        SUBROUTINE RDTREND
        INCLUDE 'REMLP.COM',NOLIST
        INTEGER I
        DO 10 I=1,NPAT
          READ(8,*) TRETST(I),DATTST(I)
 10     CONTINUE
        RETURN
        END
C
C SEQUENTIAL INPUT OF PATTERNS
C
        SUBROUTINE SEQIN(PAT)
        INCLUDE 'REMLP.COM',NOLIST
        INTEGER I,PAT
C
        DO 10 I=1,NIN
          O(I,1)=OFFSETI(I)+SCALEI(I)*INPTS(PAT,I)
 10     CONTINUE
        IF (MODE.EQ.0) THEN
          DO 11 I=1,NOUT
            TARGET(I)=OFFSETO+SCALEO*OPTS(PAT,I)
 11       CONTINUE
        ENDIF
C
        RETURN
        END
C
```

```
C FORWARD CYCLE PATTERN THROUGH NETWORK
C
        SUBROUTINE DONET
C
        INCLUDE 'REMLP.COM',NOLIST
        DOUBLE PRECISION H,SUMIN(SIZE)
        INTEGER I,J,K,S,L,LIM,KK
        INTRINSIC SIN,COS,TANH,EXP,MOD
C
        KK=0
        DO 555 L=2,LAY
C----------------------------------MAJOR LOOP START------
          DO 50 I=1,SZNET(L)-1
 50          SUMIN(i)=0.0D0
          DO 100 K=1,L-1
            S=L-K
            IF (S.LE.SLIM) THEN
                LIM=SZNET(K)
                IF (S.GT.1) LIM=LIM-1
                DO 200 I=1,SZNET(L)-1
                   DO 300 J=1,LIM
                      KK=KK+1
                      SUMIN(i)=SUMIN(i)+W(KK)*O(J,K)
 300               CONTINUE
 200            CONTINUE
            ENDIF
 100      CONTINUE
C
        DO 333 I=1,SZNET(L)-1
C----------------------------------MAJOR LOOP START------
        H=SUMIN(I)
C
        GOTO (1,2,3,4,5,6,7,8) TKEY(I,L-1)
        WRITE(6,700)
 700    FORMAT(10X,'WARNING: NO TRANSFER FUNCTION SELECTED - STOP')
        STOP
 1      CONTINUE
C          SIGMOID:
                    O(I,L)=1.0/(1.0+EXP(-GAIN(L)*H))
        GOTO 999
 2      CONTINUE
C            LINEAR:
                    O(I,L)=H
        GOTO 999
 3      CONTINUE
C              TANH:
                    O(I,L)=TANH(GAIN(L)*H)
```

```
              GOTO 999
     4        CONTINUE
C                 PIECE-WISE LINEAR:
                        IF (H.GT.CUT) THEN
                              O(I,L)=SLOPE*CUT
                        ELSE
                              IF (H.LT.-CUT) THEN
                                    O(I,L)=-SLOPE*CUT
                              ELSE
                                    O(I,L)=SLOPE*H
                              ENDIF
                        ENDIF
                 GOTO 999
     5        CONTINUE
C                   SINE:
                        H=MOD(H,TWOPI)
                        O(I,L)=SIN(H)
              GOTO 999
     6        CONTINUE
C                   COSINE:
                        H=MOD(H,TWOPI)
                        O(I,L)=COS(H)
              GOTO 999
     7        CONTINUE
C                 COSINE(PI/2+):
                        H=H+TWOPI/2.0D0
                        H=MOD(H,TWOPI)
                        O(I,L)=COS(H)
                        GOTO 999
     8        CONTINUE
C                 ACE TANH:
                        O(I,L)=ERRLVL*TANH(GAIN(L)*H)
C
 999     CONTINUE
C----------------------------------------MAJOR LOOPS END-------
 333     CONTINUE
 555     CONTINUE
C
         RETURN
         END
C
C READ WEIGHTS FROM WEI___.MAT
C
         SUBROUTINE READW
C
         INCLUDE 'REMLP.COM',NOLIST
         INTEGER K,I,J,LIM,KK,L,S
```

```
C
        KK=0
        DO 30 L=2,LAY
          DO 20 K=1,L-1
            S=L-K
            IF (S.LE.SLIM) THEN
                LIM=SZNET(K)
                IF (S.GT.1) LIM=LIM-1
                DO 10 I=1,SZNET(L)-1
                    READ(3,*) (W(KK+J),J=1,LIM)
                    KK=KK+LIM
 10             CONTINUE
            ENDIF
 20       CONTINUE
 30     CONTINUE
        RETURN
        END
C
C PROCESS INPUT PATTERNS
C
        SUBROUTINE RECALL
        INCLUDE 'REMLP.COM',NOLIST
        INTEGER J,IO
        REAL*8 CHATAR,CHAOBS,PREPER
        REAL*8 TARG,OBS,ERRRMS,ERR,RMSNRM
        EXTERNAL DONET,SEQIN
        INTRINSIC SQRT,DBLE
C
        DO 7000 IO=1,1
          ERRRMS=0.0d0
C
          DO 5000 J=1,NPAT
C-------------------------------------------
            CALL SEQIN(J)
            CALL DONET
C
            OBS=(O(1,LAY)-OFFSETO)/SCALEO
            IF (ITREND.EQ.1) THEN
                PREPER=TRETST(J)
                CHAOBS=OBS-PREPER
            ELSE
                PREPER=9999.99
            ENDIF
            IF (MODE.EQ.0) THEN
                ERR=(TARGET(1)-O(1,LAY))*(TARGET(1)-O(1,LAY))
                ERRRMS=ERRRMS+ERR
                TARG=OPTS(J,IO)
```

```
                CHATAR=TARG-PREPER
                WRITE(15,5510) DATTST(J),PREPER,TARG,OBS
      #         ,CHATAR,CHAOBS
 5510           FORMAT(I8,2X,9(E14.6,1X))
                WRITE(6,124) IO,J,TARG,OBS
                WRITE(11,124) IO,J,TARG,OBS
  124           FORMAT(1X,'o-nod=',I4,' test pat='
      #         ,I4,' tar=',e13.5,' obs=',e13.5)
                IF (ITREND.EQ.1) THEN
                   WRITE(6,125) IO,J,CHATAR,CHAOBS
                   WRITE(11,125) IO,J,CHATAR,CHAOBS
  125              FORMAT(1X,'o-nod=',I4,' test pat='
      #            ,I4,' chgtar=',E13.5,' chgobs=',E13.5)
                ENDIF
            ELSE
                WRITE(6,126) IO,J,OBS
                WRITE(11,126) IO,J,OBS
  126           FORMAT(1X,'o-nod=',I4,' test pat='
      #         ,I4,' obs=',e13.5)
                IF (ITREND.EQ.1) THEN
                   WRITE(6,127) IO,J,CHAOBS
                   WRITE(11,127) IO,J,CHAOBS
  127              FORMAT(1X,'o-nod=',I4,' test pat='
      #            ,I4,' chgobs=',E13.5)
                ENDIF
                WRITE(15,5510) DATTST(J),PREPER,OBS,CHAOBS
            ENDIF
C-------------------------------------------------------
 5000    CONTINUE
         IF (MODE.EQ.0) THEN
            ERRRMS=ERRRMS/DBLE(NPAT)
            ERRRMS=SQRT(ERRRMS)
            RMSNRM=ERRRMS/SDTS
            WRITE(6,132) ERRRMS,RMSNRM
            WRITE(11,132) ERRRMS,RMSNRM
  132    FORMAT(2X,'RMS ERROR=',E13.5,' SD NRM RMS=',E13.5)
         ENDIF
 7000    CONTINUE
         RETURN
         END
C
C PROCESS INPUT PATTERNS: STAGE-ONE
C
         SUBROUTINE RECALL1
         INCLUDE 'REMLP.COM',NOLIST
         INTEGER J
         EXTERNAL DONET,SEQIN
```

```
C
        DO 5 J=1,NPAT
           CALL SEQIN(J)
           CALL DONET
           O1(J)=(O(1,LAY)-OFFSETO)/SCALEO
  5     CONTINUE
        RETURN
        END
C
C COMBINE FIRST STAGE FORECAST WITH SECOND STAGE INPUT
C
        SUBROUTINE COMBINE
        INCLUDE 'REMLP.COM',NOLIST
        INTEGER J
C
        DO 5 J=1,NPAT
           INPTS(J,1)=O1(J)
  5     CONTINUE
        RETURN
        END
C---------------------------------------------------------
C
C COMMAND FILE: REMLP.COM
C
C---------------------------------------------------------
C REMLP.COM: COMMAND FILE: PARAMETERs AND COMMONs
C
        INTEGER BMRK,MODE,NPAT,ITREND
C
C USER SUPPLIED INPUT VARIABLES
C----------------------------
C
C BMRK: SET ACCORDING TO THE BENCHMARK
C       1 = HENON MAP; 2 = MACKEY-GLASS;
C       3 = SUNSPOTS; 4 = S&P500; 5 = BP/USD
C MODE: SET TO 0 FOR RECALL MODE WITH TARGET AVAILABLE
C                 1                        NO TARGET
C ITREND: SET TO 1 FOR EVALUATING FORECAST RISE/FALL.
C         REQUIRES DATA FILE REMLP.TRE, WHICH LISTS THE
C         UNNORMALIZED PREVIOUS ELEMENT IN TIME SERIES FOR
C         TREND EVALUATION, EACH ELEMENT PAIRED WITH DATE
C         (DATE CAN BE ANY DUMMY INTEGER).
C         TOTAL NPAT NUMBER OF LINES IN REMLP.TRE.
C NPAT: NUMBER OF INPUT PATTERNS TO BE PROCESSED
C
C=========================================================
C SET INTEGER FLAGS AS REQUIRED:
```

```
C
        PARAMETER(BMRK=4)
        PARAMETER(MODE=0)
        PARAMETER(ITREND=1)
        PARAMETER(NPAT=300)
C
C==========================================================
C CHANGE SETTINGS BELOW ONLY IF EXTRA STORAGE IS REQUIRED
C----------------------------------------------------------
C NPATX: MAXIMUM NUMBER OF INPUT PATTERNS FOR PROCESSING
        INTEGER NPATX
        PARAMETER (NPATX=500)
C
C----------------------------------------------------------
C NIMX: MAXIMUM NUMBER OF INPUT NODES
C NWMX: MAXIMUM NUMBER OF WEIGHTS
C SIZE: MAX. NO. NEUR. PER LAYER  INCLUDING BIAS
C NOUT: OUTPUT NO. NEUR. <= SIZE, EXCLUDING BIAS
C LAY:  NO. OF LAYERS, INPUT IS LAYER 1
C
        INTEGER SIZE,NOUT,NACE,LAY,NIMX,NPMX,NWMX,SLIM
        DOUBLE PRECISION TWOPI,SLOPE,CUT,EPSILON
C----------------------------------------------------------
        PARAMETER (NWMX=200)
        PARAMETER (SIZE=21)
        PARAMETER (NOUT=1)
        PARAMETER (LAY=3)
        PARAMETER (NIMX=20)
        PARAMETER (NACE=1)
        PARAMETER (SLIM=2)
C PARAMETERS FOR PIECE-WISE LINEAR TRANSFER FUNCTION
        PARAMETER (SLOPE=0.5D0)
        PARAMETER (CUT=2.5D0)
C MACHINE LIMIT
        PARAMETER (EPSILON=1.0D-10)
        PARAMETER(TWOPI=6.283185307D0)
C----------------------------------------------------------
        INTEGER SZNET(LAY),DATTST(NPATX),TKEY(SIZE,LAY),NIN
        REAL*8 GAIN(LAY),O(SIZE,LAY),W(NWMX),TARGET(NOUT)
        REAL*8 INPTS(NPATX,NIMX),OPTS(NPATX,NOUT)
        REAL*8 ERRLVL,TRETST(NPATX),O1(NPATX),SDTS
        REAL*8 SCALEO,SCALEI(NIMX),OFFSETI(NIMX),OFFSETO
C
        COMMON/I/ SZNET,NIN,DATTST
        COMMON /D/ SCALEO,OFFSETO,SCALEI,OFFSETI,ERRLVL,SDTS
        COMMON /A/ O,W,O1,TARGET,GAIN,TKEY,INPTS,OPTS,TRETST
C----------------------------------------------------------
```

```
C
C   WEI***.MAT FILES
C
C------------------------------------------------------------
C
C WEIHEN.MAT
C
  1 3 1.5
  1 3 3
  1 1 1.0
  1 1 4
  -0.094627   -2.365617    2.108923
  -0.038720   -1.117995    0.351592
  -0.438750   -0.375500    0.454308
   0.298156    5.349948
   2.576965    4.479813   -1.156457   -2.499678
   0.7830616   0.003520
   0.7830616   0.003520
   0.7830616   0.003520
   0.7103369
C------------------------------------------------------------
C
C WEIMGE.MAT
C
  4 5 1.5
  1 2 3
  3 3 4
  4 4 6
  5 5 8
  1 1 1.0
  1 1 4
   0.480526    2.072095   -0.411510    0.142323
  -0.116448    0.213659   -0.966494
  -0.389380   -0.968154   -0.025237   -0.010632
  -0.198922    0.260960   -0.707977
  -0.068195   -0.007783    0.053188    0.000638
   0.039632   -0.102619    0.075475
  -0.771201   -1.583829   -0.718458    0.097522
   0.501985    0.769532    0.131002
  -0.059636    0.107829   -0.050053   -0.030041
  -0.051974    0.017235    0.062973
   0.074206    0.359972   -0.210064    0.123915
  -0.300440    1.493312
  -1.154085   -0.727416   -0.046613    0.034191
   0.999307   -0.732971
   1.7300768    -1.3646536
   1.7300768    -1.3646536
```

```
      1.7300768      -1.3646536
      1.7300768      -1.3646536
      1.7300768      -1.3646536
      1.7300768      -1.3646536
      1.7300768      -1.3646536
      0.284675
      0.022631
C------------------------------------------------------------
C
C WEISUN.MAT
C
   1 3 1.5
   1 3 3
   1 1 1.0
   1 1 4
   -0.373935      -0.656747       1.540181       0.479106
    2.285974      -0.617044       0.193069
   -0.134413      -0.333451       1.077525       1.023802
    0.695587       1.211716       0.119085
   -0.143419       0.184473      -0.092898      -0.174056
    0.766309       0.055787       0.117436
    0.044740      -0.385976       0.271622      -0.356151
    0.243675       1.248445
   -1.404369       1.316605       0.242993       0.089731
    0.0052585      0.0000000
    0.0052585      0.0000000
    0.0052585      0.0000000
    0.0052585      0.0000000
    0.0052585      0.0000000
    0.0052585      0.0000000
    0.0052585      0.0000000
   48.626499
C------------------------------------------------------------
C
C WEISP5.MAT
C
   3 7 1.5
   1 4 3
   5 6 4
   7 7 6
   1 1 1.0
   1 1 4
   -0.004444      -0.111410       0.210965      -0.012736
   -0.060467      -0.103854      -0.093246      -0.182082
   -0.063029      -0.041359       0.077962       0.030831
    0.012416       0.060971       0.109981       0.021612
    0.045231      -0.160208
```

```
-1.106586    -0.027470    -0.602155     0.427259
 0.009112    -0.306340     0.574677    -0.520914
-0.072048     0.125607    -0.930844    -1.545488
 1.887950     0.244838     0.648763     0.497492
 0.395746    -0.083902
-0.635824    -0.355408     0.648642    -0.658621
-1.021932    -0.140636    -0.905504     1.075027
 0.714290     0.464612    -0.610478    -0.077643
-0.326404    -0.794915    -0.121374    -0.693173
-0.507819    -0.184602
 0.855900    -0.713537     0.922908     0.297566
-0.156227    -1.312171    -0.086685     0.733967
 0.339317    -0.067701    -0.882970    -1.696948
-0.645437    -0.435652     0.970332     0.404668
 0.610584    -0.489085
 0.000705    -0.083306     0.123838    -0.060778
-0.175965     0.089191     0.002927    -0.229215
-0.276198    -0.334757    -0.167653    -0.274851
-0.084684    -0.222473    -0.283565    -0.262697
-0.189650    -0.126251
-0.012488     0.059181     0.068141    -0.060242
-0.006627    -0.009168    -0.021619    -0.211453
-0.240918    -0.183626    -0.179874    -0.079393
-0.133802    -0.160670    -0.236816    -0.164900
-0.227088    -0.029539
-0.005681     0.020544     0.126208    -0.031483
 0.079548     0.042874     0.062370     0.465628
 0.668826     0.728191     0.829361     0.900641
 0.878287     0.838380     0.875632     0.851903
 0.933655    -0.228503
-0.963924     0.400541    -0.097578    -0.253480
-0.472336     0.401830    -0.396714     0.026824
 0.320564    -0.036034    -0.103207     0.236768
 1.067200     0.164905     0.103112     0.498905
 0.428585
-0.025008    -0.413872    -0.435596     0.395863
 0.257230     0.239795    -0.002380     0.103098
 1.9147157E-02     0.0000000
 1.9147157E-02     0.0000000
 7.6280333E-02     0.0000000
 5.6537297E-02     0.0000000
 5.6537297E-02     0.0000000
 5.6537297E-02     0.0000000
 5.6537297E-02     0.0000000
 8.9273758E-03    -2.9985716
 8.9273758E-03    -2.9985716
 8.9273758E-03    -2.9985716
```

```
    8.9273758E-03      -2.9985716
    8.9273758E-03      -2.9985716
    8.9273758E-03      -2.9985716
    8.9273758E-03      -2.9985716
    8.9273758E-03      -2.9985716
    8.9273758E-03      -2.9985716
    8.9273758E-03      -2.9985716
    8.9465444E-03      -3.0071572
  0.1189264E+02
C--------------------------------------------------------------
C
C WEIBPX.MAT
C
  3 5 1.5
  1 3 3
  4 4 4
  5 5 6
  1 1 1.0
  1 1 4
    0.274698   -0.633027   -0.396885    1.218696
    1.663116   -0.319191    0.251463   -0.738392
    0.473692    0.084137   -0.382421   -0.048336
    0.445808   -1.240387    0.709872   -0.020353
    0.283227   -0.450035    0.913736    1.155717
   -2.651808   -0.806475    1.019544   -0.120009
   -0.100100    0.090391    0.426639   -0.199858
   -1.390662   -0.409459    0.151885   -0.273409
   -0.189440    0.312548    0.939042    0.063852
    0.019010    0.022968   -0.031100    0.090497
    0.042838    0.079470    0.018754    0.048611
    0.265424    0.138853    0.013508    0.003932
    0.209782    0.023098   -0.268928    0.012895
   -0.012155   -0.040948   -0.032616   -0.193183
   -0.148857   -0.259053   -0.122703   -0.174991
    0.187554   -0.513914    0.754480   -0.456906
    0.303641    0.089669    0.284976    0.929684
   -1.276389   -1.123175    2.187532
    0.352600   -0.476428    0.400210   -0.079300
   -0.074545   -0.002239
    4.2149631   -2.5279241
    4.8437878   -2.4298862
    2.1645022   -3.3192641
    0.0346216    0.0000000
    0.0377937    0.0000000
    2.1717885   -3.2923227
    2.1390374   -3.2459893
    2.1301523   -3.2249441
```

```
2.1528525    -3.2820237
2.1659086    -3.2828677
2.1717885    -3.2923227
2.1390374    -3.2459893
0.1243665
3 5 1.5
1 3 3
4 4 4
5 5 6
1 1 1.0
1 1 4
-0.669060    0.285881     0.150778     0.128187
-0.254369    0.199221     1.201965    -0.227078
 0.490815   -0.481131     0.865739     0.218773
 0.211904   -0.537805    -0.421239    -0.467433
-0.048207    1.349578    -0.720218    -0.290570
-0.026665    0.346822    -0.920819     0.694380
-1.340914    0.427960     0.159900     0.352132
 0.406990    0.007493    -0.457417    -0.437758
 0.311972   -0.741371     0.729891    -0.235221
-0.253425   -0.592564    -0.533698    -0.541707
-0.218771   -0.049008    -1.009446    -0.389087
 0.014597   -0.240983    -0.040743     0.155484
-0.248157   -0.202180    -0.356268    -0.247747
-0.244111   -0.183043    -0.189593    -0.095868
 0.692759   -0.102152    -0.406709     0.540094
 0.914667    0.385536     0.400904     0.371774
 0.885788    0.911844    -1.217370    -0.443921
 0.108146   -0.332301    -0.191034
 0.516714   -1.241522    -1.145552     1.572688
-0.016664    0.278072
 2.1980846   -3.3233057
 2.1528525   -3.2820237
 2.1659086   -3.2828677
 2.1717885   -3.2923227
 2.1586616   -3.2957366
 2.1645022   -3.3192641
 0.0377937    0.0000000
 0.0346216    0.0000000
 0.1621715    0.0000000
 0.1408982    0.0000000
 0.1297870    0.0000000
 2.1390374   -3.2459893
 0.1243665
```

Bibliography

1. Abramowitz, Milton and Stegun, Irene A eds. *Handbook of Mathematical Functions*. Dover Publications, New York, 1972.
2. Adler, PA and Adler, P. *The Social Dynamics of Financial Markets*. JAI Press, Greenwich, CT, 1984.
3. Anderson, James A and Rosenfeld, Edward eds. *Neurocomputing*. MIT Press, Cambridge, MA, 1987.
4. Anderson, James A, Pellionisz, Andras and Rosenfeld, Edward eds. *Neurocomputing 2*. MIT Press, Cambridge, MA, 1990.
5. Anderson, Philip W, Arrow, Kenneth and Pines, David eds. *The Economy as an Evolving Complex System*. Sante Fe Institute Proc vol V. Addison-Wesley, Redwood City, California, 1988.
6. Ariel, Robert A. High Stock Returns before Holidays: Existence and Evidence on Possible Causes. *J. of Finance*, vol XLV, no 5, pp 1611–1626, Dec 1990.
7. Azoff, EM. Neural Network Principal Components Preprocessing and Diffraction Tomography. *Neural Computing and Applications*, vol 1, pp 107–114, 1993.
8. Azoff, EM. Reducing Error in Neural Network Time Series Forecasting. *Neural Computing and Applications*, vol 1, pp 240–247, 1993.
9. Babcock, Bruce Jr. *The Dow Jones-Irwin Guide to Trading Systems*. Dow Jones-Irwin, Homewood, Illinois, 1989.
10. Bachelier, L. Theory of Speculation. Reprinted in Cootner[36].
11. Bailey, TJ. *The Elements of Stochastic Processes with Applications to the Natural Sciences*. John Wiley, New York, 1964.
12. Balsara, Nauzer J. *Money Management Strategies for Futures Traders*. John Wiley, New York, 1992.
13. Band, RE. *Contrary Investing*. Viking Penguin, New York, 1986.
14. Battiti, Roberto. First- and Second-Order Methods for Learning, Between

Steepest Descent and Newton's Method. *Neural Computation*, vol 4, pp 141–166, 1992.

15. Battley, Nick. *An Introduction to Commodity Futures and Options.* McGraw-Hill, London, 1989.

16. Bergerson, Karl and Wunsch, Donald C. A Commodity Trading Model Based on a Neural Network-Expert System Hybrid. *Proc. IJCNN* Seattle 1991, vol 1, pp 289–293. IEEE, Piscataway, NJ, 1991.

17. Bloomfield, Peter. *Fourier Analysis of Time Series.* John Wiley, New York, 1976.

18. Blum, Adam. *Neural Networks in C++.* John Wiley, New York, 1992.

19. Boashash, Boualem. Estimating and Interpreting the Instantaneous Frequency of a Signal—Part 1: Fundamentals. *Proceedings of the IEEE.*—vol 80, no 4, pp 520–538, April 1992.

20. Boashash, Boualem. Estimating and Interpreting the Instantaneous Frequency of a Signal—Part 2: Algorithms and Applications. *Proceedings of the IEEE.*—vol 80, no 4, pp 540–568, April 1992.

21. Bourlard, H, and Kamp, Y. Autoassociation by Multilayer Perceptrons and Singular Value Decomposition. *Biological Cybernetics*, vol 59, pp 291–294, 1988.

22. Brock, William, Lakonishok, Josef and LeBaron, Blake. Simple Technical Trading Rules and the Stochastic Properties of Stock Returns. Social Systems Research Institute Workshop Series no 9022, October 1990. University of Wisconsin-Madison, Madison, WI.

23. Brock, William A. Causality, Chaos, Explanation and Prediction in Economics and Finance. In *Beyond Belief: Randomness, Prediction and Explanation in Science*, ch 10. Eds John L Casti and Anders Karlqvist. CRC Press, Boca Raton, Florida, 1991.

24. Brock, William A, Hsieh, David A and LeBaron, Blake. *A Test for Nonlinear Dynamics.* MIT, Cambridge, MA, 1990.

25. Burke, Gibbons. The Computerised Trader. *Futures*, vol XXI, p 74 May and p 68 July, 1992.

26. Burke, Gibbons. Perils, Pitfalls and Stumbling Blocks. *Futures*, vol XXII, no 3, pp 30–34, March 1993.

27. Burton, Robert M Jr, and Mpitsos, George J. Event-Dependent Control of Noise Enhances Learning in Neural Networks. *Neural Networks*, vol 5, pp 627–637, 1992.

28. Callen, Earl and Shapero, Don. A Theory of Social Imitation. *Physics Today*, pp 23–28, July 1974.

29. Casdagli, Martin. Nonlinear Prediction of chaotic time series. *Physica D*, vol 35, pp 335–356, 1989.

30. Casdagli, Martin and Eubank, Stephen eds. *Nonlinear Modeling and Forecasting.* Sante Fe Institute Proceedings vol XII. Addison-Wesley, Redwood City, California, 1992.

31. Casti, John L. *Searching for Certainty*. Morrow, New York, 1991.

32. Caudill, Maureen and Butler, Charles. *Naturally Intelligent Systems*. MIT, Cambridge, MA, 1990.

33. Chakraborty, Kanad, et al. Forecasting the Behaviour of Multivariate Time Series Using Neural Networks. *Neural Networks*, vol 5, pp 961–970, 1992.

34. Chen, JR and Mars, P. Stepsize Variation Methods for Accelerating the Backpropagation Algorithm. *Proc. IJCNN* Washington 1990, vol 1, pp 601–604. IEEE, New York, 1990.

35. Chen, Ping. Empirical and Theoretical Evidence of Economic Chaos. *System Dynamics Review* 4, pp 81–108, 1988.

36. Cootner, P, ed. *The Random Character of Stock Market Prices*. MIT, Cambridge, MA, 1964.

37. Dayhoff, Judith. *Neural Network Architectures: An Introduction*. Van Nostrand Reinhold, New York, 1990.

38. Dimson, E, ed. *Stock Market Anomalies*. Cambridge University Press, Cambridge, 1988.

39. Douglas, Mark. *The Disciplined Trader*. NYIF, New York, 1990.

40. Dreman, David M. *The New Contrarian Investment Strategy*. Random House, New York, 1982.

41. Duda, R, and Hart, P. *Pattern Classification and Scene Analysis*. Second ed. John Wiley, New York, 1993.

42. Dwyer, GP and Hafer, RW eds. *The Stock Market: Bubbles, Volatility and Chaos*. Kluwer Academic, Lancaster, 1989.

43. Eberhart, Russell C and Dobbins, Roy W eds. *Neural Network PC Tools*. Academic Press, London, 1990.

44. Efron, B. *The Jackknife, the Bootstrap and Other Resampling Plans*. SIAM, Philadelphia, 1982.

45. Elman, Jeffrey L and Zipser, David. Learning the Hidden Structure of Speech. *Journal of the Acoustical Society of America*, vol 83, pp 1615–1626, 1988.

46. Elton, E and Gruber, M. *Modern Portfolio Theory and Investment Analysis*. Fourth ed. John Wiley, New York, 1991.

47. Epstein, Richard A. *The Theory of Gambling and Statistical Logic*. Revised edition. Academic Press, New York, 1977.

48. Farmer, J Doyne and Sidorowich, John J. Predicting Chaotic Time Series. Physical Review Letters, vol 59, pp 845–848, 24 August 1987.

49. Feller, William. *An Introduction to Probability Theory and its Applications*. Third ed, vol 1. John Wiley, New York, 1968.

50. Fishman, Mark B, Barr, Dean S and Loick, Walter J. Using Neural Nets in Market Analysis. *Technical Analysis of Stocks and Commodities*, vol 9, no 4, p 18, April 1991.

51. Fishman, Mark B and Barr, Dean S. A Hybrid System for Market Timing.

Technical Analysis of Stocks and Commodities, vol 9, no 8, p 26, August 1991.

52. Freedman, Roy S. AI on Wall Street. *IEEE Expert*, pp 3-9, April 1991.

53. Goonatilake, Suran and Treleaven, Philip eds. *Intelligent Systems for Finance and Business*. John Wiley, Chichester, (forthcoming publication).

54. Greising, David, and Laurie Morse. *Brokers, Bagmen, & Moles*. John Wiley, New York, 1991.

55. Hadady, RE, Finberg, IL and Rahfeldt, D. *Winning With the Insiders*. Weiss Research, West Palm Beach, FL, 1987.

56. Hammerstrom, Dan. Working with Neural Networks. *IEEE Spectrum*, pp 43-53, July 1993.

57. Harston, Craig T. Business With Neural Networks. Chapter 24[101].

58. Haugen, Robert A and Lakonishok, Josef. *The Incredible January Effect*. Dow Jones-Irwin, Homewood, Illinois, 1989.

59. Hawley, DD, Johnson, JD and Raina, D. Artificial Neural Systems: A New Tool for Financial Decision-Making. *Finan Analy J*, p 63, Nov/Dec 1990.

60. Haykin, S. *Adaptive Filter Theory*. Second ed. Prentice- Hall, Englewood Cliffs, NJ, 1991.

61. Hebb, DO. *The Organisation of Behaviour*. John Wiley, New York, 1949.

62. Hecht-Nielsen, R. *Neurocomputing*. Addison-Wesley, Menlo Park, CA, 1990.

63. Henon, M. A Two-Dimensional Map with a Strange Attractor. *Communications in Mathematical Physics*, vol 50, p 69, 1970.

64. Hertz, John, Krogh, Anders and Palmer, Richard G. *Introduction to the Theory of Neural Computation*. Lecture Notes Volume I, Sante Fe Institute. Addison-Wesley, Redwood City, California, 1991.

65. Hirsch, Yale. *Don't Sell Stocks on Mondays*. Facts on File Publications, New York, 1986.

66. Hlawatsch, Franz and Boudreaux-Bartels, G Faye. Linear and Quadratic Time-Frequency Signal Representations. *IEEE Signal Processing Magazine*. vol 9, No 2, pp 21-67, April 1992.

67. Howrey, E Philip. A Spectrum Analysis of the Long-Swing Hypothesis. *Intrnl. Economic Review*, vol 9, pp 228-252, 1968.

68. Hsieh, David A. Testing for Nonlinear Dependence in Daily Foreign Exchange Rates. *Journal of Business*, vol 62, pp 339-369, 1989.

69. Hull, John. *Options, Futures, and other Derivative Securities*. Second ed. Prentice Hall, Englewood Cliffs, NJ, 1993.

70. Hush, Don R and Horne, Bill G. Progress in Supervised Neural Networks. *IEEE Signal Processing Magazine*. vol 10, no 1, pp 8-39, January 1993.

71. Johnson, M. *The Random Walk and Beyond*. John Wiley, New York, 1988.

72. Jolliffe, IT. *Principal Component Analysis*. Springer-Verlag, Berlin, 1986.

73. Jurik, Mark. The Care and Feeding of a Neural Network. *Futures*, vol XXI, no 12, pp 40-44, October 1992.

74. Jurik, Mark. Consumer's Guide to Neural Network Software. *Futures*, vol XXII, no 8, pp 36–42, July 1993.

75. Karlin, S and Taylor, HM. *A First Course in Stochastic Processes*. Second ed. Academic Press, New York, 1975.

76. Katz, Jeffrey Owen. Developing Neural Network Forecasters for Trading. *Technical Analysis of Stocks and Commodities*, vol 10, no. 4, p. 58, April 1992.

77. Kaufman, Perry J. *The New Commodity Trading Systems and Methods*. John Wiley, New York, 1987.

78. Kean, John. Using Neural Nets for Intermarket Analysis. *Technical Analysis of Stocks and Commodities*, vol 10, no 11, p 58, November 1992.

79. Kelly, JL. A New Interpretation of Information Rate. Bell System Technical Journal, vol 35, p 917–926, 1956.

80. Kendall, Maurice, and J Keith Ord. *Time Series*. Third ed. Edward Arnold, Sevenoaks, Kent, 1993.

81. Kindelberger, CP. *Manias, Panics and Crashes*. Basic Books, New York, 1978.

82. Klimasauskas, Casey. Neural Nets and Noise Filtering. *Dr Dobb's Journal*, pp 32–48, January 1989.

83. Knight, Sheldon. Tips, Tricks and Tactics for Developing Trading Systems. *Futures*, vol XXII, no 1, pp 38–40, January 1993.

84. Koeckelenbergh, Andre. Sunspot Index Data Center, 3 Avenue Circulaire, B-1180, Bruxelles, Belgium.

85. Kohonen, Teuvo. *Self-Organisation and Associative Memory*. Third ed. Springer-Verlag, Berlin, 1989.

86. Kolb, Robert W. *Options: The Investor's Complete Toolkit*. New York Institute of Finance, New York, 1991.

87. Kolmogorov, A. *Foundations of the Theory of Probability*. Trans. N Morrison. Chelsea, New York, 1956.

88. Korenberg, Michael J and Paarmann, Larry D. Orthogonal Approaches to Time Series Analysis and System Identification. *IEEE Signal Processing Magazine*. vol 8, no 3, pp 29–43, July 1991.

89. Kosko, Bart. *Neural Networks and Fuzzy Systems*. Prentice-Hall, Englewood Cliffs, NJ, 1992.

90. Kurkova, Vera. Kolmogorov's Theorem is Relevant. *Neural Computation*, vol 3, pp 617–622, 1991.

91. Lakonishok, Josef and Maberly, Edwin. The Weekend Effect: Trading Patterns of Individual and Institutional Investors. *J. Finance*, vol XLV, no 1, pp 231–243, March 1990.

92. Lapedes, Alan and Farber Robert. Nonlinear Signal Processing Using Neural Networks, Prediction and System Modelling. Los Alamos Report LA-UR-87-2662, Los Alamos National Laboratory, Los Alamos, NM, 1987.

93. Larrain, Maurice. Testing Chaos and Nonlinearities in T-Bill Rates. *Financial Analysts Journal*, vol 47, no 5, pp 51–62, Sep/Oct 1991.

94. Le Cun, Yann. Une Procedure d'Apprentissage pour Reseau a Seuil Assymetrique. In *Cognitiva 85: A la Frontiere de l'Intelligence Artificielle des Sciences de la Connaissance des Neurosciences*. CESTA, Paris, pp 599–604, 1985.

95. Le Cun, Yann, Denker, John S and Solla, Sara A. Optimal Brain Damage. *Advances in Neural Information Processing Systems 2*, pp 598–605. Ed D S Touretzky. Morgan Kaufmann, San Mateo, CA, 1990.

96. Lippmann, Richard P. An Introduction to Computing with Neural Nets. *IEEE ASSP Magazine*, pp 4–23, April 1987.

97. Lorenz, HW. *Nonlinear Dynamical Economics and Chaotic Motion*. Lecture Notes in Economics and Mathematical Systems No. 334. Springer Verlag, Berlin, 1989.

98. Luenberger, DG. *Introduction to Linear & Nonlinear Programming*. Addison-Wesley, Reading MA, 1973.

99. Lutzy, Ottmar and Dengel, Andreas. A Comparison of Neural Net Simulators. *IEEE Expert*. pp 43–51, August 1993.

100. Mackay, C. *Extraordinary Popular Delusions and the Madness of Crowds*. Noonday Press, New York, 1974 (Rep. of 19th century ed.).

101. Maren, Alianna, Harston, Craig and Pap, Robert. *Handbook of Neural Computing Applications*. Academic Press, London, 1990.

102. Markowitz, Harry. *Portfolio Selection: Efficient Diversification of Investments*. John Wiley, New York, 1964.

103. Marple, S Lawrence Jr. *Digital Spectral Analysis*. Prentice-Hall, Englewood Cliffs, NJ, 1987.

104. Masters, Timothy. *Practical Neural Network Recipes in C++*. Academic Press, Orlando, FL, 1993.

105. Mathews, V John. Adaptive Polynomial Filters. *IEEE Signal Processing Magazine*. vol 8, no 3, pp 10–26, July 1991.

106. McClelland, James L, Rumelhart, David E and the PDP Research Group. Parallel Distributed Processing. Vol 2: Psychological and Biological Models. MIT, Cambridge, MA, 1986.

107. McClelland, James L, and Rumelhart, David E. *Explorations in Parallel Distributed Processing*. MIT, Cambridge, MA, 1988.

108. McClish, DK. Comparing the Areas Under More Than Two Independent ROC Curves. *Medical Decision Making*, vol 7, pp 149–155, 1987.

109. McCulloch, WS and Pitts, W. A Logical Calculus of Ideas Immanent in Nervous Activity. *Bulletin of Mathematical Biophysics*, vol 5, pp 115–133, 1943.

110. McQueen, G and Thorley, S. Are Stock Returns Predictable? A Test using Markov Chains. *J Finance*, vol XLVI, no 1, p 239, March 1990.

111. Mead, WC et al. Prediction of Chaotic Time Series using CNLS-NET-Example: The Mackey-Glass equation. In *Nonlinear Modeling and forecasting*[30], pp 39–72.

112. Miller, RM. *Computer-Aided Financial Analysis*. Addison-Wesley, Reading, MA, 1990.

113. Miller, WT, Sutton, RS and Werbos, P. *Neural Networks for Robotics and Control*. MIT, Cambridge, MA, 1990.

114. Minsky, Marvin L, and Papert, Seymour A. *Perceptrons*. Expanded edition. MIT, Cambridge, MA, 1988.

115. Muller, Berndt, and Reinhardt, Joachim. *Neural Networks: An Introduction*. Springer-Verlag, New York, 1990.

116. Murphy, John J. *Technical Analysis of Futures Markets*. New York Institute of Finance, New York, 1986.

117. Newbold, Paul. *Statistics for Business and Economics*. Second edition. Prentice-Hall, Englewood Cliffs, NJ, 1988.

118. NYIF. *Futures: A Personal Seminar*. New York Institute of Finance, New York, 1989.

119. O'Hagan, Anthony. Private communication.

120. O'Reilly, Brian. Computers That Think Like People. *Fortune*, pp 58–61, 27 Feb 1989.

121. Orfanidis, Sophocles J. Gram-Schmidt Neural Nets. *Neural Computation*, vol 2, pp 116–126, 1990.

122. Owens, AJ and Filkin DL. Efficient Training of the Backpropagation Network by Solving a System of Stiff Ordinary Differential Equations. In *Proc IJCNN* Washington 1989, vol 2, pp 381–386. IEEE, New York, 1989.

123. Pardo, Robert. *Design, Testing and Optimisation of Trading Systems*. John Wiley, New York, 1992.

124. Parker, DB. Learning Logic. Technical Report TR-47, Center for Computational Research in Economics and Management Science, MIT, Cambridge, MA, 1985.

125. Pau, LF. Artificial Intelligence and Financial Services. *IEEE Trans. Knowledge and Data Engineering*, vol 3, pp 137–148, 1991.

126. Peters, Edgar E. *Chaos and Order in the Capital Markets*. John Wiley, New York, 1991.

127. Poulos, E Michael. Futures According to Trend Tendency. *Technical Analysis of Stocks and Commodities*, vol 10, no 1, p 61, January 1992.

128. Press, William H, Teukolsky, Saul A. Vetterling, William T and Flannery, Brian P. *Numerical Recipes*. Second Edition. Cambridge University Press, Cambridge, 1992.

129. Priestley, Maurice B. *Spectral Analysis and Time Series*. Academic, London, 1981.

130. Priestley, Maurice B. *Nonlinear and Nonstationary Time Series Analysis*. Academic, London, 1988.

131. Gabr, MM and Rao, T Subba. The Estimation and Prediction of Subset Bilinear Time Series Models with Applications. *J Time Series Analysis*, vol 2, pp 155–171, 1981.

132. Refenes, AN, et al. Currency Exchange Rate Prediction and Neural Network Design Strategies. *Neural Computing & Applications*, vol 1, pp 46–58, 1993.

133. Resnikoff, HL. Foundations of Arithmeticum Analysis: Compactly Supported Wavelets and The Wavelet Group. Aware Report AD890507.1, 1989. Aware, Inc, One Memorial Drive, Cambridge, MA.

134. Rioul, Olivier and Vetterli, Martin. Wavelets and Signal Processing. *IEEE Signal Processing Magazine*. vol 8, no 4, pp 14–38, October 1991.

135. Rissanen, J. *Stochastic Complexity in Statistical Inquiry*. World Scientific, Singapore, 1989.

136. Rosenblat, F. *Principles of Neurodynamics*. Spartan, New York, 1962.

137. Ruelle, David. Deterministic Chaos, the Science and the Fiction. *Proc Royal Soc London A*, vol 427, pp 241–248, 1990.

138. Rumelhart, DE, Hinton, GE and Williams, RJ. Learning Representations by Backpropagating Errors. *Nature*, vol 323, pp 533–536, 1986.

139. Rumelhart, David E, McClelland, James L and the PDP Research Group. *Parallel Distributed Processing*. Vol 1: Foundations. MIT, Cambridge, MA, 1986.

140. Rutterford, Janette. *Introduction to Stock Exchange Investment*. Macmillan, London, 1985.

141. Savit, Robert. Nonlinearities and Chaotic Effects in Options Prices. *J Futures Markets*, vol 9, pp 507–518, 1989.

142. Savit, Robert. Chaos on the Trading Floor. *New Scientist*, p 48, 11 August 1990.

143. Schiller, Robert J. *Market Volatility*. MIT, Cambridge, MA, 1989.

144. Schmerken, I. Wall Street's Elusive Goal, Computers that Think Like Pros. *Wall Street Computer Review*, vol 7, pp 61–69, June 1990.

145. Schwager, Jack D. *A Complete Guide to the Futures Markets*. John Wiley, New York, 1984.

146. Schwager, Jack D. Selecting the Best Futures Price Series for Computer Testing. *Technical Analysis of Stocks and Commodities*, vol 10, no 10, pp 65–71, October 1992.

147. Schetzen, M. *The Voltera and Wiener Theory of Nonlinear Systems*. John Wiley, New York, 1980.

148. Shanno, David F. Conjugate Gradient Methods with Inexact Searches. *Mathematics of Operations Research*, vol 3, pp. 244–256, 1978.

149. Shanno, DF and Kang-Hoh Phua. Matrix Conditioning and Nonlinear Optimisation. *Mathematical Programming*, vol 14, pp 149–160, 1978.

150. Shih, Yin Lung. Neural Nets in Technical Analysis. *Technical Analysis of Stocks and Commodities*, vol 9, no 2, p 62, February 1991.

151. Siu, Sammy and Cowan, Colin FN. Adaptive Equalization Using the l_p Back Propagation Algorithm. *Proc. Second Intl Artificial Neural Networks Conference*, Bournemouth, 1991, pp 10–12. IEE, London, 1991.

152. Sluis, A. van der and Vorst, HA van der. The Rate of Convergence of Conjugate Gradients. *Numerical Mathematics*, vol 48, pp 543–560, 1986.

153. Stokbro, Kurt and Umberger, DK. Forecasting with Weighted Maps. In *Nonlinear Modeling Forecasting*[30], pp 73–94.

154. Stokbro, Kurt. Predicting Chaos with Weighted Maps. NORDITA preprint 91/10 S.

155. Sugihara, George and May, Robert. Nonlinear Forecasting as a Way of Distinguishing Chaos from Measurement Error in Time Series. *Nature*, vol 344, pp 734–741, 19 April 1990.

156. Swales, George S Jr and Yoon, Young. Applying Artificial Neural Networks to Investment Analysis. *Financial Analysts Journal*, vol 48, no 5, Sep/Oct 1992.

157. Takens, F. Detecting Strange Attractor in Turbulence. In *Lecture Notes in Mathematics*. Eds D Rand and L Young. Springer, Berlin, 1981.

157a. Taylor, S.J. *Modeling Financial Time Series*. John Wiley, Chichester, 1986, reprinted 1994.

158. Teweles, RJ, and Jones, FJ. *The Futures Game*. Second ed. McGraw-Hill, New York, 1987.

159. Thompson, JMT, and Stewart, HB. *Nonlinear Dynamics and Chaos*. John Wiley, Chichester, 1986.

160. Thorp, Edward O. *The Mathematics of Gambling*. Gambling Times Press, Van Nuys, CA, 1984.

161. Thorp, Edward O, and Kassouf, Sheen T. *Beat the Market: A Scientific Stock Market System*. Random House, New York, 1967.

162. Tong, Howell. *Nonlinear Time Series: A Dynamical System Approach*. Oxford University Press, Oxford, 1990.

163. Tong, Howell and Lim, KS. Threshold Autoregression, Limit Cycles and Cyclical Data. *J Royal Statistical Society*, vol B 42, pp 245–292, 1980.

164. Vaga, Tonis. The Coherent Market Hypothesis. *Financial Analysts Journal*, vol 46, no 6, pp 36–49, Nov/Dec 1990.

165. Vince, Ralph. *Portfolio Management Formulas*. John Wiley, New York, 1990.

166. Vince, Ralph. *The Mathematics of Money Management*. John Wiley, New York, 1992.

167. Wallich, Paul. Wavelet Theory: An Analysis Technique that's Creating Ripples. *Scientific American*, pp 34–35, January 1991.

168. Wasserman, PD. *Neural Computing*. Van Nostrand Reinhold, New York, 1989.

169. Weigend, Andreas S, Huberman, Bernardo A and Rumelhart, David E. Generalisation by Weight-Elimination with Application to Forecasting. In

Advances in Neural Information Processing Systems 3, pp 875–882. Eds. Richard P Lippmann, John E Moody and David S Touretzky. Morgan Kaufmann, San Mateo, CA, 1991.

170. Weigend, Andreas S, Huberman, Bernardo A and Rumelhart, David E. Predicting Sunspots and Exchange Rates with Connectionist Networks. In *Nonlinear Modeling and Forecasting*[30], pp 395–432.

171. Weigend, Andreas S, Rumelhart, David E and Huberman, Bernardo A. Backpropagation, Weight-Elimination and Time Series Prediction. In *Connectionist Models, Proceedings of the 1990 Summer School*. Eds. DS Touretzky et al. Morgan Kaufmann, San Mateo, CA, 1991.

172. Weiss, Sholom M and Kulikowski, Casimir A. *Computer Systems That Learn*. Morgan Kaufmann, San Mateo, CA, 1991.

173. Werbos, P. Beyond Regression: New Tools for Prediction and Analysis in the Behavioral Sciences. PhD Thesis, Harvard University, 1974.

174. White, H. Economic Prediction Using Neural Networks, The Case of IBM Daily Stock Returns. *Proc. IEEE Int Conf on Neural Networks*, vol 2, pp 451–458. IEEE, New York, 1988.

175. Wong, FS, et al. Fuzzy Neural Systems for Stock Selection. *Financial Analysts Journal*, vol 48, no 1, pp 47–52, Jan/Feb 1992.

176. Zaremba, Thomas. Technology in Search of a Buck. Chapter 12 in *Neural Network PC Tools*[43].

177. Ziemba, William T. A Betting Simulation: The Mathematics of Gambling. *Gambling Times*, June, 1987.

Index

Index compiled by Indexing Specialists, Hove, East Sussex, UK